THE LIFE OF
MELANIA
THE
YOUNGER

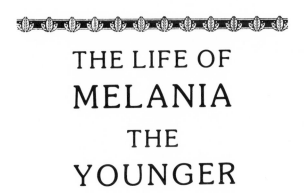

THE LIFE OF
MELANIA
THE
YOUNGER

Introduction, Translation, and Commentary

Elizabeth A. Clark

Studies in Women and Religion
Volume 14

The Edwin Mellen Press
New York and Toronto

Library of Congress Cataloging in Publication Data

Gerontius, d. 485.
   The life of Melania, the Younger.

   Translation of the Greek version of: Vita Melaniae
Junioris; notes give information on variant contents
of the Latin version.
   Bibliography: p.
   Includes index.
   1. Melania, the Younger, Saint, 385?-439.
2. Christian saints--Biography. I. Clark, Elizabeth A.
(Elizabeth Ann), 1938-   . II. Title.
BR1720.M37G4413 1984   270.2'092'4 (B)   84-20635
ISBN 0-88946-535-5

Studies in Women and Religion
Series ISBN 0-88946-549-5

Copyright   1984, Elizabeth A. Clark

Printed in the United States of America

For
Herbert W. Richardson

Editor, Mentor, Friend

TABLE OF CONTENTS

ACKNOWLEDGMENTS

Thanks are due to many individuals and groups for their assistance in the research and writing of this volume. Grants from the National Endowment for the Humanities made possible both a year free for research and a summer seminar with Alan Cameron of Columbia University on "Paganism and Christianity in the Fourth Century A.D." Dumbarton Oaks graciously allowed me the use of its excellent library. The library staffs of Mary Washington College, Union Theological Seminary, Dumbarton Oaks, and Duke University have been most helpful. Grace S. Lockwood and Beverly Wildung Harrison opened their homes to me during my research in Washington, D.C. and New York City, respectively. Among the many colleagues who have given special assistance and encouragement, I would like to thank especially Mary T. Boatwright, Peter Brown, Alan Cameron, James Charlesworth, Ann Wharton Epstein, Robert Gregg, Sidney Griffith, Dennis Groh, Diane Hatch, David Levenson, Robert Markus, Kent Rigsby, and Robert Wilken. Thanks are also due to Shelia Walker for her patient typing of the manuscript and to Amy-Jill Levine and Jay Geller for editorial assistance. The Chair of the Department of Religion at Duke University, Kalman Bland, has been exceptionally generous in making financial and other assistance available at various stages of the project.

Last, very special thanks to Ann Wharton Epstein, Susan Hanna, and Rebecca Lane Reed, whose loving friendship has sustained and enriched my life.

Elizabeth A. Clark
Duke University

June, 1984

I. INTRODUCTION TO THE TEXT

A century ago, J. G. Cunningham, the translator of Augustine's letters for the Nicene and Post-Nicene Fathers series, identified Melania the Younger for his readers:

> The name Melania, though now almost as little known to the world at large as the fossil univalve molluscs to which palaeontologists have assigned the designation, was in the time of Augustine esteemed throughout Christendom.[1]

Informing Cunningham's ascription of fossilhood to Melania is the fact that although she is mentioned in the writings of Jerome,[2] Augustine,[3] Paulinus of Nola,[4] Palladius,[5] Cyril of Scythopolis,[6] and John Rufus,[7] neither the Greek nor the Latin manuscripts on which modern editions of the *Vita Melaniae Junioris* are based had then been discovered.

Yet Cunningham also misled his readers, for Melania was known after her time not only through the notices of her contemporaries, but also through such liturgical documents as the menologies of the Eastern Church[8] and the *Synaxarium* of Constantinople.[9] Although the West was slower to include Melania in its cycle of church festivals, she is mentioned in the *Martyrology* of the ninth-century French monk, Usuard,[10] in two eleventh-century calendars of the Spanish Church,[11] and in the *Catalog of*

Saints compiled by the fourteenth-century Italian eccle-
siastic, Pietro de Natali.[12] The *Catalog* is of special
interest, for although its content proves the author
derived his information from some version of the
Lausiac History,[13] his ignorance of Melania's proper feast
day (he placed her in October, rather than on December
31) indicates that Melania was not well celebrated in
the West.

In addition to these and other brief listings,[14] a
longer recital of Melania's history was contained in the
collection of saints' *Lives* compiled by the tenth-
century Byzantine scholar, Simeon Logothetes, "the Metaphrast."[15] In the sixteenth century, a Latin translation
of the Metaphrast's *Vita Melaniae* was made and included
(without acknowledgment of its source) in Aloysius Lipomani's *De Probatis Sanctorum Historiis*.[16] Shortly after this
recovery of Melania for the Western church, her name
appeared in the *Roman Martyrology*,[17] but no new materials
pertaining to Melania were discovered for the next three
hundred years. Thus it is the Metaphrast's Greek text,
accompanied by the sixteenth-century Latin translation,
that supplied the *Life of Melania* for the *Patrologia
Graeca*.[18] The very fact that the Metaphrast's rendition
of the *Vita Melaniae* occupied twenty columns in the *Patrologia* suggests that the author had access to a more
extensive source than the scattered notices found in the
ancient and medieval documents, yet its identity
remained unknown.

Nonetheless, as early as 1709 the distinguished
French historian Lenain de Tillemont had suspected that
a Greek text of Melania's *Life* different from the Metaphrast's might someday come to light.[19] The discoveries
made by late nineteenth-century scholars surpassed
Tillemont's hopes, for they found not only an ancient
Greek but also a Latin version. The account of these

discoveries is replete with as many vagaries of fortune as Melania's own history.

In October of 1884, just twenty years after the
Patrologia Graeca published the Metaphrast's *Life of
Melania*, Mariano Rampolla del Tindaro, then papal nuntio
in Madrid, later a cardinal and Leo XIII's secretary of
state, found a Latin manuscript containing the *Vita
Melaniae* in the Escurial Library. Dating from the tenth
century, the codex (a.II.9) probably came from Oviedo.[20]
Yet Rampolla's discovery remained unknown for sixteen
years: he did not so much as announce his find until
1900, at the Second International Congress of Christian
Archeology at Rome.[21] According to the *Acts* of the
Congress, his disclosure was greeted with much curiosity
and "unanimous applause,"[22] but the scholarly world had
five more years to wait before the publication of his
monumental *Santa Melania Guiniore, senatrice romana*.

Meanwhile, although fragments of the Latin *Vita
Melaniae* had come to light elsewhere, their finders
remained unaware of Rampolla's discovery. Thus in 1885,
Augustus Molinier and Carolus Kohler spotted part of
the Latin *Vita* in codex 2178 of the new Latin acquisi-
tions in the Bibliothèque Nationale; of Spanish origin,
the manuscript dated from the eleventh century. Molinier
and Kohler immediately published the relevant parts of
this *Vita* in their work on pilgrimages to the Holy Land,
Itinera Hierosolymitana et Descriptiones Terrae Sanctae, II.[23]

In 1889, portions of the Latin *Vita* from the Paris
codex and from an eighth- or ninth-century codex found
at Chartres[24] were collated and published by the Bollandists.[25] The Chartres codex, like the one from Paris,
was incomplete; worse yet, Melania's *Vita* was interspersed with material from the *Life of St. Pelagia of
Antioch*.[26] Since the compilation still did not constitute a full *Life of Melania*, de Smedt and the Bollandists

filled in the lacunae with material from the Latin
translation of the Metaphrast's Greek version.

Only in 1900, when the Bollandists discovered in
the Barberini Library a Greek codex (III.37) dating from
the eleventh century, did they have in hand the text
Lenain de Tillemont had suspected. Not waiting for
Rampolla to publish his edition of the Latin *Vita*, they
brought out the Greek text in the 1903 *Analecta Bollandi-
ana*.[27] Their work has been criticized for faulty editing,
its sparse three-page introduction, and its dearth of
notes.[28]

Finally in 1905, Rampolla's *Santa Melania Guiniore*
appeared. The book included both Latin and Greek texts
of the *Vita*, an Italian translation of the Greek text
(but not of the Latin), and an extensive commentary in
the form of notes. Rampolla relied primarily on the
Escurial codex for his Latin text, although he also
consulted eight others, one each from Paris, Chartres,
Valencia, Brussels, Monte Cassino, Naples, and two from
Douai. The earliest of the Latin manuscripts dated
from the eighth or ninth century, the latest from the
fifteenth.[29] For the Greek text of the *Vita*, Rampolla
relied chiefly on the Barberini codex published by the
Bollandists, but corrected and re-edited by Giovanni
Mercati and Pio Franchi de' Cavallieri;[30] he also noted
the Metaphrast's Greek version.

Rampolla's publication marked the end of an
exciting era: only one other manuscript containing a
Latin version of the *Life* has since been discovered.[31]
The Greek text printed in Denys Gorce's *Vie de Sainte
Mélanie* largely reproduces the corrected version in
Rampolla.[32]

The publication of complete Greek and Latin
versions of the *Vita* opened the way to heated scholarly
controversy regarding the language of the original.

Although the two versions follow essentially the same
"story line," there are significant variations in detail
between them, often of such a contemporary flavor that
the modern historian is hard-pressed to decide on the
basis of content which is the more reliable. The
consensus of opinion holds that neither our Greek nor
our Latin version exactly replicates the original *Vita*.
Even Mariano Rampolla, staunch champion of the priority
of the Latin, conceded that neither was the original;
both derive from an "Ur-text" now lost.[33] We may assume
that in many cases, details of one version omitted in
the other were probably derived from the original *Vita*.

Not only was Rampolla convinced that the original
had been composed in Latin; he also argued that the
recension of the Latin Escurial codex was made at an
earlier date than the Greek version of the Barberini
codex.[34] Rampolla's chief argument for the priority of
the Latin recension rests on the fact that the Latin
Vita contains repetitions and confusions in chronological
order that the editor felt obliged to excuse,[35] while
the editor of the Greek text, in contrast, smoothed out
the confusions and placed the *Vita*'s episodes in correct
chronological order. Since it is highly implausible
that an editor would introduce confusions into an otherwise straightforward text, Rampolla believed he here
had evidence for the priority of the Latin recension.[36]

Others, while agreeing with Rampolla that our Greek
and Latin texts derive from an earlier version, disagreed with his claim that the Latin edition must have
been prior.[37] Adhémar d'Alès, for example, while accep-
ting Rampolla's view that the disorder of the Latin
version probably was present in the original, argued
that the mere fact the Barberini text contained no such
disorders did not prove its recension to have been later
than that of the Latin text of the Escurial codex:[38]

an editor of the Greek text could well have rectified
the chronological and other inconsistencies he found in
the "Ur-text" prior to the time the Latin version of the
Escurial codex was edited. Later editors and copyists
working with the Greek version may have had no knowledge
of the Latin text, and vice versa.

    Although, on balance, the case for the original
Vita's having been composed in Greek appears to us
stronger, Rampolla offered a variety of arguments
supporting the priority of the Latin. First, according
to Rampolla, details of content prove the Latin version
must be earlier. A few examples to illustrate Rampolla's
claim will here suffice. Far from proving Rampolla's
argument, however, they only show the subjectivity to
which such judgments are prone. For example, Rampolla
claims that the Greek text is in error (and hence later)
since it reports that Melania and Pinian visited those
condemned to the mines[39] (a point omitted in the Latin
version), because such activity would not be in accord
with the ascetic solitude they had espoused even at
Rome.[40] Yet, we could counter, why does Rampolla not
question the testimony of the Latin version that the
couple visited prisoners,[41] an activity that also seems
to accord poorly with ascetic solitude?[42] The omission
from the Latin version of Melania and Pinian's visit to
the mines hardly constitutes a case for its priority.

    According to Rampolla, the Latin text exhibits
greater precision of detail than the Greek at many
points. For example, the Latin *Vita* correctly identi-
fies Lausus as "ex praepositus sacri cubiculi,"[43]
whereas the Greek version calls Lausus "ὁ πρεπόσιτος,"[44]
thus revealing (to Rampolla) that its author was unaware
that Lausus had not served in this office for many
years.[45] Yet, we can argue, the Latin *Vita* does not
have exclusive claim to precision of language; it, too,

can waver, as when it variously designates Theodosius
II as "Augustus," "imperator," and "rex."[46] Precision
of detail provides no sure clue to the priority of
either version, for each contains detail not found in
the other. Such divergences will be noted in the commentary below.

A third example concerning content used by Rampolla
to argue the priority of the Latin *Vita* is the notice
given in the Greek text that Melania's father, Valerius
Publicola, had other children.[47] This point is not
mentioned in the Latin *Vita*, which proceeds on the assumption that Melania was an only child. Although Rampolla
declares that the Latin version is correct,[48] the matter
cannot be settled by a simple assertion of preferences,
especially when another ancient source explicitly states
that Melania had a sibling or siblings.[49] The question
of whether Melania was an only child is important for
the discussion to follow,[50] but it cannot be decided in
the manner Rampolla attempts.

A last example regarding content raised by Rampolla
to argue the priority of the Latin text is that Valentinian III, the Western emperor, is referred to as
"imperator noster,"[51] whereas the Eastern emperor Theodosius II is not; according to Rampolla, the more personal reference to Valentinian indicates that the author
of the original *Vita* was a Westerner.[52] Yet d'Alès'
counter-explanation seems at least plausible: Valentinian III was still alive when the *Vita* was composed,
whereas Theodosius II was not[53] (Theodosius II died in
A.D. 450; Valentinian III was murdered in 455). Such
examples as these illustrate the problems inherent in
Rampolla's attempt to mount an argument on the basis of
content. Rampolla, however, appeals to other types of
arguments as well.

He claims, for instance, that misspellings and

wrong divisions of words in the Greek text indicate
that the Latin was earlier (e.g., σὺν κάμνειν for συγ-
κάμνειν, κατεσπέραν for καθ᾿ ἐσπέραν, θεράπεναν for
θεράπαιναν).[54] Here his argument is likewise unconvin-
cing, for such errors can easily be attributed to copyists and redactors rather than to the original author.
Nor does the awkwardness of the Latin style, when
compared with the smoothness of the Greek,[55] prove the
Latin's originality, as Rampolla argues;[56] the clumsier
Latin could just as well indicate a poor translation
from the Greek.

A third argument Rampolla uses to claim the priority of the Latin is based on citations from the Bible
and the *Lausiac History*. Rampolla argues that the Greek
Barberini text has translated two Scriptural quotations
from the Latin *Vita* rather than taken them directly from
the Septuagint. The examples Rampolla cites are these:

Escurial Text (ch. 7)	Barberini Text (ch. 7)	Septuagint Ps 44:11-12
Audi, filia, et vide et inclina aurem tuam et obliviscere populum tuum et domum patris tui. Et con-cupiscet rex speciem tuam.	῎Ακουσον, θύγατερ, καὶ ἴδε καὶ κλῖνον το οὖς σου, καὶ ἐπιλάθου τοῦ λαοῦ σου καὶ τοῦ οἴκου τοῦ πατρός σου. Καὶ ἐπιθυμήσει ὁ βασιλευς τοῦ κάλλους σου.	῎Ακουσον, θύγατερ, καὶ ἴδε καὶ κλῖνον το οὖς σου καὶ ἐπιλάθου τοῦ λαοῦ σου καὶ τοῦ οἴκου τοῦ πατρός σου ὅτι ἐπεθύμησεν ὁ βασιλευς τοῦ κάλλους σου.
(ch. 64)	(ch. 63)	Jer 48:10
Maledictus qui facit opus Domini negligenter.	᾿Επικατάρατος ὁ ποιῶν το ἔργον Κυρίου ἀμελῶς.	᾿Επικατάρατος ὁ ποιῶν τα ἔργα Κυρίου ἀμελῶς.[57]

Yet we would argue against Rampolla that the variations between the Barberini text and the Septuagint
are exceedingly minor: the splitting of a complex sentence into two sentences and the use of a singular
rather than a plural do not constitute a strong case
that the Greek was translated from the Latin *Vita* rather

than taken directly from the Septuagint. Quite the opposite: it would be almost inconceivable that the composer of the Greek text could have managed such a close correspondence with the Septuagint reading if he had not had it in mind when he set down the Scriptural quotations given above.

A second citation to which Rampolla gives much importance, found in chapter 1 of the *Vita*, comes from the *Lausiac History*. It relates how Melania pleaded with Pinian to adopt a life of chastity with her, but asked that if he felt unable to do so, would he leave her body "free," in return for which favor she would grant him all her possessions. Rampolla argues that the wording of the Latin text of the *Vita* is much closer to Palladius than is that of the Greek Barberini text, thus again suggesting that the Latin is prior. The texts are as follows:

Escurial Text	Palladius, *Lausiac History* 61	Barberini Text
Si volueris habitare mecum secundum legem castitatis et continentiae, dominum meum te cognoscam et dominatorem vitae meae esse confiteor. Si autem grave tibi hoc quasi adulescenti videatur, omnes meas facultates suscipe, et tantum corpus meum liberum effice ut perficiam, quod est secundum Deum, desiderium.	Εἰ μὲν αἱρῆσαι συνασκηθῆναι κἀμοὶ κατα τον τῆς σωφροσύνης λόγον, καὶ δεσπότην σε οἶδα καὶ κύριον τῆς ἐμῆς ζωῆς· εἰ δε βαρύ σοι τοῦτο καταφαίνεται ὡς νεωτέρῳ, πάντα μου λαβὼν τὰ πράγματα ἐλευθέρωσόν μου το σῶμα, ἵνα πληρώσω μου την κατα θεον ἐπιθυμίαν κτλ.	Εἰ μεν βούλει, φησίν, κύριέ μου, ἀγνεύειν συν ἐμοὶ καὶ κατα τον τῆς σωφροσύνης συνοικισθῆναί μοι νόμον, καὶ κύριόν σε καὶ δεσπότην τῆς οἰκείας ζωῆς ἐπιγράφομαι· εἰ δε τοῦτό σοι ἐπαχθες καταφαίνεται καὶ οὐκ ἰσχύεις ἐνέγκαι την πύρωσιν τῆς νεότητος, ἰδοῦ πρόκεινταί σοι ἅπαντά μου τα ὑπάρχοντα, ὧν ἐντεῦθεν ἤδη δεσπότης γενόμενος χρήσει καθως βούλει· μόνον το σῶμά μου ἐλευθέρωσον, ἵνα τοῦτο σον τῇ ψυχῇ μου ἄσπιλον παραστήσω τῷ Χριστῷ κατα την ἡμέραν ἐκείνην την φοβεράν· οὕτω γαρ πληρο-

φορήσω την κατα θεόν
μου ἐπιθυμίαν.[58]

Rampolla's argument was challenged within one year
of the publication of *Santa Melania Guiniore* by Dom Cuthbert Butler, editor of the *Lausiac History*.[59] Butler admits that the Barberini text of the *Vita* represents a
paraphrase of the passage, but contends that it nonetheless "preserves a considerable element of Palladius's
actual phraseology."[60] He notes the following corres-
pondences in phraseology:

Palladius

Εἰ μεν αἱρῆσαι συνοικισ-
θῆναί μοι κατα τον τῆς
σωφροσύνης λόγον, και δεσ-
πότην σε οἶδα και κύριον
τῆς ἐμῆς ζωῆς ὁμολογήσω σε.

Και μόνον το σῶμά μου
ἐλευθέρωσον, ἵνα πληροφορήσω
μου την κατα θεον ἐπιθυμίαν.

Barberini Text

Εἰ μεν βούλει ... κατα τον
τῆς σωφροσύνης συνοικισθῆναί μοι
νόμον, και κύριόν σε και δεσ-
πότην τῆς οἰκείας ζωῆς ἐπι-
γράφομαι.

μόνον το σῶμά μου ἐλευθέρωσον ... οὕτω γαρ πληροφορήσω την
κατα θεόν μου ἐπιθμίαν.[61]

Butler concludes, "It is evident that a retranslation
of the Latin back into the Greek could not have repro-
duced in this way the words of Palladius." The *Vita*,
he asserts, was originally composed in Greek, but "the
Barberini MS contains a rewritten and somewhat para-
phrased text."[62] Again, Butler's case seems more
convincing than Rampolla's.

The most telling arguments for the probable priority
of the Greek, however, are based on an analysis of three
other passages, and Rampolla summons no compelling
counterarguments against them. The first example is
found in chapter 20, which describes the arrival in
North Africa of Melania, Pinian, and Albina, and the
advice given them by the "great bishops." In the Greek
version, the latter are described in the following

words: "λέγω δὴ ὁ μακάριος Αὐγυστῖνος καὶ ὁ τούτου
ἀδελφὸς ᾿Αλύπιος καὶ Αὐρήλιος ὁ Καρταγέννς."[63] An
illustrious group indeed: Augustine of Hippo, his
"brother" (presumably meaning his brother in the faith)
Alypius of Thagaste, the town where the family had
settled, and Aurelius of Carthage.

The Latin version, on the other hand, introduces
the name of an unknown person to the list, "Brother
Jovius"; for the Latin editor, the group of ecclesias-
tics includes "beatus Augustinus et Alypius, Iovius
frater et Aurelius carthaginensis."[64] Rampolla is
aware of the divergence between the Latin and Greek
texts but maintains the priority of the Latin, puzzling
over how τούτου and ᾿Ιόβιος could have been confused by
the Greek translator.[65] But an ingenious explanation
has been provided by d'Alès, who champions the priority
of the Greek text: the τούτου would have been translated into the Latin as HVIVS: a scribe misreading the
text deformed the HVIVS into IOVIVS (Jovius), thus
bringing into existence an otherwise unknown priest,
and aligning him with ecclesiastical giants such as
Augustine.[66] If d'Alès' hypothetical reconstruction of
events is correct -- and it seems entirely plausible --
we have a clue to the probability of the Greek as the
Vita's original language.

A second example, taken from chapter 26 of the *Vita*,
is equally illuminating. In the Greek version, the
entire chapter pertains to Melania's intellectual and
spiritual exercises: she reads and makes copies of
Scripture, performs the divine office, and reads treatises of the saints, managing Greek and Latin equally
well.[67] The Latin version describes similar activities
and expands the chapter with a few lines on her fasting
practices.[68] Most curious in the Latin version, however, is the discordant note contained in the sentence

detailing her study of Scripture: that with her own
hands, she made *calciamenta* (shoes) for the saints.   The
sentence reads: "Legebat autem novem et vetus testamen-
tum per annos singulos quater, scribens sufficienter,
et de manibus suis praebens calciamenta sanctis,
reddens etiam psalterium singulariter et regulam per-
ficiens cum sororibus suis."[69]   It may well be that
Melania worked with her hands (another document of the
time reports that she did woolwork),[70] but such information does not fit the context of the sentence.

The Greek version, by contrast, reads: "Ἀνεγίνωσ-
κεν δὲ ἡ μακαρία τὴν μὲν παλαιὰν καὶ καινὴν διαθήκην
τοῦ ἐνιαυτοῦ τρίτον ἢ τέταρτον, (καὶ) καλλιγραφοῦσα τὸ
αὔταρκες παρεῖχεν τοῖς ἁγίοις ἐκ τῶν ἰδίων χειρῶν ὑποδείγματα."[71]   Although Rampolla champions the priority
of the Latin,[72] the counterargument seems stronger:
that the Latin translator read ὑποδείγματα (copies) as
ὑποδήματα (shoes) and thus understood Melania to be
making footwear for the saints in the midst of her
Scripture reading.[73]   The priority of the Greek, we
think, here receives additional support.

Chapter 38 of the *Vita* contains an example of a
different sort.   The chapter describes how the desert
fathers and mothers were reluctant to accept Melania's
money, despite her determination to present them with
it, and concludes, "since many other anchorites and
very devout virgins did not want to take anything, the
blessed woman, through a spiritual ruse, left the gold
in their cells."   In Greek, the sentence begins with a
genitive absolute construction ("Καὶ ἄλλων δὲ πολλῶν
ἁγίων ἀναχωρητῶν καὶ σεμνοτάτων παρθένων μὴ βουληθέντων
λαβεῖν") and proceeds on to its subject, "ἡ μακαρία,"
at its end.[74]   There is no grammatical reason for the
Latin writer to begin his sentence with a genitive, yet
he does so, producing this awkward construction:

"Plurimorum autem monachorum et virginum accipere
nolentium hanc occultam offerebat oblationem: tanto
enim desiderio accendebatur, ut omnes quos viderat ex
eius datis acciperent."[75] The most probable explanation for this peculiar construction is that the Latin
translator simply borrowed the genitive clause from the
Greek, disregarding the fact that he produced a sentence that has been deemed "grammatically inex-
plicable."[76]

These last three examples lend weight to the
hypothesis that Greek was the original language of the
Vita. Although wary commentators agree that the final
word has not been pronounced on the issue and that new
manuscripts may be needed to solve the problem definitively,[77] Greek has, at present, the strongest claim
to be the original language. Other variations in the
two versions of the *Vita* and their possible significance
will be discussed in the pages below.

Given the major disagreement over the original language of the *Vita*, it is surprising to discover that
all modern commentators agree on the identity of the
anonymous author: Gerontius. The first hints regarding
authorship are supplied by the text itself: in both
Greek and Latin versions, the writer indicates that he
was the priest who spent many years at Melania's side.
Despite his professed unworthiness, he was favored by
the saint, whom he considers his spiritual mother.[78]

Early in the eighteenth century, Tillemont posited
that the *Vita* had been composed by a monk in Melania's
Jerusalem monastery.[79] The monk was identified as
Gerontius by de Smedt,[80] and outside sources have
corroborated his thesis. Cyril of Scythopolis, a
sixth-century writer of saints' *Lives*, reports that
Gerontius assumed the direction of Melania's monasteries for forty-five years after her death and died

during the reign of the emperor Zeno[81] (A.D. 474-491).
In Cyril's *Life of St. Euthymius*, Gerontius is described
as an ardent Monophysite. He was sent on an embassy
to convince the desert monk Euthymius that Chalcedonian
doctrine was heretical, but could not overcome Euthymius' impassioned attachment to Chalcedon. Although
the other delegate, Elpidius, was won to Euthymius'
side, Gerontius steadfastly held to his Monophysite
position[82] and remained a Monophysite to the end. He
was finally driven from his monastery for his heterodox
views, forced to wander in the desert, and died outside
the Catholic communion.[83] Gerontius' Monophysitism is
also noted in Cyril's *Life of St. Sabas*.[84]

John Rufus, bishop of Maiouma, provides further
information. In his *Plerophoria*, he reports that Gerontius was a deacon in Melania's monastery.[85] In a second
work now ascribed to him, the *Life of Peter the Iberian*,[86]
more is revealed about Gerontius. According to this
Life, its hero Peter was a Georgian prince who had been
taken as a hostage to the court of Theodosius II in
Constantinople when he was about twelve years old.[87]
Yearning to be monks, he and a friend escaped and made
their way to Jerusalem where they were aided by Melania
and Pinian.[88] In Jerusalem they received the monastic
habit from Gerontius, priest and abbot of the Mount of
Olives monastery.[89] The author adds that although
Gerontius originally came from Jerusalem, he had been
brought to Rome as a boy and raised by Melania and
Pinian for the holy life.[90] There he learned the distinctive practices of the Roman church (Peter's *Life*
reveals that on the Mount of Olives, Gerontius celebrated mass three times on Sundays and held private
masses for Melania daily, "as was the custom of the
Roman church").[91] John Rufus confirms Cyril of Scythopolis' report that Gerontius was an avid anti-Chalcedo-

nian. He broke with Juvenal, the bishop of Jerusalem, whom he considered a Judas-like "traitor" for assenting to the Chalcedonian formula.[92] Probably it is safe to infer that Gerontius was among those who worked to have Juvenal deposed as bishop of Jerusalem and replaced by the anti-Chalcedonian monk Theodosius, a partisan of Dioscorus of Alexandria. From Cyril's *Life of St. Euthymius* we learn that it was this heterodox bishop, Theodosius, who sent Gerontius on the embassy to convince Euthymius of Chalcedon's error.[93]

Rampolla makes much of the statement in the *Life of Peter the Iberian* that Gerontius was part of Melania and Pinian's household in Rome, for it bolsters his claim that the author of Melania's *Vita* was an eyewitness to nearly all the incidents reported in the account. Gerontius' years in Rome and North Africa would then explain (for Rampolla) his knowledge of Latin and of such details as the construction of San Lorenzo in Rome[94] and the ecclesiastical customs of the West.[95]

Rampolla's easy confidence in this aspect of the *Vita Petri Hiberii* has been questioned by both d'Alès and Gorce. As d'Alès correctly notes, of the early chapters of the *Vita Melaniae Junioris*, only in chapter 12, which describes Melania and Pinian's visit to Serena, does the author insert himself into the account (he speaks of "we," "us," "our").[96] Nowhere else in the sections of the *Vita* prior to the Jerusalem episodes does the author represent himself as a witness to the events described.[98] Moreover, in the earlier sections of the *Vita*, the author confesses that he is confused about the order of events.[99] Given these data, d'Alès concludes that it is doubtful Gerontius as a child lived with Melania and Pinian.[100] Gerontius' participation in the events described in chapter 12 can also be questioned, for the very fact that the Latin text

reports that Melania later ("postea") told the author
about the gifts she and Pinian took to Serena[101]
suggests that Gerontius was not himself present at the
occasion.[102]   Gorce offers this explanation for how the
first person plural references might have found their
way into chapter 12: the Greek original, no longer
extant, probably put the recitation of events into the
mouth of Melania, who would have used the first person
plural to describe the adventures she and Pinian
shared; in composing his biography, the author of the
Latin version forgot that he should switch to indirect
discourse.[103]

To these arguments against the presence of Gerontius
with Melania in Rome and North Africa we can add the
point that the author does not seem very well-informed
about Melania's earlier life. For example, while the
writer of the Greek version refrains from detailing the
activities of Melania's mother Albina ("her virtuous
life requires another person to write about it"),[104]
the Latin editor bluntly states that he will not write
about Albina because he "doesn't know" ("quia nec
novi").[105]   Such disclaimers of eyewitness information,[107] when coupled with a surprising thinness of
detail in some early sections of the *Vita*,[108] lead the
contemporary reader to assume that Gerontius was not
present at the episodes described.

To be sure, the partisans of a Latin original can
contend that it is not necessary to posit that Gerontius lived in Rome and North Africa as a youth in order
to theorize that the *Vita* was composed in Latin. As
Franz Diekamp argued decades ago, the *Life* itself provides evidence that Melania was fluent in both Greek
and Latin, and Gerontius' years of association with her
could have given him the linguistic competence to compose a *Life* in Latin.[109]   The probability remains, how-

ever, that if Gerontius was originally from Jerusalem,
Greek would have been his native tongue.[110]

The question of the *Vita*'s original language has
consequences for our suppositions about its recipient
and its dating. Although both versions of the *Life*
indicate in their prologues that the account is being
written for a churchman,[111] commentators have disagreed
on his identity. Rampolla, championing Latin as the
language of the original, posits that the *Vita* was composed for a Western, perhaps North African bishop, a
plausible hypothesis for him to hold given Melania's
seven-year sojourn in North Africa and her generous
donation of monasteries to the area.[112] Rampolla
believes that the *Vita* was composed between A.D. 440-
442, that is, within three years of Melania's death.[113]

The conclusions of those favoring a Greek original
of course differ. D'Alès posits that the Greek *Vita*
was composed within eleven years of Melania's death
(i.e., before the Council of Chalcedon in A.D. 451)
for an Eastern bishop of either Catholic or Eutychian
sentiment who was strongly anti-Nestorian: Dioscorus
of Alexandria is proposed as a candidate.[114] According
to d'Alès, in A.D. 452 or shortly thereafter, a Latin
translation was made that adds to the Greek version
several notices relating to the life of the Roman
Church,[115] perhaps a reference to the bishop of
Rome,[116] and (we think more dubiously) one to the
Council of Chalcedon.[117]

D'Alès' suggestion regarding recipient and dating
of the Greek *Vita* has three points in its favor: (1)
that there is no reference to the Council of Chalcedon
in the Greek text (and, we may add, the author had a
perfect opportunity to mention the council, had it
occurred and he wished to refer to it, for Melania on
her way to Constantinople stopped at the Church of St.

Euphemia where the council was held);[118] (2) that it is
not unlikely, given Gerontius' doctrinal sympathies,
that he composed the *Vita* for a Monophysite bishop; and
(3) that the bishop of Rome is nowhere mentioned in the
Greek *Vita*. His absence is striking, considering that
Melania was from Rome,[119] and is even more striking
when we recall that the bishop of Rome before the Council of Chalcedon was Leo the Great, whose letter had
been passed over by the Council of Ephesus in 449.[120]
Yet questions can be raised both about the recipient
(Dioscorus) and the dating of the *Vita* (pre-Chalcedon),
as hypothesized by d'Alès.

Although Dioscorus appears to be a suitable candi-
date, given Gerontius' Christological opinions, one
jarring note leads us to question d'Alès' hypothesis.
We know from other sources that Dioscorus behaved badly
toward the friends and relatives of his predecessor
Cyril of Alexandria after Cyril's death in A.D. 444.
A nephew of Cyril named Athanasius complained to the
Council of Chalcedon about Dioscorus' "persecution" of
Cyril's heirs and asked the council to intervene.[121]
In addition, an Alexandrian deacon named Theodore
brought charges against Dioscorus that he had expelled
or executed relatives and friends of Cyril.[122] Allowing for ecclesiastical hyperbole, we are still left
with evidence that Cyril was in disfavor with Dioscorus.
If Dioscorus were the recipient of the *Vita*, surely
Gerontius would not refer to Cyril as "the most holy
bishop" who greeted Melania, Pinian, and Albina on
their first visit to Alexandria in A.D. 417 "in a manner worthy of his holiness."[123]

Yet on the other hand, Cyril is conspicuously
absent from two scenes in which we might have expected
him to appear: in the passage depicting Melania and
Pinian's return trip to Egypt, where they visited with

holy men in Alexandria,[124] and in that depicting the
dedication of Melania's martyrion on Olivet[125] (according to the *Life of Peter the Iberian*, Cyril presided at the
deposition of the relics).[126] In neither instance is
Cyril named as present. It could be hypothesized that
Gerontius was suppressing evidence relating to Cyril
out of courtesy to the recipient of his work, Dioscorus,
if Gerontius had not already made much of Cyril's "holiness." As it stands, the evidence provides no clear
solution if we imagine Dioscorus to be the recipient of
the *Vita*.

Another detail of the text leads to an alternate
hypothesis. Nowhere in the *Vita* is Juvenal, the bishop
of Jerusalem from 422-458 (except from late 451-453),
named. The omission is striking, when we consider that
throughout the *Life*, Melania is represented as honoring
and being honored by bishops; the lack of recognition
given to Juvenal suggests that the author may have purposely relegated his name to silence. Even in the
scene depicting Melania's death, we are told only that
"the bishop dearest to God" attends her,[127] but the
person is not named, nor is he even said to be the
bishop of Jerusalem. When he comes to her a second
time, he arrives in the company of anchorites who are
said to live near Eleutheropolis,[128] and in Codex
Parisinus 1553, which contains Simeon the Metaphrast's
version of the *Vita Melaniae*, the person is explicitly
called "the chief priest of Eleutheropolis."[129] The
latter detail is not without interest, since Eleutheropolis was known at Gerontius' time as a refuge for
Monophysites.[130] Thus the bishop visiting Melania on
her deathbed was possibly not Juvenal of Jerusalem,
but a bishop of Eleutheropolis not identified in the
text, but known to Palestinian readers.

What would Gerontius' attitude toward Juvenal have

been? Up to October 451, the month that the Council of
Chalcedon met, he would have deemed Juvenal Christolog-
ically correct. After all, Juvenal was one of the
ringleaders at the Council of Ephesus in A.D. 449 [131]
(the famous "Robber Synod") who there passed over reading a letter from Bishop Leo of Rome into the council's
records.[132] Indeed, before the Council of Chalcedon,
Juvenal was known to have called Leo's Tome "Jewish,"[133] i.e., its Christology was too low for his
theological tastes. Yet under pressure of deposition
at Chalcedon[134] (or lured by an extension of his ecclesiastical jurisdiction if he would switch sides),[135]
Juvenal did an about-face and affixed his signature to
the Chalcedonian Creed,[136] a creed that weeks earlier
he would have considered Nestorian.

If we allow, with Ernest Honigmann, that the *Vita*
may have been composed in the immediate aftermath of
Chalcedon[137] rather than before, we have a cogent explanation for why Juvenal is never named in the text:
he is the subject of a *damnatio memoriae*.[138] The recipient
probably shared Gerontius' view of the matter. Again,
Dioscorus of Alexandria presents himself as a candidate
for consideration. Although Dioscorus was sent into
exile in Paphlagonia as a result of decisions made at
Chalcedon,[139] this fact would not have deterred Gerontius from considering him a "holy father," indeed a
martyr for the truth, and thus a worthy recipient for
his *Vita*. Yet the evidence presented above pertaining
to Dioscorus encourages us to look for a possible
recipient of Melania's *Vita* other than either Dioscorus
or his successor as bishop of Alexandria Proterius, for
he was a Chalcedonian.[140]

A more likely recipient of the *Vita* is the Monophysite Theodosius[141] who succeeded Juvenal when the
latter was ousted from his see by Palestinian monks and

clergy enraged by his change of position at Chalcedon.[142] That Theodosius not only knew Gerontius but
considered him his theological supporter is indicated
by the fact that it was Theodosius who sent Gerontius
on the abortive mission to convert Abba Euthymius from
Chalcedonianism to Monophysitism.[143] And although
Theodosius reigned only twenty months as bishop of
Jerusalem before imperial forces restored Juvenal to
the see,[144] this was a long enough period for him to
ordain several Monophysite bishops for Palestine, including Peter the Iberian.[145] Theodosius was supported
during his brief tenure as bishop of Jerusalem by the
empress Eudocia,[146] who was loath to accept Juvenal as
bishop for several years after his re-instatement.[147]
The absence of Juvenal's name from the text of the *Vita*
and the praise accorded Eudocia therein[148] take on
added significance if we imagine that the recipient of
the *Vita* might have been the Monophysite bishop of
Jerusalem, Theodosius.

We also would find a good explanation for why the
"holy father" who received the *Vita* requested Gerontius
to compose a *Life of Melania*:[149] assuming Jerusalem's
episcopal throne, Theodosius wished to know more about
one of the holy city's famous religious women who had
constructed two flourishing monasteries, a chapel, and
a martyrion on the Mount of Olives, and had been the
intimate friend of his supporter Gerontius. The request for the *Vita* could be said to bespeak an interest
in "local history." Moreover, the fact that the recipient of the *Vita* had "again" ("πάλιν") promised Gerontius to help him in his task through his "holy prayers"
suggests that he was someone known to the author who
had earlier requested Gerontius to compose a *Life of
Melania.*[150] The identity of the *Vita*'s recipient, however, is not definitely resolvable with the evidence

we currently possess, and Theodosius' candidacy, however attractive, is admittedly a conjecture.

Several features of the Latin version of the *Vita*,
on the other hand, suggest that its editor wished to
minimize aspects of Gerontius' account that would be
offensive to Westerners scandalized by the disrespect
paid to Bishop Leo of Rome at the Council of Ephesus
and, more generally, by the Monophysite dissension in
the East. The Latin editor appears ever eager to note
that Melania's religious practices were explicitly
Roman, a theme not contained in the Greek *Vita*. Thus
when he speaks of Melania's daily communion as the custom of the Roman church, he tells his audience that
the practice came down from the time of its originator,
"the most blessed of the apostles, Peter, who ruled as
bishop, and then from the blessed Paul," who preserved
the tradition.[151]

A second probable reference to the Roman see in
the Latin *Vita* occurs in Melania's speech to her nuns
on the necessity of obedience. The Latin editor adds
an illustration of obedience not found in the Greek
text, namely, that in the holy church of God, the bishops are "sub principe episcoporum," while the "princeps episcoporum" is himself "sub synodo."[152] In
d'Alès' opinion, the "princeps episcoporum" is the
Roman pontiff, a likely hypothesis, and the council is
Chalcedon[153] with which Leo was indeed in sympathy.

Moreover, the editor of the Latin text omits the
explicitly anti-Nestorian tenor of Melania's teaching
at the Constantinople court, which the Greek *Vita* reports as follows:

> Just then the Devil, through the polluted
> doctrine of Nestorius, threw the souls of
> simple people into great trouble. There-
> fore many wives of senators and some of

the men illustrious in learning came
to our holy mother in order to investigate the orthodox faith with her.
And she, who had the Holy Spirit indwelling, did not cease talking
theology from dawn to dusk. Many who
had been deceived she turned to the
orthodox faith, and sustained others
who doubted; quite simply, she benefited all those who chanced to come
to her divinely-inspired teaching.[154]

In the Latin *Vita*, on the other hand, Melania simply
exhorts the noble women[155] to "constancy of faith"
("constantia fidei"),[156] a phrase vague enough to en-
compass any doctrinal preference. Nor does the Latin
version mention, as does the Greek, that Melania also
"edified the most pious emperor Theodosius,"[157] who,
we may recall, later favored the decisions of the Council of Ephesus.[158]

Still another aspect of the Latin *Vita* may relate
to the doctrinal divisions plaguing the period. The
Latin *Life* includes a story unflattering to the empress
Eudocia, well-known as a Monophysite supporter: when
she attempts to woo some of Melania's nuns away from
their ascetic seclusion, Melania appears in visions to
threaten the nuns and warn Eudocia, with the result
that Eudocia sends word for the women to return to
their monastery.[159] Eudocia is here presented as in-
sensitive to the need for the cloistering of nuns, a
necessity (it is implied) that any truly devout person
would have understood without being chastized by
Melania in a vision. The omission of this story from
the Greek *Vita* may well indicate that its recipient
shared Eudocia's religious views and would not be
pleased to hear a story critical of her.

Such additions and subtractions in the Latin text
suggest that its editor wished to remove Melania from
any association with Monophysite tendencies and to max-
imize her Romaninity, presenting her as a model of
orthodoxy suitable for emulation by Westerners. The
Latin editor both "corrected" passages in the Greek
original that might be understood to align Melania
with the later Monophysites and highlighted her funda-
mental Romaninity, despite her years spent in the East.

On such a reading of the *Vita Melaniae Junioris*, we
thus hypothesize that the text's original language was
Greek, that its author was Gerontius, that its recipient was an opponent of Juvenal of Jerusalem, possibly
his Monophysite successor Theodosius, and (if so) that
the dating of the *Vita* might be assigned to A.D. 452 or
453, when Theodosius was bishop of Jerusalem.

II. TRANSLATION: THE LIFE OF MELANIA

Bless me, father.[1]

Prologue

God be blessed, who has aroused your honored
Reverence, holy priest, to seek an account from my lowly self concerning the life of our holy mother, Melania
the Roman, who has her home with the angels. Since I
spent not a little time with her, I know in an indis-
tinct way the story of her senatorial family, and how
she entered upon the angelic life, putting under foot
all the pride of worldly glory. But since I am keenly
aware of my own lack of skill, I deemed myself inadequate to the narration of these great contests. I
decided, rather, that it was less dangerous for me to
refuse, imagining that I could better extol the noble
servant of God through my silence than insult her
splendid feats through my own unskilled speech. But
since you once again, holy priest, have promised to
suffer with us through your holy prayers, I took heart
in the power of the Spirit. I prepared to cast myself
into the boundless sea of recitation, seeing clearly
the heavenly reward from my obedience. It is not so
amazing if I, an amateur author and slow of speech,
lose heart at the undertaking of such a task, for by my
reckoning not even the philosophers themselves have
ventured too far on so great an assignment, so it seems.
For who would be able to recount in a clear and worthy
manner the manly deeds of this blessed woman? I mean
of course her utter renunciation of worldly things, her

25

ardor for the orthodox faith (an ardor hotter than
fire), her unsurpassable beneficence, her intense
vigils, her persistence in lying on the ground, her
ill-treatment and ceaseless ascetic discipline of her
soul as well as of her body, her gentleness and temper-
ance that vie with the incorporeal powers, the cheapness
of her clothing, and even more than these, her humility,
the mother of all good things. Each one of this
woman's virtues steers us to a boundless sea of thoughts
and the composition of an entire book, a task which
surpasses our ability by far. Since, then, I have my
doubts about the interminable length of the narrative,
I shall try to become like fishermen. They know that
they will be unable to catch all the fish, yet for all
that they do not abandon their undertaking; rather,
each one according to his own ability carries home
whatever luck affords. Or again, I shall try to become
like those who enter a garden, where they experience
every kind of fragrance and pungent flower: even if
they are not able to pick flowers from the entire meadow, they nonetheless leave only when they have selected
a sufficient number. So using this comparison as well,
and strengthened by the prayers of Your Holiness, I
shall approach the spiritual meadow of our holy mother
Melania's deeds, and gathering there what can be
readily plucked, I shall offer those flowers to the ones
who are fond of hearing recitations that inflame their
virtue and to those who wishing the greatest benefit,
offer their souls to God, the savior of us all.

     Then with which of her great combats shall I be-
gin? Or with what songs of praise shall I repay the
woman who has praise in the heavens, since I am an amateur writer, of slow speech, as I have already said?
What shall I offer to the one who has labored so hard

over the hope of my salvation, except merely to call
upon her holy prayers for assistance? For these
prayers contributed to my salvation while she lived in
the flesh, and I appeal to them also after her death,
so that I may recall her holy instructions and cast off
all sluggishness, forgetfulness, sleepiness, irresolu-
tion, and lack of faith. I can thus recount in part
her most magnificent virtuous acts that she, according
to the manner of the Gospel, was eager to hide.[2] Yet
since it is the voice of the Lord himself that says,
"Thus what you have heard with the ear shall be broad-
cast from the housetops,"[3] for this reason the saints'
virtues cannot be hidden. Even if those who perform
good deeds would prefer to hide them all, God, on the
other hand, who strives for everyone's salvation and
edification, reveals their greatest virtuous deeds, not
only for the profit of those who hear them, as we have
already mentioned, but also for the glory of those who
for his sake have contested up to the very point of
death. Thus I write a few of the numerous things that
I have seen with my own eyes as well as those about
which I have been carefully instructed by others. I
shall leave the rest for you, with your zeal for
learning, to discover, just as is written, "Give an opportunity to a wise man and he will increase his
wisdom."[4]

1.   This blessed Melania, then, was foremost among the
Romans of senatorial rank. Wounded by the divine love,
she had from her earliest youth yearned for Christ, had
longed for bodily chastity. Her parents, because they
were illustrious members of the Roman Senate and expected that through her they would have a succession of
the family line, very forcibly united her in marriage

with her blessed husband Pinian, who was from a consular family, when she was fourteen years old and her spouse was about seventeen. After she had had the experience of marriage and totally despised the world, she begged her husband with much piteous wailing, uttering these words: "If, my lord, you consent to practice chastity along with me and live with me according to the law of continence, I contract with you as the lord and master of my life. If, however, this seems burdensome to you, and if you do not have the strength to bear the burning passion of youth, just look: I place before you all my possessions; hereafter you are master of them and may use them as you wish, if only you will leave my body free so that I may present it spotless, with my soul, to Christ on that fearsome day. For it is in this way that I shall fulfill my desire for God."

At first, however, he neither accepted her proposal nor did he, on the other hand, completely rule out her plan. Rather, he replied to her in these words: "If and when by the ordinance of God we have two children to inherit our possessions, then both us together shall renounce the world." Indeed, by the will of the Almighty, a daughter was born to them, whom they promptly dedicated to God for the virginal estate.

2.   But Melania's heart burned even more strongly with the divine fire. If, as was the custom, she sometimes was sent to the baths by her parents, she went even though she did not want to. When she entered the hot air room, in order to show her obedience, she washed her eyes with warm water, and wiping them with her clothes, she bribed with gifts those who accompanied her so that they would not tell anybody what she had

done. Thus the blessed woman constantly had the fear
of God before her eyes.

3.   The young man, however, was still desirous of
worldly glory. Although she frequently asked him to
keep bodily chastity, he would not agree, saying that
he wanted to have another child.

4.   Therefore the saint kept trying to flee and to
leave him all her possessions. When this matter was
brought to the attention of the holy men, they advised
her to wait a short while longer, so that through her
patience she might fulfill the apostolic saying, "Wife,
how do you know if you will save your husband?"[5] Under
her silken clothing she began to wear a coarse woolen
garment. Her aunt noticed this and pleaded with her
not to be so rash as to clothe herself in such a garment. Melania, however, was exceedingly distressed
that she had not escaped notice and begged her not to
reveal to her parents what she had done.

5.   Later on, when the prayers of the saint had taken
effect and she was about to give birth to her second
child, the feast of Saint Lawrence arrived. Without
taking any rest and having spent the whole night kneel-
ing in her chapel, keeping vigil,[6] at dawn the next day
she rose early and went with her mother to the Church
of the martyr. With many tears she prayed to God that
she might be freed from the world and spend the rest of
her days in the solitary life, for this is what she had
yearned for from the beginning. And when she returned
from the martyr's shrine, she commenced a difficult
labor and gave birth prematurely to a child. It was a
boy, and after he was baptized, he departed for the Lord.

6.   After this, when her blessed husband saw that she
was exceedingly troubled and was giving up on life, he
lost courage and was himself endangered.[7] Running to
the altar, he cried aloud with tears to the Lord for her
life. And while he was sitting next to the altar, the
saint declared to him: "If you want me to continue
living, give your word before God that we will spend
the rest of our lives in chastity, and then you will
see the power of Christ." And since he was very fear-
ful that he might never see her again alive in the
flesh, he promised this joyfully. Because of grace
from on high and the young man's promise, she was
cheered; she got better and completely regained her
health. She took the occasion of her child's death to
renounce all her silk clothing.

At this time, their daughter who was devoted to
virginity also died. Then both Melania and Pinian hastened to fulfill their promises to God. They would not
consent to their parents' desires, and were so unhappy
that they refused to eat unless their parents would
agree with them and consent to release them so that
they could abandon their frivolous and worldly mode of
life and experience an angelic, heavenly purpose.

But their parents, whom we mentioned before, were
wary of peoples' reproaches and would not agree to
their children's wishes. Melania and Pinian suffered
much pain since they were unable to take up the yoke of
Christ freely because of their parents' compulsion.
They planned with each other to go into seclusion and
flee the city. As the blessed woman told us for our
edification, while they were plotting these things, as
evening was coming on, immediately and suddenly a heavenly perfume descended on them and changed the sadness
of their grief to inexpressible joy. Thanking God,

they were emboldened against the schemes of the Enemy.[8]

7. After the passage of some time, her father's last
illness finally came upon him. As he loved Christ
greatly, he called the blessed ones and said, "Forgive
me, my children. I have fallen into a great sin because of my enormous folly. Because I feared the
abuses of blasphemous men, I have pained you, by
keeping you from your heavenly calling. But now see
that I am going to the Lord, and from now on you have
the power to gratify your desire for God as you please.
May you only intercede on my behalf with God, the ruler
of all." They heard these words with much joy. Right
away they felt free from fear; they left the great city
of Rome and went to her suburban property where they
devoted themselves to training in the practice of the
virtues. They clearly recognized that it was impossible for them to offer pure worship to God unless they
made themselves enemies to the confusions of secular
life, just as it is written, "Hear, daughter, and see;
turn your ear and forget your people and your father's
house, and the king will desire your beauty."[9]

8. When they began the angelic way of life, the
blessed Melania was twenty years old and Pinian, who
was henceforth her brother in the Lord, was twenty-four
years old. Although at the time they were not able to
practice rigorous asceticism because of their pampered
youth, they clothed themselves in cheap garb. Thus the
blessed woman wore a garment that was exeedingly cheap
in value and very old, trying in this way to extinguish
the beauty of youth. As for Pinian, he then once and
for all rejected the magnificent clothes and luxury of
his recent life, and garbed himself in Cilician

clothes.[10] The blessed woman was immeasurably saddened
to see that he had not yet completely scorned the em-
bellishments of dress. She feared to censure him
openly, however, because he was yet unproven in years
and experienced the ardor of youth; she saw that he
was still vigorous in body. She therefore changed her
approach with him and said to him, "From the time when
we began to carry out our promise to God, has your
heart not been receptive to the thought of desiring
me?" And the blessed man, who knew well the rectitude
of his thoughts, affirmed in the Lord's presence,
"From the time when we gave our word to God and entered
the chaste life, I have looked on you in the same way
as your holy mother Albina." Melania then exhorted
him, saying, "Then be persuaded by me as your spiritual
mother and sister, and give up the Cilician clothes; it
is not fitting for a man who has left behing worldly
frivolities for the sake of God to wear such things."
And he saw that her exhortation was for his own good.
Straightway he obeyed her excellent advice, judging
this to be advantageous for the salvation of them both.
And changing his Cilician garments, he clothed himself
in those of the Antiochene style that were natural-
colored and were worth one coin.

9.   Thus by God's grace having successfully accomplished this virtue, they turned anew to another one.
Together they wisely considered the matter and said,
"If we take upon ourselves an ascetic discipline that
is beyond our strength, we will not be able to bear it
because of the softness of our way of life. Our body
will not be able to bear it, will weaken completely,
and later we will be likely to surrender ourselves to
sensuality." For this reason they chose this righteous

practice for themselves. They went around to simply
all who were sick, visiting them in order to attend to
them. They lodged strangers who were passing through,
and cheering them with abundant supplies for their
journey, sent them on their way. They lavishly assisted all the poor and needy. They went about to all
the prisons, places of exile, and mines, setting free
those who were held because of debt and providing them
with money. Like Job, the blessed servant of the Lord,
their door stood open to any of the helpless.[11] Henceforth they began to sell their goods, remembering the
saying of the Lord that he uttered to the rich man:
"If you would be perfect, sell your goods and give them
to the poor, and you will have treasure in heaven.
Take your cross and follow me."[12]

10. While they were planning these things, the Devil,
the enemy of truth, subjected them to an enormous test.
Since he was jealous at the great zeal these young people showed for God, he prompted Severus, the brother of
the blessed Pinian, and he persuaded their slaves to
say, "We realize we haven't been sold yet, but if we
are forced to be sold, rather than be put on the open
market, we prefer to have your brother Severus as our
master and have him buy us." Melania and Pinian were
very upset by this turn of events, at seeing their
slaves in the suburbs of Rome rising in rebellion.,...

11. The devout empress Serena understood clearly about
the lustre of the blessed Melania's present life.
Since she had heard of her great deeds of virtue and of
her transformation from worldly frivolity to piety, she
very much desired to see her, having in mind the verse
from Psalms that goes, "Here is the change of the right

hand of the Most High."[13] But Melania, completely
scorning worldly glory, had refused to visit Serena.

   Afterwards, when their slaves in the suburbs revolted, Melania said to her blessed husband, "Perhaps
the occasion calls us to see the empress. For if our
slaves who are nearby have rebelled against us in this
way, what do you think those outside the cities will to
us--I mean those in Spain, Campania, Sicily, Africa,
Mauretania, Britain, and the other lands?" Thus because of this problem they were eager to pay a visit to
the most holy empress, a visit that took place with the
holy bishops intervening on their behalf.

   And since we deem it very beneficial to relate
some few things pertaining to their visit, things that
Melania told us many times for our edification, I shall
write them with utter truthfulness for the benefit of
those who read them. According to Melania, when many
people said that she ought to uncover her head during
the visit, according to the custom of those Romans of
senatorial rank, she affirmed with noble resolution
that she would not change her garments, for it is written, "I have put on my clothes. How shall I take them
off?"[14] Nor would she uncover her head, because of the
apostolic saying, "A woman should not pray with uncovered head."[15] She said, "No, even if I am likely to
lose all my goods, for it is preferable to me not to
neglect one jot of Scripture, nor to violate my con-
science before God, than to gain the whole world." For
those clothes were garments of her salvation, and all
her life was considered to be a prayer. Thus she would
not uncover her head even for a short while, lest she
grieve the angels who were with her.[14]

   They took with them precious ornaments of great
value and crystal vases as gifts for the pious empress,

and other ornaments, such as rings, silver, and silken
garments to give to the faithful eunuchs and court
officers. Melania presented herself at the palace, and
when they had been announced, they were summoned to
enter.

12. Straightway the devout empress went to meet them
at the entrance to the porch with great joy. She was
greatly moved when she saw the blessed woman in that
humble garment, and having welcomed her, she had her
sit on her golden throne. Serena called together all
the servants of her palace and began to speak to them
in this manner: "Come, see the woman who four years
ago we beheld vigorous in all her worldly rank, who has
now grown old in heavenly wisdom. Let us learn from
her that pious judgment conquers all the pleasures of
the body. Behold, she has trod underfoot the softness
of her upbringing, the massiveness of her wealth, the
pride of her worth, and, quite simply, all the delight-
ful things of this life. She does not fear weakness of
the flesh nor voluntary poverty, nor any other things
of this sort at which we shudder. She has rather even
bridled nature itself and delivered herself to death
daily, demonstrating to everyone by her very deeds that
before God, woman is not surpassed by man in anything
that pertains to virtue, if her decision is strong."
        Truly, the servant of the Lord did not become
arrogant at hearing these praises. Rather, the more
the empress praised her, the more she humbled herself,
fulfilling that prophetic saying, "All the glory of man
is like the flower of the field."[17] The empress em-
braced her and kissed her eyes, reciting once more to
those present how much Melania and Pinian had suffered
in their renunciation, and how they had been persecuted

by their father, who had completely prevented them from
associating with the saints and from hearing the word
of salvation concerning God's way. For the Devil had
led her father to such an extent (as we said above)
that he, a man of such virtue, had committed a great
sin under the pretext of good. It was suspected that
he wanted to take their possessions and give them to
the other children, because he was eager to hinder them
from their heavenly project, as we related earlier.
The empress again remarked how both of them were
blessed, how much trouble they had endured through the
machinations of Severus, lord Pinian's brother, who
wanted to take all their goods for himself, their numerous and great possessions, and how every one of
their senatorial relatives had schemed for their goods,
wanting to make themselves richer from them. And
Serena said to them, "Do you wish me to make Severus
submit to justice, and when he is chastened, he will
learn no longer to take advantage of those who conse-
crate their souls to God?"

     But the saints answered the empress in this way:
"Christ commanded us to be wronged and not to do
wrong; to be struck on the right cheek and turn the
other one; to be pressed into service for one mile and
go two; and to the person who takes our tunic, to give
our cloak as well.[18] It is thus unfitting for us to
repay wrong with wrong, and this also when those who
try to take advantage of us happen to be our relatives.
We trust in Christ that with his support and with the
patronage of you, our pious empress, even our modest
possessions will be rightly spent."

     When the empress heard these things, she was much
edified and straightway informed her truly pious, devout
brother, the very blessed emperor Honorius, who issued

a decree in every province that their possessions
should be sold by the agency of the governors and min-
isters, and that by their enterprise, the money
deriving from them should be remitted to Melania and
Pinian. The Christ-loving emperor thus did this,
eagerly and with every joy, so that orders were given
to the executors while Melania and Pinian were sitting
there.

13. Amazed at such liberality in the holy emperor and
empress, Melania and Pinian glorified God, the highest
Savior. They brought out the ornaments along with the
crystal vases and offered them to their Pieties,
saying, "Accept from us small blessings, just as the
Lord received the widow's two coins."[19] Serena,
smiling kindly at this speech, answered them in this
fashion: "May the Lord persuade Your Saintliness that
I judge the man taking any of your possessions, except
for the saints and the poor, to be sacrilegious. The
person who does this heaps the eternal fire on himself,
because he takes what has been consecrated to God."
The empress then ordered the *prepositus*[20] and two other
illustrious eunuchs to accompany them home with every
honor, having made the former swear by the welfare of
her most blessed brother that neither they nor anyone
else from the palace would consent to take even one
coin from them. And the Christ-loving servants of the
Christ-loving rulers carried out the orders with every
joy and eagerness.

14. The saints departed with great happiness, as they
had gained a spiritual benefit. They had as a pledge
the Lord's saying, "Well done, good servant, you were
faithful over small things, so I will set you over great

ones. Enter into the joy of your master."[21] They
looked forward to scattering on the earth whatever they
believed would store up unsullied treasure in heaven.
They went back to their own place of lodging and considered what sort of thanks they might render the
empress who had done so much for them. Since none of
the senators in Rome had the means to buy the house of
the blessed Pinian, they let the empress, of whom we
have spoken, know through the holy bishops that she
might buy it. She did not want to do this however, and
said to the intermediaries, "I do not think I have the
means to buy the house at its true value." They requested that she at least accept some of the precious
statues from the saints as a token of friendship. Serena
reluctantly acquiesced, for she did not wish to grieve
them any further. The saints were not able to sell the
house, and after the barbarian invasion they let it go
for less than nothing since it was burned.

15. I shall report on their property by just skimming
the surface of things I heard from the mouth of the
blessed Pinian. He said that he had as an annual income 120,000 pieces of gold, more or less, not counting
that derived from his wife's property. Their movable
goods were such that they were too many to be counted.
Immediately they began, with zeal, to distribute these,
entrusting to the holy men the administration of alms.
They sent money to different regions, through one man
40,000 coins, through another 30,000, by another 20,000,
through another 10,000, and the rest they distributed
as the Lord helped them do.

The saint herself said to her blessed husband and
brother, "The burden of life is very heavy for us, and
we are not competent in these circumstances to take on

the light yoke of Christ. Therefore let us quickly
lay aside our goods, so that we may gain Christ."
Pinian received the admonition of the blessed woman as
of it came from God, and with generous hands they distributed their goods.

16. Once, when we strongly urged her to tell how they
could come from such great heights to such lowliness,
Melania began by saying, "Not few were the problems and
struggles we endured in the beginning from the Enemy
who is hostile to good, until we could divest ourselves
of the burden of so much wealth. We were vexed and distressed because our battle was not against flesh and
blood, but, as the apostle says, against the principali-
ties, against the world rulers of this realm of
darkness."[22]
    "One night we went to sleep, greatly upset and we
saw ourselves, both of us, passing through a very narrow place in a wall. We were totally discomposed in
the narrowness, so that all that remained was to give
up our souls. When we came through that pain with
great suffering," she said, "we found abundant great
relief and ineffable joy. God manifested this to us,
comforting our faintness of spirit, so that we might be
brave concerning the future repose that we would
receive after such suffering."

17. "And then again," the highborn and magnanimous
servant of Christ said, "one day we had collected a
massive, extraordinary amount of gold to send for the
service of the poor and the saints: 45,000 pieces of
gold. When I went into the triclinium, it seemed, by
the operation of the Devil, as if I were lighting up
the house with fire from the multitude of gold pieces.

In my thoughts, the Enemy said to me, 'What sort of
place is this Kingdom of Heaven, that it can be bought
with so much money?'" Melania said, "As I was upset,
fighting against the Devil, I immediately ran, sober-
minded, for the invincible assistance. Falling on my
knees, I prayed to God that he drive the Adversary away
from me. After the prayer I was strengthened and said
in my mind, 'With these corruptible things are purchased
those others, about which the Holy Scripture says,
"Things which eye has not seen, nor ear heard, nor has
entered into the heart of man, are what God has prepared for those who love him."'"[23]

18. Melania said that the same thing occurred a second
time. She taught us about the various strategems of
the Devil, that it is necessary for those souls who wish
to please the Lord always to be vigilant and never to
be totally relaxed. She said, "We had an extraordinary
piece of property, and on it was a bath that surpassed
any worldly splendor. On one side of it was the sea,
and on the other, a forest with diverse vegetation in
which wild boar, deer, gazelles, and other animals used
to graze. From the pool, the bathers could see boats
sailing on one side and the animals in the wood on the
other. Therefore the Devil found in this another op-
portune pretext. He set before me," she said, "the
variety of statues there and the inestimable income
that derived from the estate itself." For there were
sixty-two households around the bath.[24]
     The blessed woman again lifted up her eyes to God
in pious meditation and repelled the Enemy by saying,
"O Devil! You will not thwart my journey in this way!
For, to put it briefly, how can these things that today
exist and tomorrow will be destroyed by the barbarians,

or by fire, or by time, or by some other circumstance,
that which is bought by means of these corruptible
things, be compared to eternal goods that exist forever
and will remain through infinite ages?" The Devil then
realized that he could not overcome her, but that he
himself was rather being defeated and that he was providing her with even more abundant crowns. Disgraced,
he no longer dared to trouble her.

19. Furthermore, they fearlessly gave away the remainder of their possessions in Rome, as we have said
before--possessions that were, so to speak, enough for
the whole world. For what city or country did not have
a share in their enormously good deeds? If we say
Mesopotamia and the rest of Syria, all of Palestine,
the regions of Egypt and the Pentapolis, would we say
enough? But lest we continue on too long, all the West
and all the East shared in their numerous good deeds.
I myself, of course, when I traveled the road to Constantinople, heard many old men, especially lord
Tigrius, the priest of Constantinople, give thanks to
the holy ones. When they acquired several islands, they
gave them to holy men. Likewise, they purchased monasteries of monks and virgins and gave them as a gift to
those who lived there, furnishing each place with a
sufficient amount of gold. They presented their
numerous and expensive silk clothes at the altars of
churches and monasteries. They broke up their silver,
of which they had a great deal, and made altars and
ecclesiastical treasures from it, and many other
offerings to God.

When they had sold their properties around Rome,
Italy, Spain, and Campania, they set sail for Africa.
Just then Alaric set foot on the property the blessed

ones had just sold. Everybody praised the Lord of all
things, saying, "Lucky are the ones who anticipated
what was to come and sold their possessions before the
arrival of the barbarians!" And when they left Rome,
the prefect of the city, who was a very ardent pagan,
decided along with the entire Senate to have their property confiscated to the public treasury. He was eager
to have this accomplished by the next morning. By
God's providence, it happened that the people rebelled
against him because of a bread shortage. Consequently
he was dragged off and killed in the middle of the city.
All the others were then afraid and held their peace.

They set sail from Sicily to the most holy bishop
Paulinus, to whom even at the beginning they also bade
farewell. By the dispensation of God, adverse winds
prevented their ship from sailing; a great and sudden
storm came upon them. Since there were many people on
the boat, a water shortage developed, and for a brief
while they were all in danger. When the sailors claimed
that this had come about by the wrath of God, the
blessed woman said to them, "It is certainly not God's
will for us to go to the place we had intended. Therefore give the boat over to what carries it and do not
struggle against the winds." They took the saint's advice, stretched the sail, and came to a certain island
that the barbarians had blockaded after having carried
off the most important men of the city with their wives
and children. The barbarians had demanded from them a
certain sum of gold which, if they gave it, they would
be freed, but if they did not, they themselves would be
murdered and the city would be burned by the barbarians.
As the saints were disembarking from the ship, the
bishop heard of their arrival. He came to them with
others, fell on his knees, and said, "We have as much

gold as the barbarians want except for 2500 coins."
Melania and Pinian willingly presented them with this
amount, freeing the whole city from the barbarians.
They also gave them an extra 500 coins, and the bread
and other provisions they were carrying with them, thus
rescuing the suffering people from both famine and distress. And not only did they do this; they provided 500
coins to ransom one distinguished woman in their midst
who had been captured by the barbarians.

20. Then they departed from the island and sailed
toward Africa, as we mentioned before. When they arrived there, they immediately sold their property in
Numidia, Mauretania, and in Africa itself.[25] Some of
the money they sent for the service of the poor and some
for ransoming captives. Thus they distributed the money
freely and rejoiced in the Lord and were gladdened, for
they were fulfilling in action what had been written,
"He has given funds; he gave to the poor; his righteousness remains from age to age."[26]

When the blessed ones decided to sell all their
property, the most saintly and important bishops of
Africa (I mean the blessed Augustine, his brother
Alypius, and Aurelius of Carthage) advised them, saying,
"The money that you now furnish to monasteries will be
used up in a short time. If you wish to have memorial
forever in heaven and on earth, give both a house and
an income to each monastery." Melania and Pinian eagerly accepted the excellent counsel of the holy men and
did just as they had been advised by them. Henceforth,
advancing toward perfection, they tried to accustom
themselves to complete poverty in their living arrangements and in the food they ate.

21.   The town of the very blessed bishop Alypius, named
Thagaste, was small and exceedingly poor.   The blessed
ones chose this as their place to live,[27] especially because this aforesaid holy man Alypius was present, for
he was most skilled in the interpretation of the Holy
Scriptures.   Our blessed mother held him dear, for she
was a friend of learning.   Indeed, she herself was so
trained in Scriptural interpretation that the Bible
never left her holy hands.   She adorned the church of
this holy man with revenue as well as offerings of both
gold and silver treasures, and valuable veils, so that
this church which formerly had been so very poor now
stirred up envy of Alypius on the part of the other
bishops in that province.

22.   They also constructed two large monasteries there,
providing them with an independent income.   One was inhabited by eighty holy men, and the other by 130 virgins.   The holy woman made progress in the virtues.   She
saw herself become a little lighter from the burden of
possessions.   Fulfilling the work of Martha, she began
henceforth to imitate Mary, who was extolled in the
Gospel as having chosen the good part.[28]   Indeed, in the
beginning, Melania would just taste a little oil and
take a bit of something to drink in the evening (she
had never used wine during her worldly life, because the
children of the Roman senatorial class were raised in
this way).   Then after that she began to mortify her
body with strenuous fasting.   At first she took food
without oil every two days, then every three days, and
then every five, so that it was only on Saturday and
Sunday that she ate some moldy bread.   She was zealous
to surpass everyone in asceticism.

23. She was by nature gifted as a writer and wrote
without mistakes in notebooks. She decided for herself
how much she ought to write every day, and how much she
should read in the canonical books, how much in the col-
lections of homilies. And after she was satisfied with
this activity, she would go through the *Lives* of the
fathers as if she were eating dessert. Then she slept
for a period of about two hours. Straightway after
having gotten up, she roused the virgins who were
leading the ascetic life with her, and said, "Just as
the blessed Abel and each of the holy ones offered
first-fruits to God, so we as well in this way should
spend the first-fruits of the night for God's glory. We
ought to keep awake and pray at every hour, for, just
as it is written, we do not know at what hour the thief
comes."[29] She gave strict rules to the sisters with
her that no idle word or reckless laughter should come
forth from their mouths. She also patiently inquired
about their thoughts and refused to allow filthy imagi-
nations to dwell in them in any way.

24. As we said earlier, she fasted from the week of
holy Pentecost until Easter, not taking oil at all.
Many who knew her well testified that she never slept
outside her sackcloth nor ate on Saturday before she
finished the entire divine office.

25. After she had lived in this ascetic routine for
many years, Melania began to fast on the holy day of
Christ's resurrection as well. Her blessed mother, who
imitated the holy women of old (her virtuous life requires another person to write about it), was greatly
grieved. It is enough for me to say this about Albina,
that from the fruit the tree is known, and a glorious

fruit comes from a good root. Albina used to make such
comments as these to Melania: "It is not right for a
Christian to fast on the day of our Lord Jesus Christ's
resurrection; rather, we should refresh our body just
as we also refresh our spirit." By saying these things,
she scarcely persuaded her blessed daughter to take oil
for the three days of the holiday and then return once
more to her usual ascetic discipline, just as the excellent farmer who owns a fertile field hastens to his own
happy task.

26. The blessed woman read the Old and New Testaments
three or four times a year. She copied them herself
and furnished copies to the saints by her own hands.
She performed the divine office in company with the
virgins with her, reciting by heart on her own the remaining Psalms. So eagerly did she read the treatises
of the saints that whatever book she could locate did
not escape her. To the contrary, she read through the
books that were bought, as well as those she chanced
upon, with such diligence that no word or thought remained unknown to her. So overwhelming was her love of
learning that when she read in Latin, it seemed to
everyone that she did not know Greek, and, on the other
hand, when she read in Greek, it was thought that she
did not know Latin.

27. She showed an inexpressible sweetness to those who
trained themselves in philosophy.[30] She had such zeal
for the name of our Lord Jesus Christ and the orthodox
faith that if she heard that someone was a heretic, even
in name, and advised him to make a change for the better, he was persuaded....But if he was not persuaded,
she would in no way accept anything from him to give for
the service of the poor.

28. Thus there was a certain woman of high status who ended her life in a foreign country, at the Holy Places. I mentioned her name in the holy eucharistic offering along with those of saints now dead, for it is our custom to do this, so that in that fearsome hour they may intercede on our behalf. Since that woman in communion with us was said by some of the orthodox to be a heretic, the blessed Melania was so disturbed that she said this to me very directly and on the spot: "As the Lord lives, if you name her, I will no longer be in communion with you at the eucharist." When I gave my word at the holy altar that I would not mention her again, she said, "This once was too much. Since you have named her, I am not communing." Thus she believed it was a transgression against the orthodox faith to name heretics during the holy eucharist.

29. Melania yearned so exeedingly for chastity that by money and admonitions she persuaded many young men and women to stay clear of licentiousness and an impure manner of life. Those whom she encountered, she taught with these words: "The present life is brief, like a dream in every way. Why then do we corrupt our bodies that are temples of the Lord, as the apostle of God states?[31] Why do we exchange the purity in which Christ teaches us to live for momentary corruption and filthy pleasures? Truly, the value of virginity is so great that our Lord Jesus Christ deemed it worthy to be born of a virgin." Many who heard these things were zealous for purity and leaped into the arena of virtue. Only the Lord himself knows how many saints' feet she washed, how many servants of God she served, some through money and some through the exhortation of the word, how many Samaritans, pagans, and heretics she persuaded through

money and exhortations to come back to God! Through
him she accomplished such great and numerous feats.

30. It was as if she hoped that by the virtuous practice of almsgiving alone she might obtain mercy; as the
Lord said, "Blessed are the merciful, for they shall
obtain mercy."[32] Her love for poverty exceeded everyone else's. As she testified to us shortly before her
departure for the Lord, she owned nothing at all on
earth except for about fifty coins of gold for the offering and even this she sent to a certain very holy
bishop, saying, "I do not wish to possess even this much
from our patrimony." Not only did she offer to God that
which was her own; she also helped others to do the
same. Thus many of those who loved Christ furnished
her with their money, since she was a faithful and wise
steward. She commanded these monies to be distributed
honestly and judiciously according to the request of the
donor.

31. Melania made for herself a garment, a veil, and a
hood of haircloth, and did not abandon these clothes
from the time of holy Pentecost until the fifth day of
the festival of holy Easter, not by day or by night.
Such was her burning love for God, even though she had
been delicately raised as a member of such an important
senatorial family. Those who knew well how she had been
reared as a child said that when she still was wearing
worldly clothes, it once happened that the embroidery of
the expensive dress she was wearing touched her skin
and an inflammation developed from it, because of her
extreme delicacy. But the Lord who says, "Ask and it
shall be given to you, seek and you shall find it,
knock and it shall be opened unto you,"[33] gave her the
strength from on high for which she asked.

32. Since she had been wounded by the divine love, she
could not bear to live the same life any longer, but
prepared herself to contend in even greater contests.
She decided to shut herself up in a tiny cell and to see
no one at all, spending her time uninterruptedly in
prayer and fasting. This was impossible to carry out
because many profited from her inspired teaching and for
this reason everyone bothered her. Thus she did not
carry out her plan, but rather set specific hours for
herself when she would help those who had come to her
for good conversation. For the remaining hours, in contrast, she spoke to God in prayer and accomplished her
spiritual work. She had a wooden chest built for herself of such dimensions that when she was lying in it,
she could turn neither to the right nor to the left, nor
was she free to extend her body. Although she possessed
such great and numerous virtues, she never became proud
about her own righteous deeds, but always made herself
lowly, called herself a useless servant.

33. And sometimes when her mother, full of compassion
for her daughter, went to enter Melania's little cell
when she was writing or reading, Melania would not even
recognize her or speak to her until she finished her
usual office. Then she would speak to her as much as
was necessary. Albina, embracing Melania in such a manner, said amid tears, "I trust that I, too, have a share
in your sufferings, my child. For if the mother of the
seven Maccabean children, who in a single hour saw the
tortures of her sons, had eternal joy with them,[34] how
is it not that I, who have been more tortured every day
than she was, will have that joy, when I see you thus
wearing yourself out and never giving yourself any
pause from such labors?" And again Albina said, "I

thank God that I have received a daughter such as this
from the Lord, unworthy as I am."

34.[35] When they had remained in Africa for seven years
and had renounced the whole burden of their riches,
they at last started out for Jerusalem, for they had a
desire to worship at the Holy Places. They set sail
from Africa and headed eastward, arriving at Alexandria,
where the most holy bishop Cyril received them in a
manner worthy of his holiness. At that time, it just
happened that the holy abba Nestoros, a man who possessed prophetic gifts, was in the city. This holy man
was accustomed to come once a year to the city for the
purpose of curing the sick. He also possessed this
gift from the Lord, that he could deliver from diverse
diseases those who came to him, using oil that had been
blessed. As soon as the saintly ones, who were great
friends of the holy men, heard about him, they immediately set out to receive spiritual profit. Because of
the immense crowd of people who came to him, they got
separated from one another. The first to enter with
the limitless crowd was Pinian, the most blessed brother
of the saint. He was eager to receive the blessing so
that he could leave. The holy man, however, looking
intently at him with his spiritual eyes, recognized the
beauty of his soul, seized him, and made him stand
alongside him. Then Melania, the servant of Christ,
also came in with a great crowd. When Nestoros saw her,
he recognized her with his spiritual eyes and made her
stand with her brother. Thus when Melania's holy mother
came in third, Nestoros stopped her and made her stand
with the two. After he had dismissed the whole crowd,
he began to tell them first with exhortation and prophetic speech what diverse troubles they had endured in

their renunciation. He counseled them like his own
children and exhorted them not to lose heart, since the
goal of affliction is to have unutterable bliss. He
said, "For the sufferings of the present time are not
worthy to be compared to the coming glory that is to be
revealed to us."[36]

35. Thus being much encouraged and praising God even
more, they set sail for Jerusalem and hastened on to
their destination. They stayed in the Church of the
Holy Sepulcher. Since they themselves did not want to
distribute with their own hands the gold left to them,
they gave it to those who were entrusted with adminis-
tering charity for the poor. They did not wish for
people to see them doing good deeds. They were in such
a state of poverty that the holy woman Melania assured
us of this: "When we first arrived here, we thought of
inscribing ourselves on the church's register and of
being fed with the poor from alms." Thus they became
extremely poor for the sake of the Lord, who himself
became poor for our sakes and who took the form of a
servant.

It happened that Melania was sick when we were
first in Jerusalem and had nowhere to lie down except
in her sackcloth. A certain well-born virgin presented
her with a pillow as a gift. When she became healthy
again, she spent her time in reading and prayer, sincerely serving the Lord.

36. Thus Melania and her mother lived together by themselves. Melania was not quick to see anyone except the
holy and highly reputed bishops, especially those who
stood out for their doctrine, so that she might spend
the time of their conferences inquiring about the divine

word. As we said before, she wrote in notebooks and
fasted during the week. Every evening, after the Church
of the Holy Sepulcher was closed, she remained at the
cross until the psalm-singers arrived. Then she departed for her cell and slept for a short while.

37. Because of the barbarian invasion, they could not
sell all their property, and hence some of it remained
unpurchased. A certain believer whose heart God had
awakened was able to sell part of it in the area of
Spain where peace prevailed. Having collected a little
gold from the sales, he took it to the blessed ones in
Jerusalem. Melania seized it as if from the lion's
mouth and dedicated it to God, saying to her spiritual
brother in the Lord, "Let us go to Egypt to inquire
after the holy men," And he, who did not hesitate to
perform such works, obeyed her cheerfully, as she was a
truly good teacher.

When she was about to depart on this spiritual
journey, Melania asked her holy mother to have a little
cell built for her near the Mount of Olives, with its
interior made from boards, where she might dwell peace-
fully in the near future. They arrived in Egypt and
toured the cells of the holy monks and the very faithful
virgins, supplying to each as he had need (as it is
written),[37] for they were indeed wise administrators.

38. In doing this, they arrived at the cell of the holy
man, abba Hephestion, as he was called, and asked him to
receive from their hand a little gold. He vehemently
proclaimed that they should not do this. The blessed
woman went around to the holy man's cell and looked over
his equipment. She discovered that he had no possessions on earth except a mat, a basket containing a few

biscuits, and a small basket of salt. She was greatly
moved at the inexpressible and heavenly richness of the
saint, and hid the gold amid the salt. Then she hastened to leave, fearing lest what she had done might be
discovered by the old man. They asked for his blessing
and then departed in haste, but not unnoticed. After
they had crossed the river, the man of God ran toward
them, holding the gold and shouting, "Why do I want
this?" Holy Melania said to him, "In order to give it
to those in need." He solemnly swore that he would not
keep it nor give it away, chiefly because the place was
a desert and none of the needy was able to come there.
Because they could not persuade him to accept their
gold, the holy man threw it into the river after a long
discussion. Since many other anchorites and very devout
virgins did not want to take anything, the blessed woman,
through a spiritual ruse, left the gold in their cells.
She thought that the refreshment of the holy people was
a great spiritual gain, a substantial benefit to the
soul.

39. Thus when they had made their tour, they came once
more to Alexandria and were honored by not a few holy
men. Among those with whom they met was the superior
of the Tabennisi monastery, and the very holy abbot
Victor, and the most God-loving fathers and superiors
called Zeugetes,[38] and a certain other most holy priest
named abba Elias, and many others, whose names cannot
be repeated because of their number. The blessed woman
was eager to reap the benefit and the blessing from each
of the holy men in her own person and to partake in
their virtue. Leaving Alexandria, they came to the
mountain of Nitria and to the place called "the Cells,"
in which the fathers of the most holy men there received

the saint as if she were a man. In truth, she had been
detached from the female nature and had acquired a mas-
culine disposition, or rather, a heavenly one. They
associated with the holy fathers and were blessed; after
they stayed with them in this way, they departed and
were conducted by all of them with much gladness.

40. The blessed ones returned to Jerusalem carrying a
full cargo of piety. Having completed the work of our
Lord Jesus Christ's service with much eagerness, they
both fell ill due to the bad quality of the air. The
blessed woman found the little cell on the Mount of
Olives already finished through the effort of her saintly mother. There, after the day of Holy Epiphany, she
shut herself in, and sat in sackcloth and ashes, seeing
nobody, with the exception that on some days she met
with her very holy mother and her spiritual brother.
Her cousin, the blessed virgin Paula, also came to see
her. The holy woman Melania had guided Paula in all the
commandments of God, and had brought her back to much
humility from great vanity and the Roman way of thinking. She also had as a servant one virgin who often
assured us, "At the time of Holy Easter, when the
blessed woman emerged from that exceedingly narrow cell,
we shook the sack that lay under her and enormous lice
fell out." Melania lived in this kind of ascetic regime
for fourteen years.

41. When the Lord called her holy mother, she departed
to his saints to receive the promised goods. When they
had carried Albina's remains to the Mount of Olives with
much honor and singing of Psalms, Melania straightway
remained there in the dark cell, no longer wishing to
live in the city. She spent that year in great grief,

ascetic discipline, and fasting, and at the end of it
she had a monastery built for herself and decided to
save other souls along with herself. She asked her
brother to gather some virgins for her. So there arose
a monastery of ninety virgins, more or less, whom she
trained as a group from the first not to associate with
a man. She constructed for them a cistern inside the
monastery[39] and supplied all their bodily needs, saying
to them, "I myself will properly attend to everything
for you, as a servant would, and I will not let you lack
any necessities. Only be warned about associating with
men." She laid hold of women from places of ill-repute
and by her admonitions brought them as a sacrifice to
God, for she was aware of what was written: "If you
bring out the honored from the worthless, you will be as
my mouth."[40] She constantly addressed them on matters
concerning their salvation.

In her excess of humility, she would not accept the
superiorship of the monastery, but chose another woman
for this task who was spiritual and burning with emotion
for God, while Melania spent her time only in prayer and
in serving the saints. When the superior was a bit too
unbending, Melania busied herself greatly to take care
of the nuns' physical needs. Thus she took heed for the
weaker sisters, secretly took them the things they
needed, and arranged to place them in each woman's cell
under the bed. When the women entered, they would find
every refreshment readied for them, without their mother
superior learning of the situation. The sisters, however, knew from the manner in which it was done that the
saint was the one who had provided these things, and
they were eager to cleave to her to a remarkable degree,
to obey her in all things, for they knew her boundless
compassion.

42. I am not able to relate the continual and inspired
teachings she used to put to them, but I shall attempt
to report a little about some of them. Her whole concern was to teach the sisters in every way about spiritual works and virtues, so that they could present the
virginity of their souls and the spotlessness of their
bodies to their heavenly Bridegroom and Master, Christ.

        First she taught that it was necessary to stay
vigilant during the night office, to oppose evil
thoughts with sobriety, and not to let their attention
wander, but to focus their minds on singing the Psalms.
She would say, "Sisters, recall how the subjected stand
before their mortal and worldly rulers with all fear and
vigilance; so we, who stand before the fearsome and
heavenly King, should perform our liturgy with much fear
and trembling. Just keep in mind that neither the
angels nor any intelligible and heavenly creature can
worthily praise the Lord who needs nothing and is beyond praise. If then the incorporeal powers, who so
much surpass our nature, fall short in worthily celebrating the God of all things, as we have already said,
how much more ought we, useless servants, to sing Psalms
in all fear and trembling, lest we bring judgment upon
ourselves for our lack of care in glorifying our Master
instead of reward and benefit."

43. "As for pure love to him and to each other, we are
taught by the Holy Scriptures that we ought to guard it
with all zeal, recognizing that without spiritual love
all discipline and virtue is in vain. For the Devil can
copy all our good deeds that we seem to do, yet, in
truth, he is conquered by love and by humility. I mean
something of this sort: we fast, but he eats nothing at
all; we keep vigil, but he never sleeps. Let us thus

hate arrogance since it was through this fault that he fell from the heavens and by it he wishes to carry us down with him. Let us also flee the vainglory of this age that fades like a plant's flower. And before all else, let us guard the holy and orthodox faith without deviation, for this is the groundwork and the foundation of our whole life in the Lord. Let us love the holiness of our souls and bodies because apart from this, no one will see the Lord."

And since she feared that one of them might fall out of pride in excessive mortification, she said, "Of all the virtues, fasting is the least. Just as a bride, radiant in every kind of finery, cannot wear black shoes, but adorns even her feet along with the rest of her body, so does the soul also need fasting along with all the other virtues. If someone is eager to perform the good deed of fasting apart from the other virtues, she is like a bride who leaves her body unclothed and adorns only her feet."

44. Concerning obedience to God, she frequently exhorted them saying, "Without obedience, the affairs of the world could not go on, for even worldly rulers are submissive and obedient to each other. When you speak of him who wears the diadem, in most and in very important circumstances, he does nothing by himself, nor does he try to command without first seeking the counsel of the Senate. If in worldly houses you were to remove obedience, the greatest possession, you would take away the whole order of things, and where order does not exist, the limbs of peace are crippled.[41] Thus we all ought to render obedience to each other. And this is obedience: that you do what you do not want to do, to give repose to the one who ordered you, so that you

force yourself for the sake of the one who said, "The
Kingdom of God suffers violence, and the violent seize
it forcibly."[42]

She used to tell them the story of an old holy man
that concerned the necessity of submitting onself to
everyone, a situation that is likely to be the lot of a
person who lives in the midst of humans: "Someone went
to an aged holy man wanting to be instructed by him, and
the holy man said to him, 'Can you obey me in everything
for the sake of the Lord?' And he answered the father,
'I will do everything that you order me to do with great
zeal.' The holy man said, 'Then take a scourge, go over
to that place, and hit and kick that statue.' The man
returned having willingly done what he was commanded.
The old man said to him, 'Did the statue protest or
answer back while it was being struck or kicked?' And
he replied, 'Not at all.' The father said, 'Then go
again; hit it a second time and add insults as well.'
When he had done this still a third time at the command
of the father and the statue did not answer--for how
could it, since it was stone?--then at last the old
saint said to him, 'If you can become like that statue,
insulted but not returning the insult, struck but not
protesting, then you can also be saved and remain with
me.' Thus let us, too, O children, imitate this statue
and nobly submit to everything--to insult, reproach,
contempt--in order that we may inherit the Kingdom of
Heaven."

45. In regard to exerting oneself in fasting, Melania
repeated the apostolic words, "Not from grief or from
necessity, for God loves a joyful giver,"[43] and left
this matter of fasting to everybody's own personal decision. Concerning love, humility, gentleness, and the

other virtues, in contrast, she said, "A person does
not blame either his stomach or any other part of his
body, but it is inexcusable for any human not to keep
the Lord's commandments. Thus I exhort you to wage
your contests in patience and longsuffering, for the
saints enter into eternal life through the narrow gate.
The labor is very small but the refreshment is grand
and eternal. Just endure a little, that you may be
crowned with the wreath of righteousness."

46. During the night hours she awakened the sisters
for a service of praise, in accordance with the prophetic saying, "I have come so late and have cried," and
again, "In the middle of the night I arose in order to
confess to you."[44] She said, "It is not helpful to
arise for the nightly liturgy after we have sated ourselves with sleep. Rather, we should force ourselves
to rise, so that we may receive the reward for the force
we have exerted in the age to come." After they had
completed their customary office, Melania provided them
with a little time to get some sleep, by which they
might rest from the toil of the vigil and renew their
bodies for the day's psalmody.

47. Their nightly office had three responses and three
readings and near the hour of daybreak, fifteen antiphons. They chanted at the third hour, she said, "because at this hour the Paraclete descended on the
apostles,[45] and at the sixth, because at that hour the
patriarch Abraham was deemed worthy to receive the
Lord,[46] and at the ninth, because according to the tradition of the holy apostles, at the ninth hour, Peter
and John, while going up at the hour of prayer, healed
the lame man."[44] She also listed other testimonies

from Holy Scripture in accordance with the practice,
for example, the most holy prophet Daniel who knelt to
pray three times a day,[48] and the parable in the holy
Gospel that tells about the householder who went out at
the third, the sixth, and the ninth hours to engage
workers for his vineyard.[49]

"As for evening prayers," she said, "we ought to
undertake them in all zeal, not only because we have
passed the course of the day in peace, but also because
in that hour Clophas and the one with him were deemed
worthy to travel in the company of the Lord after his
resurrection."[50] She exhorted them to be especially
zealous on Sundays and the other important feast days
to give themselves to uninterrupted psalmody. She said,
"If in the daily liturgy it is good not be negligent,
how much more ought we on Sundays and the remaining
feasts to chant something beyond the customary office."

48. By thus saying these things, she affirmed the sisters' zeal through her teaching, so that when the
blessed woman wished to spare them in their vigil, because of the great toil which they had had....They would
not agree and said, "Since you are ceaselessly concerned
with our physical needs every day, thus we ought so much
the more to be concerned with spiritual things, so that
we leave nothing out from the customary office." And
the blessed woman rejoiced mightily when she saw their
good decision in the Lord. Thus she was eager to have
an oratory built in the monastery and to have an altar
erected in it, so that they would always have the honor
of participating in the holy mysteries. Melania arranged for the sisters to accomplish two eucharistic
sacrifices each week, apart from the feast days, one on
Friday and one on Sunday. She placed in the oratory

the relics of the holy martyrs, I mean those of the
prophet Zechariah, the holy protomartyr Stephen, the
holy Forty Martyrs of Sebaste, and others, whose names
God knows.

49. While our holy mother Melania was waging her contests, her most blessed brother completed the measure
of his life in the flesh. Having fought the good fight,
he was crowned with a wreath because of his voluntary
poverty and obedience to the divine precepts, and joyfully departed to the God of all things, eight years
before Melania's own death. It was God who arranged
matters thus to be in accord with Melania's good purpose, so that the blessed woman, contesting even more,
might more illustriously carry out her way of life in
the Lord.

         After her brother, whom we have mentioned, fell
asleep in the Lord, Melania remained in the Aposteleion
that she had constructed a short time before and in
which she had also deposited the remains of the blessed
man. She remained here for about four years, very much
wearing herself out in fasting, vigils, and constant
sorrow. After these things occurred, aroused by divine
zeal, she wished to build a monastery for holy men that
they might carry out their nightly and daily psalmody
without interruption at the place of the Ascension of
the Lord and in the grotto where the Savior talked with
his holy disciples about the end of time. Some people
balked at her good proposal, however, alleging that she
would not be able to complete such a great undertaking
because of her extreme poverty. But the Lord, who is
rich in everything, fulfilled the wishes of that holy
soul by arranging for a certain man who loved Christ to
offer her two hundred coins. Receiving them with great

joy, she called the priest with her, whom she had taken
from the world and presented to God as an offering--and
that man was my own pitiable self--and said to him,
"Since you believe that you will receive the compensa-
tion for this labor from the Lord in the ages to come,
take these few coins and buy stones for us, so that we
may begin the construction of the men's monastery, in
the name of our Lord Jesus Christ. Thus while I am
still in the flesh I may see both the divine service
being offered without interruption in the church and the
bones of my mother and my master find rest through their
chanting."

And when, under God, she began this project, the
Lord who worked with her in all things completed the
vast undertaking in one year, so that everyone was as-
tounded to learn that truly it was by a heavenly influence that the work had been accomplished. She lodged
there holy men, lovers of God, who cheerfully performed
the divine service in the Church of Christ's Ascension
and in that of the Apostles, where the blessed ones were
also buried.

50. Immediately, other battles fell to her, greater
than the earlier labors. For when the monastery was
finished and she was catching a little breath, straightway letters arrived from her uncle Volusian, ex-prefect
of greater Rome, stating that he was going to Constantinople on a mission to the most pious empress Eudoxia,
who had been pledged in marriage to our Christ-loving
emperor Valentinian. There arose in Melania a desire
to see her uncle. She was spurred by grace from above
to entertain this desire so that she might save his
soul through her great effort, for he was still a pagan.
She struggled mightily, lest she do something contrary

to God's pleasure. She told all the holy men about the
matter and exhorted them to pray earnestly that her
journey might be in accordance with God's will. And
after she entrusted the monasteries to the Lord, she
left Jerusalem.

51. From the beginning of her journey, the holy men of
every city and country (I mean the bishops and clergy)
gave her glory and indescribable honor. The God-loving
monks and pious virgins, when they had seen her whose
illustrious virtues they had heard about for a long
time, were separated from her with many tears.

52. I do not consider it without risk to pass over in
silence the miracle that God did on her behalf in Tripoli, because, as the Scripture says, "It is good to
hide a king's secret, but the works of God are glorious
to reveal."[51] When we arrived there, we stayed in the
martyrion of Saint Leontius, in whose shrine not a few
miracles took place. Since many who were traveling
with her did not have the prearranged document, the official proved to be very difficult about releasing the
animals. His name was Messala. The blessed woman was
very upset about this; she remained in prayer and kept
vigil by the relics of the holy martyr Leontius from
evening until the time when the animals arrived. We
left Tripoli and had traveled about seven miles when
the aforementioned official came after us, in total
confusion, and asked, "Where is the priest?" Since I
was inexperienced about traveling, I was afraid lest he
had come to retrieve the animals. Getting down, I asked
him why he was upset, and he replied, "I am eager to
have the honor of meeting the great woman." Then, when
he saw her, he fell down and seized her feet amid many

tears and said, "I beg your pardon, O servant of Christ, that I, not knowing your great holiness, held back the release of the animals." And Melania replied, "God bless you, child, that you did indeed release them, even if belatedly." He straightway took out the three coins that we had given him as a tip and begged us to take them back from him. Since I was not of a mind to do so, he started to confess to the saint: "All night long, both I and your servant, my wife, were strongly tested by the holy martyr Leontius. Thus we got up immediately and both ran to the martyrion. When we did not find you, she returned, because she was not able to run any further, but I, who have overtaken you, beg your holiness to pray for us both, in order that the God of all things may deign to be gracious to us." When we heard this, we accepted the coins, offered a prayer, and let the official go in peace, rejoicing. Since all those traveling along with us were amazed by what had happened, the saint said, "Take courage, for our journey is in accordance with God's will." And when all of us asked her to teach us openly the reason why, the saint answered, "All night I prayed to the holy martyr Leontius that he might show us an auspicious sign for this trip. And behold, though I am unworthy, my request has been fulfilled." Then we joyfully traveled on and were welcomed by everyone.

53. When we finally arrived near the Christ-loving city of Constantinople, the saint was anxious, since she was about to enter this sort of an imperial city after so much ascetic discipline and solitude. We came to the martyrion of Saint Euphemia in Chalcedon where the Victorious One greatly comforted the saint, providing her with much cheer and encouragement. Then strengthened

in the Lord, she entered Constantinople. The lord
Lausus, the *prepositus*, received her as was fitting for
someone of his virtuous way of life.[52] She also found
her uncle who, by God's dispensation, had fallen ill.
When he, who carried himself about in such dignity of
worldly glory, saw her in that extremely simple and
shabby clothing, with many tears he began to tell my
humble self, "Perhaps you don't know, lord priest, how
delicately she was brought up, more so than the rest of
our family? And now she has humbled herself to such a
degree of austerity and poverty!"

The blessed woman took from his words an opportunity for her discourse, and answered him, "Then you
have realized from me, my lord, that which concerns the
future and eternal good, which the Creator and Ruler of
the whole world cheerfully gives to those who sincerely
trust him. I have despised glory, possessions, and
every pleasure of this present life. I beg you, approach the bath of immortality, so that you may obtain
eternal goods, just as you have enjoyed temporal things.
Free yourself from the error of demons who will be
burned in eternal fire along with those who are won
over to them."

And when he perceived that she wished to take the
matter to the emperors, he was cut deeply to the heart,
and said to her, "I exhort Your Holiness not to take
from me the gift of self-determination with which God
has honored us from the beginning. For I am completely
ready and long to wash away the stain of my many errors.
But if I should do this by the command of the emperors,
I would gain it as if I had come to it through force
and would lose the reward of my free decision."

But Melania was not patient enough to keep silent
and through some highly-ranked persons she submitted

the matter to the holy bishop Proclus, who came to Volusian and benefited him greatly by speaking at length
about his salvation. Volusian, however, since he was a
very sharp-minded man, saw that the archbishop had come
to him through the suggestion of the blessed woman, and
he disclosed to her, "If we had three men in Rome like
lord Proclus, no one there would be called a pagan."

54. Just then the Devil threw the souls of simple people into great trouble through the polluted doctrine of
Nestorius. Therefore many of the wives of senators and
some of the men illustrious in learning came to our holy
mother in order to investigate the orthodox faith with
her. And she, who had the Holy Spirit indwelling, did
not cease talking theology from dawn to dusk. She
turned many who had been deceived to the orthodox faith
and sustained others who doubted; quite simply, she
benefited all those who chanced to come to her divinely-
inspired teaching. Thus the Devil, the enemy of truth,
was very jealous both on account of those who came to
her for edification and on account of her uncle's salvation. He changed into a young black man, came to her,
and said the following: "For how long do you destroy
my hopes through your words? Know, then, that if I am
strong enough to harden the hearts of Lausus and the
emperors...if not, I inflict on your body such tortures
that you will fear even for your life, so that you may
be kept silent by necessity." After she had made him
disappear by calling on our Lord Jesus Christ, she sent
for my most humble self to tell me the threats of the
Black One. And she had not yet finished speaking to me
when she began to feel a pain in her hip. Suddenly her
suffering was so strong that she remained mute for
three hours. After we had made an offering on her

behalf, she scarcely recovered herself. She spent six
days in that unspeakable suffering, feeling far greater
pain at that hour when she had seen the Black One. And
when on the seventh day it seemed as if she would be
released from this temporal life, someone came to announce that her uncle was in danger of dying, and he
was still a catechumen.

55. Melania's grief at this announcement was greater
than her suffering and her pains. She kept repeating
to us, "Take me to him before I die." But we feared
even to touch her because her foot was like dry wood.
She lay there saying, "Carry me to my uncle, for if you
don't, I am in more danger from that affliction." So
according to her command we brought a litter and with
much labor we hoisted her on it. I arrived before them
at the palace and inquired how the ex-prefect was. And
some of the famous people answered me, "Yesterday he
asked for the saint and upon learning that she was
seriously ill, he called lady Eleutheria, the nurse of
Eudoxia the most pious empress, and through God he was
enlightened." When I heard these things, I was cheered
in the Lord and speedily sent off a horseman so that it
might be announced to the blessed woman. When she heard
that her uncle had been baptized, she was able to move
her foot without pain because of her great joy. The
Devil, disgraced, withdrew at that hour and with him all
the pains totally left the blessed woman, so that she
who had not been able to raise herself up, walked up all
the stairs and through the side door of the palace, and
entered the dwelling of the friend of Christ, the empress Eudoxia. Everyone was amazed and glorified the
Lord because of the defeat of the Enemy of our salvation.

Melania herself sat all night at her uncle's bed-
side comforting him by saying things such as these:
"You are truly blessed, my lord, because you have been
sufficiently glorified in this life, and in the future
one you are going towards the Lord, justified in having
received the holy bath of incorruption." She had him
participate three times in the holy mysteries and at
dawn--it being the feast of Holy Epiphany--she joyfully
sent him on in peace to the Lord. And while everybody
was giving thanks to the One who did great wonders, the
blessed woman said, praising his unutterable love for
humans, "How great is his concern for even one soul,
that in his goodness he arranged for Volusian to come
from Rome and moved us to come from Jerusalem, so that
a soul who had lived an entire lifetime in ignorance
should be saved!"

56.   Melania remained at Constantinople until she had
done her time of forty days. She greatly benefited all
who were there, most particularly the Christ-loving imperial women. She also edified the most pious emperor
Theodosius. And since his wife had a desire to worship
at the Holy Places, Melania begged him to let her go.
We departed from there at the end of the month of
February.

At that time the winter was so fierce that the
Galatian and Cappadocian bishops asserted that they had
never seen such a winter. And although we were completely covered with snow all day, we made our journey
without faltering. We saw neither the ground nor the
mountains, nothing except the hostels in which we
stayed at night. Melania, who was like adamant, did
not let up on her fasting at all. She said, "We ought
now to fast more and to give thanks to God, the ruler

of everything, because of the great wonders he has accomplished with me." Persevering in her unceasing
prayer, she prevented both herself and us from suffering
anything disagreeable in that most terrible cold. She
showed that the prayer of a just person is a very strong
weapon through which even the very elements are moved
and overcome.[53]

While all the holy men tried to delay us en route,
she was not persuaded by any of them to do so, but had
one wish, to celebrate Christ's Passion in Jerusalem.
This God granted to her, according to the trustworthy
promise he spoke through his most holy prophet, "He will
do the desire of those who fear him and will hear their
prayer."[54]

57. We arrived at the Holy Places the third day of the
week before the Savior's Passion.[55] Having celebrated
Easter in a spiritual manner and the Holy Resurrection
in great cheerfulness among her own sisters, she again
submitted to the customary rule, taking care of both
monasteries. And when she saw how well the psalmody
was performed in the church by the God-loving monks,
another pious desire came to her: she wanted to have
built a small martyrion. Thus she said to my own humble
self, "This is the place in which the feet of the Lord
stood. Therefore let us build here a holy oratory, so
that after my journey from this world to the Lord, an
offering on behalf of my soul and those of my masters
can also be offered unceasingly in this place." Since
every wish and desire of hers satisfied the God of all
things, the work was completed in a few days. She again
gathered other holy men and established them there.

58. When this had taken place, it was announced that
the most pious empress was coming to Jerusalem and had
already gotten as far as the city of Antioch. Thus
Melania considered within herself what then she might
do both to glorify God and to benefit human beings. She
said, "If I go out to meet her, I fear lest I bring reproach by traveling through the cities in this humble
attire. But if I remain here, I must beware that this
behavior not be thought arrogant on my part." So finally, having gone over this matter in pious reflection,
she set out, saying, "It is fitting that we who have
taken on the yoke of Christ, and were strong enough to
do so, should carry on our own shoulders such a faithful empress, exulting in the power of the Lord because
he has established such a Christ-loving empress."

   She then went to meet Eudocia at Sidon, repaying
with gratitude the extreme love the empress had showed
to her in Constantinople. She stayed in the martyrion
of Saint Phocas, which is said to have been the dwelling
of the faithful Canaanite woman who said in the holy
Gospel of the Lord, "Yes, Lord, for even the little dogs
eat the crumbs that fall from the table of their masters."[56] Thus the blessed woman was zealous to please
the Lord even in the matter of a dwelling, as well as
in conversation and every other activity.

   When the God-loving empress saw her, she fittingly
received her with every honor, as Melania was a true
spiritual mother. It was a glory for her to honor the
woman who had so purely glorified the heavenly King.
The saint, acknowledging her faith and the burden of her
journey, exhorted her to proceed still further in good
works. The pious empress answered her with this speech,
worthy of remembrance: "I am fulfilling a double vow to
the Lord, to worship at the Holy Places and to see my

mother, for I have wished to be worthy of Your Holiness
while you still serve the Lord in the flesh."

In an excess of spiritual love, the Christ-loving
empress was eager to get to the saint's monastery.
Having arrived there, she regarded the virgins as if
they were her own sisters. And since she had been
greatly benefited, the empress desired also to go to the
monastery of the men and be blessed.

The deposition of the relics in the martyrion
newly-built by Melania, as we mentioned earlier, was
about to occur. The empress requested that the festival
take place while she was present.

59. And the Enemy of good, again envious of such spiritual love, prepared to twist the empress' foot at the
deposition of the holy remains, and there resulted from
this incident extraordinary trouble. This probably occurred as a contest for the faith of the holy woman.
For at the very hour that Melania had escorted Eudocia
to the Church of the Holy Sepulcher, she had seated herself by the relics of the holy martyrs. Not standing
aloof from them, she had prayed earnestly in much sorrow and fasting along with the virgins until the time
the empress summoned her and the pain had stopped.[57]
When the pain had improved, the blessed woman did not
cease fighting against the Devil, who had desired to
make such a difficulty in their midst. When Melania
had spent a few days with the empress and had benefited
her immeasurably, she escorted her as far as Caesarea.
They were scarcely able to be separated from one
another, for they were strongly bonded together in spiritual love. And when she returned, the saint gave
herself anew to ascetic discipline, praying thus up to
the end that the pious empress would be returned to her

husband in good health, which the God of all things
granted to her.

60. I shall try to recall a few of the many miracles
that the Lord performed through her, for I am not capable of relating all of them, both because of their
great number and because of my personal incapacity.
Now one day a certain young woman was seized by a very
evil demon. Her mouth and her lips were shut for many
days. It was completely impossible for her either to
talk or to take nourishment, so that quite soon she was
in danger of starvation. Many doctors had lavished a
number of drugs on her but were not able to make her
move her lips even a bit. When medical skill had
proven to be incapable of driving out the demon, then
at last they carried her with an escort to the saint,
with her parents following along. The blessed woman,
who shunned the glory of men, said to them, "Since I am
a sinner, I am incapable of doing this. Let us bring
her to the holy martyrs and by their direct intercession, the God who loves humankind will cure her." As
they arrived there, the saint earnestly called upon the
Master of all things. She took the oil consecrated from
the relics of the holy martyrs and with this she touched
the mouth of the sick woman three times, saying in a
clear voice, "In the name of our Lord Jesus Christ, open
your mouth." And straightway at the calling on the
Lord, the demon, who was disgraced or rather frightened,
fled, and the woman opened her mouth. The saint gave
her something to eat and all who saw this glorified God.
The woman who had been cured returned home with great
joy, praising the Lord. Likewise another woman who had
suffered from the same sickness was cured by Melania.

61.[58] Once again, a woman had a very difficult labor and the fetus died in the mother's womb. The wretched woman could neither live nor die. When the true servant of the Lord heard about this, she was very sympathetically grieved. Pitying the woman, she said to the virgins with her, "Let us go to visit the sick woman, so that by seeing the suffering of those who live in the world, we can also thus understand from how many difficulties God has relieved us." When they arrived at the house where the woman was who was dangerously ill, they said a prayer. Immediately the suffering woman, scarcely able to whisper in a weak voice, said to the saint, "Have pity on me." Melania stood there a long time supplicating God earnestly on the woman's behalf. She loosened her own belt which bound her around and placed it on the woman, announcing, "I have received this blessing from a great man, and I believe that his prayers will cure her speedily." Immediately the dead fetus emerged. Having fed the woman, Melania straightway returned home. And God was glorified, as usual. Melania said in humility, "The belt belongs to a saint, whose prayers cured the endangered woman." Thus she always attributed her virtuous deeds to the saints.[59]

62. And once a certain one of the virgins with her asked her if, since she practiced such a high degree of asceticism and virtue, she were not troubled by the demon of vanity and arrogance. Melania began to utter these things for the edification of us all: "I am not aware of anything completely good in myself. If, however, I notice that the Enemy is sowing in me thoughts of arrogance under the pretext of fasting, this is how I might answer him: 'What is so great if I fast for a week, when others do not eat for forty whole days? If

I do not take any oil, there are others who do not sat-
isfy themselves even with water.' And if the Enemy
prompted me to become proud about my renunciation, I,
made bold by the power of God, would oppose his unspeakable wickedness by thinking like this: 'How many
prisoners taken by the barbarians have been deprived
of their very freedom? How many who have fallen under
the imperial anger have lost their lives along with
their possessions? And how many have been left poor
even by their parents? And then there are others who
have suddenly been reduced to poverty from their former
wealth because they fell afoul of a false accusation
and robbery? It is no great thing if for the sake of
incorruptible and undefiled goods we despise those of
the earth.' And again, when I see the Evil One suggesting a vainglorious thought to me (for example, that
far from linen and numerous dresses of silk, I now wear
haircloth), I think of myself as very lowly. I bear in
mind that there are those who lie in the marketplace
naked, or only on mats, freezing in the cold. Thus God
would drive the Devil from me."

"They say that the plots of the Enemy are manifest.
But in my case, the people who have born the outward
garment of sanctity have made more serious trouble for
me than the Enemy. They observed that I was eager to
fulfill in sincerity the word that the Lord said to the
rich man, 'If you would be perfect, sell your goods,
give to the poor, and take your cross and follow me.'[60]
They said to me, 'Indeed, it is all right to become
poor and to practice asceticism in the Lord, but do so
in moderation.' Yet I thought about those who in this
world do their service under mortal rulers and how, always grasping for greater honors, they are endangered
to the point of death. So if they thus toil wearily

for the flower of the field--for such is worldly glory--
how much more should I be eager so as to attain the
greater honor in heaven?" Such was her spiritual
teaching that assisted the soul.

    She had acquired such gentleness and quietness that
if when, as usually happened, a sister who had made a
problem for her came seeking pardon, the saint would say
such things: "The Lord knows that I am unworthy, and I
do not judge myself to be good compared to a worldly
woman. But I believe that the Enemy will not accuse me
on the Day of Judgment of having gone to sleep holding
a grievance against someone."[61]

63. After a certain time had passed, Melania, like an
expert runner who having come round the stadium desires
the trophy, was also eager to be released to be with
Christ. For she groaned (in the apostle's phrase), desiring "to clothe herself in the garment of heaven."[62]
And when the holy Nativity of the Savior arrived, she
said to her cousin, lady Paula, "Let us go to holy
Bethlehem, for I do not know if I will hereafter see
this festival in the flesh." Thus they went there and
kept the whole vigil; at dawn they participated in the
fearsome mysteries.

    Finally the saint, as if she had received an answer
from God, said the following to her cousin: "Pray on
my behalf, for henceforth you will be celebrating the
birth of the Lord alone. For me, the goal of bodily
life is to be finished after a short while." When Paula
heard this, she was greatly disturbed. After they returned from holy Bethlehem to the monastery, the saint,
not reckoning at all the labor of the vigil and the
journey, straightway went out into the grotto and
prayed intensely.

64. On the next day we went to the martyrion of the
holy protomartyr Stephen--for the memorial of his falling asleep had arrived--and after we had held a service
there, we returned to the monastery. During the vigil,
I read first, then three sisters read, and last of all
Melania herself read from Acts about the death of the
holy Stephen. When she had completed the extent of the
reading, all the sisters said to the holy woman, "Be in
good health for many years, and may you celebrate many
memorials of the saints." But Melania, as if she had
received complete assurance from on high, answered them,
"You stay in good health, too, for you will no longer
hear me read." At this word all the women were deeply
moved, for they believed that she said these words as a
prophecy. And as if she were already passing from this
world to the Lord, she left them a spiritual testament,
saying these things: "I exhort you to be eager after my
departure to perform the office in fear and vigilance,
for it is written, 'The one who does the work of the
Lord in negligence is convicted.'[63] If I am to be separated from you in body in a short while and will no
longer be with you, God who is eternal and who fulfills
all things will dwell with you, and he knows the depths
of every heart. Thus have him before your eyes constantly and keep your souls in love and purity to the
end, knowing that all of us must appear before his
fearsome throne and that each one will receive either the
reward of his labors or the judgment for his sins."

All were grieving greatly because they were about
to lose such a good guide and divinely-inspired teacher. She left them and said to my own humble self, "Let
us go to the martyrion of the men's monastery in order
that we may pray, for there too are laid away the relics
of Saint Stephen." With deep sorrow I did according to

the command of the holy woman and followed her.

    When we entered the martyrion, she, as if she were already in conversation with the holy martyrs, prayed with tears, saying, "God, the Lord of the holy martyrs, who knows all things before they come to pass, you know what I chose from the beginning, that I love you with all my heart, and from fear of you, my bone has been glued to my flesh. For I have given my soul and body to you, who formed me in my mother's womb, and you have taken my right hand to guide me in your counsel. But being human, I have sinned against you many times both in word and in deed, against you who alone are pure and without sin. Therefore accept my prayer, which I offer to you with these tears, through the intercession of your holy athletes,[64] and purify me, your servant, so that in my coming to you, the steps of my soul may be unfettered and the evil demons of this air not hold me back, but that I may go to you spotless, guided by your holy angels. May I be deemed worthy of your heavenly bridal chamber, when I have heard your blessed voice by which you will say to those who please you, 'Come, the blessed of my Father, inherit the Kingdom prepared for you from the creation of the world.'[65] For to you belongs inexpressible compassion and abundant pity; you will save all those who hope in you."

    Next she entreated the holy martyrs, saying, "Athletes of the Lord who shed your honored blood in order to confess him, be compassionate to your humble servant who always reverenced your holy relics. Just as you have always listened to me, do so also now, you who speak openly, be my ambassadors to the God who loves mankind, so that he may receive my soul in peace and guard the monasteries up to the end in the fear of him."

She had scarcely finished her prayer when right
away her slight frame began to shiver. When we returned
to the monastery of the virgins, we came upon the sisters still celebrating the psalmody. And I, who was in
anguish at being overwhelmed by distress, could not
stand up any longer and went away to rest for a while,
but Melania once again went to the divine office.

When the sisters saw that hence she had become
weaker, they strongly begged her and said, "Rest yourself a bit, for you are not strong enough to stand."
She did not agree to that and replied, "Not until we
have completed the morning hymns." After the entire
liturgy was completed, she departed and lay down. Gripped by a pain in the side, she became much weaker. She
sent for my humble self and all the sisters, and began
to speak to me: "Behold, I am going to the Lord.
Therefore pray for me." And I was deeply pained in my
heart when I heard this.

65. Once more she said to the virgins, "I beg you to
pray for me, because I have never wished evil on any of
you. Even if I at any time spoke a harsh word to one
of you, I did it out of spiritual love. Therefore consider yourselves as true servants of Christ. Spend the
remainder of your lifetimes in all knowledge, in order
that you may have bright lamps on that day and be pleasing to the heavenly Bridegroom.[66] Therefore behold, I
entrust you to God who can guard your souls and bodies.
I entrust you also to the lord priest and exhort you not
to distress him in anything, but submit to him in all
humility, knowing that he too carried your burden for
the sake of God, and that she who resists him and does
not submit to him causes grief to God." Having said
these things, she desired to be placed in the oratory,
and said, "Carry me close to the holy martyrs."[67]

66. Then when her pains increased even more, she said to us, "The day has been fulfilled." All lamented bitterly, especially the virgins who mourned, since they were being deprived of a truly tender mother. When the saint saw that my heart as well was very pained, she said to me, on the fifth day of her illness, which was also the day she died, "My child, as much as you may pray and weep, it benefits nothing. For I have heard a voice saying in my heart that it is necessary that I be completely freed from the bonds of the body and go out to the Lord, according to his command." When the Lord's day was dawning, she said to me before sunrise, "Do me the honor of celebrating for us the holy offering." And while I was performing the offering, because of my great grief I was not able to speak up. When Melania did not hear the epiclesis,[68] she, who was in total agony, indicated to me while I was standing at the altar, "Raise your voice so that I will hear the epiclesis."

67. When she had thus received the divine mysteries, the bishop dearest to God arrived with the clergy. He spoke words appropriate to the salvation of the soul and finally the blessed woman said to him, "I commend to you the priest and the monasteries; oversee all as a good shepherd looks after flocks endowed with reason, imitating your own master." When he saw how great a good was about to depart the earth, he was very much troubled. The saint asked for communion from him, too, and bade him farewell in peace.

68. Finally the God-loving monks from her monastery entered and she said to them, "I take leave of you, as I am about to depart from this present life. I exhort you to give relief to the priest in all ways, knowing

that in this you give rest to the God of all things,
for he, although he was free from all things, became
your servant for the sake of the Lord, and although he
was not under any necessity, he bore our burdens."

Then people came from the rest of the monasteries
and from the city. She was a truly noble woman, for
despite the fact that severe pain gripped her body, she
was not neglectful in any way, but with undisturbed
heart and with great patience bade farewell to everyone, as was fitting.

After these events, her cousin Paula came in to
her, with all her household. Melania admonished everybody, cheering her who was so grieved at being separated
from her, and after many blessings and prayers, she dismissed them.

Last of all she spoke these words to my humble
person: "It is superfluous to ask a friend of God such
as you to look after the monasteries, for while I was
still living in the flesh, you were the person who carried the care and burden of all things, and helped me
in everything. That is why I now entrust the monasteries to you and exhort you, in my absence, to be even
more solicitous to submit to toil for their sakes. May
God give you a reward for doing so in the age to come."

And as she had given instructions to everybody in
peace, she said, "Do pray." Thus she dismissed all of
them, saying, "Leave me now to rest." About the ninth
hour she began to lose consciousness. We assumed that
she had died and tried to stretch her legs, but she recovered a little and whispered in a weak voice to my
humble person, "My hour has not yet come." As for me,
I was not able to bear the grief that overcame me, and
answered her, "When the hour comes, will you tell us?"
And she replied, "Yes." She said this, I think, to

indicate that there was no need to adjust her body after
her death. And some holy men remained with me, for that
had always been her prayer, to give over her spirit in
the midst of holy men.[69]

Again came the Christ-loving bishop, and the anchorites who lived around Eleutheropolis, most holy men,
who said to the blessed woman, "You have fought the good
fight on earth. Go with joy to the Lord, as all the
angels rejoice. But we are greatly distressed that we
will be separated from your beneficient presence." And
she uttered to them her last word, "As the Lord has
pleased, thus has it come to pass." And immediately she
gave over her holy soul to her Master, gently and
peaceably, in joy and exaltation, on the evening of the
same holy Lord's day, in order that she might show in
this her great love for the Lord and for his holy
resurrection.

Her holy remains needed no further adornment, for
her legs were found stretched, both her hands were
folded on her chest, and her eyelids had naturally
closed. As she had ordered, the holy fathers who had
gathered from different places later buried her, after
they passed the entire night in solemnly singing Psalms
and readings.

69. Her burial garments were worthy of her holiness.
I think it necessary for me to describe them for the
benefit of those who may read this account. She had the
tunic of a certain saint, the veil of another servant of
God, another garment without sleeves, the belt of
another which she had worn while she was alive, and the
hood of another. Instead of a pillow she had a hood
made from the hair of another saint, which we made into
a cushion and placed under her honored head. For it was

fitting that she be buried in the garments of those
whose virtues she had acquired while she was living.
She had no burial cloth, except the linen with which we
wrapped her from without.

70.   The saint received the answer to her prayer and
rose to the heavens with joy, having clothed herself in
virtues as a garment.   Therefore the hostile powers did
not trouble her, for they were able to find nothing of
their own in her.   And the holy angels joyously received her, for in her corruptible body she had copied
their passionlessness.   Likewise, the holy prophets and
apostles, whose lives and teachings she had fulfilled
in deeds, welcomed her rejoicing into their own choir.
The holy martyrs, whose memory she had glorified, and
whose combats she had voluntarily endured, came to greet
her, rejoicing.

     Thus she is receiving in heaven "what eye has not
seen, nor ear heard, nor has entered into the heart of
man, what God has prepared for those who love him."[70]
To him be glory and power forever and ever.   Amen.

III. COMMENTARY

A. Melania's Ancestry and Family

The *Vita Melaniae Junioris* provides an instructive
example of the disruption that the vocation to Christian
asceticism brought to aristocratic Roman families of
the late imperial period: the issues of continuance of
family line and inheritance of property were not taken
lightly by those who numbered consuls and prefects in
their ranks and whose possessions included palaces in
Rome, suburban villas, and vast estates scattered
throughout the empire. Yet the ascetic resolution of
Melania the Younger was not novel even within her own
family: her grandmother, Melania the Elder, after whom
the *Vita's* heroine was named, had followed the same
course some three decades earlier.[1] According to
Palladius, she provided the inspiration and example
that spurred her granddaughter to desire a life of renunciation.[2]

Although numerous details of genealogy and dating
are irretrievably lost, we can posit that Melania the
Elder stemmed from the *gens Antonia* on the paternal side;
her grandfather, Antonius Marcellinus, was consul in
A.D. 341.[3] According to Palladius, she was of Spanish
descent,[4] most likely on her mother's side of the
family.[5] Melania the Elder's husband, of the *gens Valeria*,
was perhaps the Valerius Maximus who served as praetorian prefect in the early 360s.[6] Palladius reports

that Melania was widowed at twenty-two;[7] other sources
add that she had already borne three sons, two of whom
died within months of their father's death.[8] The remaining son, Valerius Publicola (the father of Melania
the Younger), was abandoned in Rome by his mother when
she went on pilgrimage to Egypt and Palestine, not to
return West until Publicola himself had a daughter of
marriageable age.[9]

    Melania the Younger's mother Albina was also of
aristocratic descent. A member of the Ceionii Rufii,
she was the daughter of the Ceionius Rufius Albinus who
served as prefect of Rome from A.D. 389-391.[10] Although
Ambrose of Milan wrote a treatise for an Albinus,[11]
probably Albina's father, there is no compelling reason
to assume that he was a Christian: bishops of the period often engaged in correspondence with members of
the pagan aristocracy, as is illustrated by Augustine's
correspondence with and concerning Albina's pagan
brother Volusian.[12] Even if Albina's father was pagan,
she may have been raised by her mother as a Christian.
Certainly by her middle years she was known for her
Christian piety, as is evidenced by Augustine's letter
dating from A.D. 412.[13] Nonetheless, her family must
have adopted Christianity rather recently: her grandmother, Caecina Lolliana, was a priestess of Isis;[14]
her uncle, Publilius Caeionius Caecina Albinus, was the
pagan pontifex known from such sources as Jerome's letters[15] and Macrobius' *Saturnalia*;[16] and the paganism of
her brother, Rufius Antonius Agrypnius Volusianus, is
the focus of an interesting episode in Melania's *Vita*
(to be discussed below).[17] To Albina and Valerius
Publicola was born a daughter, Melania, in approximately
A.D. 385.[18]

From another branch of the *gens Valeria*, the Valerii
Severii, came Melania the Younger's husband, Valerius
Pinianus.[19] That Christianity had penetrated this
family by the middle or late fourth century is demon-
strated by the bronze lamp found on the Coelian Hill
where the palace of the Valerii had stood: the lamp, in
the form of a ship, bears the figures of (presumably)
Peter and Paul and the inscription "Dominus legem dat
Valerio Severo."[20] The son of Valerius Severus who was
prefect of Rome in A.D. 382, Pinian had a brother
Severus,[21] whom the *Vita* casts in the role of villain.[22]
According to Paulinus of Nola, Pinian's family could be
traced back to the first consul of Rome, P. Valerius
Publicola (Paulinus relishes the thought that the first
Valerius Publicola, a pagan, was now in "the black pit
of hell," while his descendant Pinian was "Christ's
consul").[23] The marriage of Pinian and Melania the
Younger, in about A.D. 399,[24] effected a reunion of two
branches of the Valerii. If relatives hoped that this
union would produce inheritors for the family's vast
wealth, they were to be sadly disappointed: when the
couple's two children died in infancy,[25] Melania and
Pinian took a vow of celibacy.[26]

Yet such a straightforward presentation of
Melania's genealogy masks perplexities occasioned by the
Vita. We would, for example, expect Melania's illustrious ancestors and relatives to be lauded by the
author, even if he, like Jerome, desired to exploit a
woman's aristocratic descent in order to highlight her
ascetic renunciation.[27] Instead, we find that Melania
the Elder is totally overlooked in the *Vita*: she is not
named once. We would never know from the *Life* that (as
Palladius reports) her example served as the chief inspiration for Melania the Younger's asceticism[28] and

that the elder Melania had journeyed back from Jerusalem
as "an old woman of sixty" to rescue her now-married
granddaughter from "bad teaching or heresy or bad
living."[29] And despite the fact that Melania the
Younger was to build monasteries on the Mount of
Olives,[30] her grandmother's foundations on Olivet go
completely unmentioned in the *Vita*.[31] The significance
of this omission and its possible relation to the taint
of heresy that clung to the name of Melania the Elder
will be discussed below.[32]

A second striking feature of the *Vita* is the hostility with which its author views Melania's father,
Valerius Publicola. Publicola is represented as for-
bidding Melania to adopt the ascetic life, which
prompted the chagrined couple to retaliate with a hunger
strike.[33] In describing the couple's interview with
Serena, mother-in-law of the emperor Honorius and wife
of Stilicho, Gerontius claims that the Devil had led
Valerius Publicola astray to the point where he considered disinheriting Melania; he is even said to have
"persecuted" the couple in their quest for ascetic renunciation.[34] Moreover, in the Latin version of the
Vita, Melania's father sends servants as spies to ensure
that his daughter is not keeping vigils when she should
be sleeping (Melania bribes them to report what her
father wished to hear).[35] In both versions of the *Vita*,
Valerius Publicola on his deathbed repents his error of
attempting to prevent Melania's renunciation.[36]

The picture of Valerius Publicola sketched in the
Vita does not correspond to that presented in other
sources. Palladius, for example, reports that Publicola
and other members of the elder Melania's family provided
the funds that enabled her to make "donations to
churches, monasteries, guests, and prisons."[37] He adds

that Publicola "attained a high degree of education and character, made a good marriage, and became great by worldly standards."[38] The latter point is corroborated by an inscription revealing that Publicola was the *patronus* of Beneventum, a town in southern Italy.[39]

Paulinus of Nola, describing the joy with which the elder Melania's family (presumably Publicola and Melania the Younger, among others) greeted her upon her return from Jerusalem, comments that they believed their kinship with her "cleansed them from the pollution of their riches."[40] Although he reports that Melania the Elder grieved at her son's death because he had not adopted asceticism,[41] Paulinus affirms that Publicola was nonetheless "rich through works"; he inwardly espoused Christian humility even though he still wore worldly clothing. His "striking" sense of religious duty and devotion to Christ endeared him to Paulinus.[42]

A fourth possible source for Valerius Publicola can be dismissed from consideration, namely, the correspondence between Augustine and a certain Publicola (letters 46 and 47 of Augustine). This Publicola is concerned, among other things, with problems occasioned by the tribe of the Arzuges, who lived on the borders between Byzacena and Tripolitania.[43] The geographical detail might suggest that Augustine's correspondent was Melania's father, for we know that the Valerii had a connection with Byzacena: bronze tablets from the atrium of the Valerian mansion unearthed in the sixteenth century are dedicated to Q. Aradius Rufinus Proculus, governor of Byzacena in A.D. 321, by the inhabitants of Thaena and Hadrumetum.[44] Yet other points stand against identifying the Publicola of epistle 46 with Valerius Publicola, Melania's father.

First, we hear nothing in the *Vita* about Melania or
her father possessing property in this region, although
we are told much about other properties. Moreover,
epistle 46 implies that its author was living at the
scene of the disturbances: the letter dates to A.D.
398, and, as far as we know, Valerius Publicola lived
in Rome with his family at this time.[45] Most telling,
however, is the content of the letter: it is difficult
to believe that Melania's urbanely aristocratic father
was paralyzed by anxiety over oaths to "idols" taken by
his pagan workers, or by fear of contamination either
from eating food offered to pagan gods or from going to
baths where pagan sacrifices might have been offered.[46]
As Van der Meer observes, Publicola's questionnaire to
Augustine reveals him "to be almost pathologically concerned with the question of defilement."[47] This Publicola's worries seem very different from those of
Melania's father, who, just at the time epistle 46 was
written, was forcing his recalcitrant daughter to visit
the public baths in Rome.[48] Last, we question whether
the Valerius Publicola who Palladius claimed had received "a high degree of education"[49] could write what
Van der Meer calls the "execrable" Latin of epistle
46.[50] Thus we conclude with Thouvenot that the Publicola of the letter is probably not Valerius Publicola.[51]
Far from attempting to limit conflict between pagan and
Christian so that social life could proceed in normal
fashion, as did many late ancient men of cultivation,[52]
the author of the letter exacerbates it. The nugatory
concerns of epistle 46 contrast sharply with the shrewd
theological objections posed by Valerius Publicola's
brother-in-law, Volusian (to be considered below).[53]
Thus epistles 46 and 47 can be eliminated from consideration in our discussion of Valerius Publicola, and we

may return to the evidence provided by Gerontius, Palladius, and Paulinus of Nola.

　　Two explanations may be proffered for the discrepancy between the picture of Valerius Publicola in the
Vita and that given by Palladius and Paulinus. On the
one hand, the contrasting protrayals may simply reflect
the differing perspectives of the authors. We have no
reason to doubt that Valerius Publicola gave generously
to Christian causes or that as a wealthy layman, his
contributions were not in accord with what churchmen
and ascetic leaders, such as Palladius and Paulinus,
might hope them to be. But there is also no reason to
doubt that (as the *Vita* reports) he may have balked when
his daughter, perhaps his only heir, attempted to flee
her marriage, renounce childbearing (thus depriving him
of descendants), and disperse the vast patrimony.[54]
Having spent much of his childhood as a virtual orphan
because of his mother's ascetic enthusiasms, Valerius
Publicola may well have wished his daughter to adopt a
mode of life in which Christian concern was not divorced
from the usual societal expectations for aristocratic
maidens.

　　But a second hypothesis may be posed concerning the
Vita's hostility to Valerius Publicola: the very fact of
his association with Melania the Elder may have damaged
him in the author's eyes. As C. P. Hammond has suggested, the exaggerated picture of the enmity prevailing
between Melania the Younger and her relations "is caused
partly by a desire to exalt Melania herself at the ex-
pense of her family, partly by a fear of the taint of
heresy"[55] such as clung to the reputation of her grandmother. To be sure, emphasizing parental opposition
heightens Melania the Younger's heroism and thus can be
understood as a typical hagiographical device,[56] but we

suspect that the denigration of Valerius Publicola bears
upon the text's total disregard for Melania's paternal
grandmother. To this point we shall return.

A third puzzle regarding Melania's family, occasioned by the divergent testimony of the sources and
important for understanding her renunciation, is whether she had siblings. The Latin *Vita* gives no clue that
she did: there is an unspoken assumption throughout
that she was an only child, a view that adds poignancy
to Valerius Publicola's desire for his daughter to marry
and bear children. Although the Greek *Vita* does not explicitly mention siblings, it does report that Melania's
desire for asceticism so enraged Valerius Publicola that
he considered disinheriting her and giving his possessions "to the other children."[57] Although this is the
first and only reference to Melania's possible siblings
in the Greek *Vita*, we should not dismiss this testimony
out of hand, since the *Lausiac History* lends it support.
In Palladius' report on Melania the Elder, he mentions
that her son Valerius Publicola had two children,[58] and
adds that Melania the Elder "taught (κατηχήσασα) the
younger son of Publicola and led him to Sicily,"[59] presumably meaning that she attempted to woo him to
Christian asceticism.

Some scholars argue that Palladius (or at least
Butler's Greek text of the *Lausiac History*) is wrong on
this point,[60] since the *Vita* never mentions a brother
for Melania. Yet if the Greek text of the *Lausiac History*
is here suspect, we possess an ancient Syriac translation that provides a check on the reading.[61] The Syriac
version, however, gives only mixed assistance. Like
its Greek counterpart, it contains two references that
might shed light on a possible brother. In the first,
found in a chapter on Melania the Elder, her son,

Valerius Publicola, is said to have had "two children, a male and a female."[62] This reference is more specific as to sex than is the Greek version, which merely reports "two children."[63] However, in the passage corresponding to the Greek account that Melania the Elder taught "the younger son" of Publicola and led him to Sicily,[64] the Syriac version reads, in literal translation, "but her [Melania the Elder's] son, Publicola, the young one, she taught him and brought him to Sicily."[65] (René Draguet translates the line, "Quant à sons fils Publicola, qui était un jeune homme, elle l'instruit et le mena en Sicile.")[66] If the Syriac rendition of this second passage is accepted as preferable to the Greek, we lose a reference to a brother for Melania the Younger, but gain the information that Valerius Publicola accompanied his mother on a Sicilian sojourn in the opening years of the fifth century.[67]

Thus we must conclude that the Syriac version of the *Lausiac History* does not lend definitive assistance in resolving the question whether Melania had a brother. If she did, we can posit two possible reasons why he does not appear in the *Vita Melaniae Junioris*: either he died young, before the time when the inheritance was passed to Melania, or his association with Melania the Elder led to his mention being likewise suppressed in the text, along with hers. It is of course possible that Melania never thought to tell Gerontius about a brother who died while young, yet given the importance of problems concerning inheritance in the *Vita*, this possibility seems unlikely. We agree with Denys Gorce, translator of Melania's *Vita* into French, that there is no reason to rule out the possibility that Melania had a brother,[68] especially considering Palladius' testimony.

One consideration in particular leads us to defend
Palladius' information about Melania the Younger: although he wrote the *Lausiac History* some years after the
events described, namely, in A.D. 420[69] and in his
chapter on Melania the Younger includes no references to
activities later than about A.D. 409,[70] he was person-
ally acquainted with her. He had enjoyed hospitality
at her Roman mansion when he journeyed West to plead
on behalf of Constantinople's exiled bishop, John
Chrysostom, from approximately September 404 to early
405.[71] He describes his mission in his biography of
Chrysostom[72] and explicitly comments on Melania's hospitality in the chapter of the *Lausiac History* devoted to
her.[73] Given the revised dating of Valerius Publicola's
death to (probably) A.D. 406,[74] it is likely that
Palladius met him as well as other members of Melania's
family. He obviously knows details concerning her life
in this period, for example, that Pinian was the son of
Severus, former prefect of Rome.[75] Thus whatever crit-
icisms can be made about the historical accuracy of
Palladius' work in general, we see no reason to reject
out of hand the veracity of his report that Melania had
at least one brother[76]--but even if she did, we must
acknowledge that he plays no part in the *Vita*. Melania's
inheritance and subsequent renunciations, to which we
now turn, are not complicated in Gerontius' account by
the presence of a male sibling.

B. Melania's Early Renunciations

Melania's renunciations can best be understood
when viewed in the context of the ascetic devotion that
swept Christian Rome, especially its women, in the late
fourth century. Asceticism was not so ancient a

phenomenon in Rome as in Asia Minor[1] or in Egypt,[2] yet
by the mid-fourth century, Romans, too, had been struck
by enthusiasm for the ascetic life. Jerome dates the
origin of Christian asceticism in the Western capital
to about A.D. 340, when his friend Marcella heard
stories of the desert fathers from Athanasius' companions in exile and yearned for a similar renunciation.[3] Yet he probably dates Marcella's ascetic
interest too early: since she lived until A.D. 410,[4]
she would have been a child in 340.[5] However, in the
third quarter of the fourth century Marcella was prac-
ticing "house asceticism" in her palace on the
Aventine,[6] prior to her retreat to a more secluded setting.[7] This date well fits the evidence that in the
350s and 360s noble Roman women began to adopt asceticism: Pope Damasus' epitaph for his sister Irene
suggests that she espoused the ascetic life around 360;[8]
Ambrose's sister Marcellina dedicated herself to virginity at the time of Pope Liberius, probably around
353;[9] and Jerome represents both Asella[10] and Lea[11] as
among the older generation of female ascetics in Rome.

A few years later, Jerome's friend Paula adopted
ascetic practices after being widowed, and she gathered
about her a group of like-minded women.[12] After Melania
the Elder's bereavements, she departed in 372 or 374[13]
for a life of asceticism in the East.[14] Augustine reports that when he was in Rome (presumably in 383 or
388), he saw women ascetics who lived together and
worked with their hands to support themselves.[15] And in
the years when Melania the Younger was residing at
Thagaste, the renunciation of the adolescent Roman
heiress Demetrias of the *gens Anicia* took place in North
Africa.[16] Such examples illustrate the interest in ascetic devotion among Roman women, especially among the
aristocracy.

Two points should be registered about the phenomenon of asceticism in Rome. First, the type of renunciation originally practiced by Roman women was "house
monasticism": they went into ascetic retreat in their
own homes or palaces, adopting such renunciatory practices as fasting, vigils, and constant prayer.[17] Only
after this initial stage were monasteries established.
Melania the Elder's monasteries in Jerusalem marked the
beginning of the movement;[18] Paula's in Bethlehem were
founded a decade later.[19] Thus Melania the Younger repeated an established pattern in first espousing asceticism at home,[20] then retreating to the suburbs,[21]
and, finally, founding monasteries in North Africa[22]
and Jerusalem.[23] A second point worth reflection is
that women were the primary diffusers of the ascetic
ideal in Rome.[24] Since Jerome did not arrive in the
Western capital until A.D. 382, he was not the instiga-
tor of ascetic devotion among Roman women, as is sometimes implied in the scholarly literature.[25]

According to Melania the Younger's *Vita*, she had
been so "wounded by divine love" from an early age that
she wished to devote herself to virginity.[26] When her
young husband refused her request that they live in
chastity,[27] Melania more than once attempted to flee
the marriage,[28] but was restrained by "holy men" who
reminded her of Paul's words, "Wife, how do you know if
you will save your husband?"[29] Only after Melania's
brush with death at the birth of her son did Pinian re-
lent and agree to a chastity vow.[30] Melania's concern
for celibacy continued throughout her life: she counseled young people to retain their virginity and to shun
"filthy pleasures."[31] In addition, her refusal to
bathe,[32] choice of rough clothing,[33] and sleepless
vigils[34] are all attested from her early years, even

before her father's death opened the way for greater renunciations. Throughout the *Vita*, Melania's fasts, sleeplessness, coarse garments, and other deprivations receive ample attention.[35]

Her most spectacular renunciations, however, and those that by her own confession proved the greatest temptation,[36] were concerned with wealth. The problems Melania and Pinian faced in their journey from riches to rags centered on three issues: the dispersal of their annual discretionary income, the liquidation of their enormous estates scattered throughout empire, and the sale or manumission of their slaves. Although these three divestments are indeed linked, since the couple's income was largely derived from the revenues of the great estates worked by slaves, they may be separated for purposes of discussion.[37]

The Greek version of the *Vita* reports that Pinian's annual income was 120,000 "pieces of gold, more or less, not counting that derived from his wife's property."[38] The Latin version, on the other hand, ascribes the figure of 120,000 to Melania, apart from her husband's income.[39] Two problems here confront us: whose income the number represents, and whether the phrase "pieces of gold" means pounds of gold or gold *solidi*.

Rampolla, while noting that the texts do not state whether the gold was measured in pounds or in *solidi*, assumes the larger amount.[40] As was pointed out shortly after the publication of Rampolla's *Santa Melania Guiniore*, his calculation would give Melania a yearly income far in excess of all of Switzerland's revenues for the year 1904![41] If, on the other hand, the "pieces of gold" are understood as *solidi*, the income translates into 1,666 pounds of gold annually.[42] This figure, however, poses a further puzzle, for Melania would then not be as affluent as her *Vita* implies.

Our knowledge of senatorial wealth in the period
is aided by Olympiodorus' valuable report that the
richest senators had incomes of 4,000 pounds of gold
yearly, and the "middle level" of senators, 1,000 to
1,500 pounds.[43] Of course, if Melania and Pinian each
had annual incomes of about 1,700 pounds of gold they
might well be among the more affluent senators. But
even if we rank them among the moderately wealthy senators, as defined by Olympiodorus, they would have enjoyed a style of life comparable to that of Symmachus,
who owned nineteen houses and estates[44] and spent 2,000
pounds of gold on the games he sponsored for his son's
praetorship.[45] Thus even a moderate senatorial income
would be considered enormous wealth by modern standards.
Recalling that at the time of Gregory the Great[46]
eighty pounds of gold were deemed sufficient to support
3,000 nuns for a year,[47] we can instantly calculate that
an annual income of 1,666 pounds of gold more than suf-
ficed to provide a luxurious lifestyle for one person.

A second question is whether the *Vita* describes
Melania's or Pinian's income. Here we receive unex-
pected assistance from a letter of Symmachus. Although
undated, the letter must have been written several years
before Melania and Pinian made their renunciations, for
Symmachus died in about A.D. 402.[48] The letter, addressed to a certain Patruinus, asks the recipient to
intercede for the sons of Severus "of illustrious
memory" who had been subjected to plunder and injustice
at someone's hands.[49] If we assume that the Severus in
question is Valerius Severus, the letter provides the
important information that Pinian's father was already
dead and the family fortune under attack. (That Symmachus may have had some personal contact with the family
suggested by the fact that Pinian's uncle, Valerius

Pinianus, succeeded him as city prefect in A.D. 385.)[50]
Thus if the 120,000 "pieces of gold" described in the
Greek *Vita* were Pinian's income in *solidi*, the figure
could signify the reduced circumstances to which he and
his brother Severus had fallen through the unspecified
"plunder and injustice" mentioned by Symmachus. There
can be no doubt, however, that the *Vita* seeks to represent Melania and Pinian as the wealthiest people in
Rome: it reports that not one senator, not even Serena,
the mother-in-law of Honorius, could afford to buy their
Roman mansion.[51] Gerontius emphasis on the couple's
staggering wealth serves mainly to highlight the spectacular nature of their renunciations.

The amount of gold dispensed by Melania and Pinian
early in their ascetic careers functions as a barometer
of their riches. On one occasion, they sent 45,000
pieces of gold to the poor and to the saints;[52] they
distributed funds to "Mesopotamia, Syria, Palestine,
Egypt," indeed, to "all the West and all the East."[53]
At another time, they sent 100,000 coins to various
regions.[54] Paulinus of Nola notes that Pinian ransomed
children from prison with his gold,[55] and Palladius
reports that Melania gave 500 coins to the desert father Dorotheus.[56]

Much of the couple's wealth was derived from their
extensive properties scattered throughout the empire.
Their Roman palace on the Coelian Hill is mentioned
several times in the *Vita*, although modern commentators
disagree whether it belonged to Melania's family or to
Pinian's.[57] (Rampolla assigns it to Melania on the basis of an inscription found near the property that names
L. Valerius Poplicola Balbinus Maximus, whom he believes
to be an ancestor of Melania's father, Valerius Publicola;[58] De Rossi and Gatti judge the palace to be

Pinian's on the basis of a lamp inscription found at the
site pertaining to Valerius Severus, who was either
Pinian's father or his brother.)[59] From the *Vita* we
learn that this mansion, which at one time no one could
afford to buy,[60] was let go "for less than nothing"
after it was burned in the Gothic sack of Rome.[61]
In the sixth century, the Valerian palace probably became a hospice: a *xenodochium Valerii* is mentioned in two
letters by Gregory the Great.[62] Somewhat later, perhaps
in the seventh century, the monastery of St. Erasmus was
located on the site.[63] The Norman invasion of A.D. 1084
marked the end of the properties on the Coelian Hill,
all of which were destroyed by fire.[64]

Archeology has contributed much to our knowledge
of Melania and Pinian's palace. As early as A.D. 1554,
the atrium of a Roman house on the Coelian Hill was excavated, and bronze tablets found therein honoring L.
Aradius Valerius Proculus and Q. Aradius Valerius Proculus indicate that it belonged to the Valerii.[65]
Inscriptions discovered in 1561 add confirmation to the
assignment.[66] Seventeenth-century excavations at the
site uncovered a courtyard, vestiges of paintings that
depicted scenes of Rome, statues, busts, and the famous
lamp, now in the Archeological Museum in Florence,
bearing the inscription, "Dominus legem dat Valerio
Severo Eutropi vivas."[67] De Rossi posited that the lamp
commemorated the baptism of Valerius Severus,[68] Pinian's
father or brother.[69] The inscription in any case con-
firmed that some of the Valerii were Christians by the
later fourth century, a confirmation strengthened by
eighteenth-century finds of silver household vessels
with Christian emblems in the ruins of the Valerian
palace.[70] During construction of the Hospital of the
Addolorata between 1902 and 1904, more remains of the

Valerian mansion were unearthed, among them an atrium
with a colonnaded portico, three marble herms, mosaic
pavements (including one labeled "obscene" by Colini),
a walled rectangular area bounded by tiers, and a foun-
tain.[71] The *Vita's* testimony to the richness of the
house has thus received ample archeological support.

In addition to their Roman mansion, Melania and
Pinian also owned suburban property (perhaps a villa
along the fifth mile on the Appian Way)[72] to which they
retired immediately after her father's death.[73] The
Vita mentions another villa on the seacoast with an elaborate bath positioned between the sea and the forest,[74]
large enough, according the Latin version of the *Life*,
to be surrounded by sixty houses sheltering four hundred
agricultural slaves;[75] this may have been either the
estate in Sicily to which Melania and Pinian retired
shortly after Alaric's attack on Rome or one they owned
in Campania.[76] Their Italian property also included
some islands that they donated to "holy men."[77]

Italy, however, was only one area in which Melania
and Pinian owned land. The *Vita* reports estates in
Spain, Africa, Mauretania, Britain, and Numidia,[78] and
Palladius adds Aquitania and Gaul to the list.[79] When
Melania, Pinian, and Albina fled to North Africa, they
settled near Thagaste on one of their estates, which
the Latin *Vita* claims was larger than the town itself,
had a bath, and was inhabited by numerous artisans who
worked in gold, silver, and copper.[80] From this notice
we learn that the family's income was derived not just
from agricultural produce, but also from manufacture.
Melania's property might serve as a good illustration
of Olympiodorus' observation that Roman senatorial man-
sions were like small cities, containing their own hip-
podromes, public areas, temples, fountains, and baths.[81]

The *Vita* does not reveal the precise number of slaves Melania and Pinian owned.[82] Although the editor of the Latin *Life* reports that they freed "thousands" of slaves, he declines to give a number for fear of "vainglory": the couple and God know how many there were![83] Palladius, on the other hand, relates that at the beginning of her renunciations, Melania freed eight thousand of her slaves who desired manumission, and sold the rest to "her brother"[84] (presumably Pinian's brother Severus, whom the *Vita* depicts as laying claim to the couple's property and as stirring up their slaves to rebel).[85] Probably Melania drew her first core group of nuns from her former slaves.[86] Despite the lack of precise figures, we can readily calculate that the number of slaves she owned bespoke great wealth: John Chrysostom reports that a man who owned between one and two thousand slaves was rich.[87]

The dispersal of Melania and Pinian's property occasioned a number of dilemmas described in the *Vita*. For instance, the couple had not reached their legal majority (age twenty-five) when they began their renunciations: she was twenty, he was twenty-four.[88] A minor who wished to sell his property could apply for a special dispensation, the *venia aetatis*,[89] but even with this exemption, family members could insist that a minor have a guardian appointed for him if they could prove that he was given to prodigality or suffered mental derangement,[90] as Melania's relatives might with justification have claimed. Although the state wished to ensure that wealth did not leave senatorial families or at least the senatorial class in general,[91] Christian literature rarely represents imperial officials prohibiting ascetically inclined aristocrats' dispersal of their wealth.[92] Nonetheless, Valerius Publicola's

deathbed speech in which he freed Melania to disperse
her inheritance as she pleased [93] probably carried no
legal value. [94] Thus when the *Vita* indicates that
Melania's senatorial relatives, as well as Pinian's
brother Severus, tried to prevent the alienation of the
family property, [95] we must acknowledge that they were
within their legal right to do so, even though Gerontius
views the couple's renunciations as blessed acts.

A slave revolt proved another obstacle in their
renunciatory endeavor, prompting Melania and Pinian to
seek imperial assistance with their case. According to
the *Vita*, the Devil worked through Pinian's brother
Severus to agitate the slaves: the slaves did not wish
to be sold, but if sold they were going to be, they preferred to have Severus as their master than be "put on
the open market." [96] Although the process by which the
slaves' request developed into a revolt is not detailed
in the *Life*, the couple's fear of further slave uprisings on their other estates is said to have led them to
seek Serena in order to secure imperial intervention. [97]

Their visit in late 407 or early 408 [98] to Serena,
wife of Stilicho and mother-in-law of the emperor
Honorius, forms one of the more detailed episodes in the
Vita. We learn from it that four years had passed since
Serena had seen Melania: [99] this notice gives a clue to
dating, for the imperial entourage, usually resident in
Ravenna, was in Rome during January 404 for the celebration of the sixth consulship of Honorius. [100] In the
four years that followed, Melania had begun her earnest
renunciations, a development elaborated upon by
Serena. [101] The schemes of Severus and of Melania's
senatorial relatives who wished to enrich themselves
from her inheritance are here said to have been the
cause of the couple's difficulty in dispersing their

property. Although Serena offered to punish Severus,
the couple, in the spirit of Christian forgiveness, refused to seek revenge.[102] Oddly enough, the issue of
the slave revolt is not directly mentioned in the interview: Melania and Pinian rather received from Serena
her intercession with Honorius that resulted in a decree
mandating public officials in the provinces where the
couple owned land to sell their possessions and remit
the money to them.[103] Thus Melania and Pinian not only
received the highest authorization for the liquidation
of their property; they also were relieved of the burden
of having to dispose of it themselves.

The *Vita* provides another interesting detail related to the sale of the family property: an unnamed
city prefect, described as "a very ardent pagan," attempted along with the Senate to confiscate Melania and
Pinian's possessions for the public treasury. Soon
thereafter, reports Gerontius, the prefect felt the
hand of "God's Providence": he was killed in a riot
precipitated by a bread shortage, the couple's property
was, for the moment, preserved intact.[104] The fact that
Melania and Pinian would have been required to petition
this city prefect in order for them, as minors, to receive a dispensation allowing the sale of their property[105] raised the interesting possibility (not
addressed in the *Vita*) that the prefect became aware of
their intentions when they applied for a *venia aetatis*.

These events transpired in the context of Alaric's
advance on Rome. Information supplied by Zosimus,
Sozomen, and other contemporary historians sheds light
on three points in the *Vita* pertaining to this event:
Serena's intervention to help the couple liquidate their
property, the slave revolt, and the attempt of the city
prefect and the Senate to confiscate the couple's

property for the city treasury. A brief review of historical events is helpful in our reconstruction of Melania's exodus from Rome.

Barbarians under Radagaisus invaded northern Italy in A.D. 405; in late 406 and early 407, barbarian troops crossed the Rhine and ravaged Gaul.[106] According to Zosimus, in the midst of Gaul's devastation, Honorius canceled the proposed campaign that would ally Stilicho and Alaric for the West's conquest of Illyria.[107] It was necessary to pacify Alaric on this occasion, but the Senate was reluctant to pay the 4,000 pounds of gold suggested.[108] Realizing the military weakness of Rome, Stilicho throughout pursued a policy of peace with Alaric; this plan has been judged more realistic by modern commentators than the war-mongering enthusiasms of the Senate.[109] Stilicho's concessive measures toward the Gothic chief,[110] when coupled with the rumor that he desired to place his own son Eucherius on the Eastern throne[111] after the death of the Eastern emperor Arcadius on 1 May 408, no doubt contributed to his downfall.[112] Inflamed by fears and rumors, the troops massacred Honorius' officials at Ticinum on 13 August.[113] Against the advice of his barbarian advisors, Stilicho marched to Ravenna, where he was executed on 22 August.[114] When the report of Stilicho's death reached Roman soldiers stationed in the cities, they engaged in a bloodbath, cutting down the wives and children of barbarian men and confiscating their possessions. This massacre, Zosimus says, led the relatives of the murdered barbarians to ally themselves with Alaric against Rome and raise a force ready to support the barbarian chief.[115]

After Stilicho's execution, his partisans were in a dangerous position. Laws from September and November

of 408 order their property to be confiscated, among
other reprisals;[116] Zosimus relates that Stilicho's
friends were tortured and put to death, in addition to
the confiscations.[117] The "anti-German" mood was
clearly manifest.

        The fate of Serena, however, was not immediately
clear. Honorius had sent his new bride Thermantia,
daughter of Stilicho and Serena, back to her mother at
the time of Stilicho's execution;[118] this act could be
interpreted to mean that Honorius did not intend to
move against Stilicho's wife and daughter.[119] The mood
at Rome, however, was far from irenic: as Alaric moved
south toward the end of 408, suspicion arose that
Stilicho's widow was in collusion with him. Whether
Honorius in Ravenna could have stayed the chain of
events that followed is unclear. In any case, the
Senate, together with Honorius' sister Galla Placidia,
accused Serena of collaborating with Alaric in his first
attack on the city and had her executed.[120] Although
no date is given for Serena's execution, it must have
occurred at the end of 408 or the very beginning of 409.
To what extent Serena's Christian enthusiasm (and im-
piety toward the pagan gods) played a role, as well as
to what extent the will of Galla Placidia, has been debated.[121] According to Zosimus, the Senate naively
assumed that with Serena gone, Alaric would retreat in
the belief that no one else would betray the city to
him.[122]

        Alaric, of course, did not abandon Rome. After a
short reprieve, he blockaded the Tiber, thereby pre-
venting food and other supplies from reaching the
city.[123] Famine and plague abounded; rumors of canni-
balism were rife.[124] According to Zosimus' ordering of
events, an embassy from Rome to Alaric returned bearing

his first request: that all the city's gold, silver, movable goods, and barbarian slaves be given to him.[125] The city prefect, Gabinus Barbarus Pompeianus,[126] suggested that Etruscan rituals be performed to ward off the Gothic danger. Although Pompeianus allegedly had the connivance of Pope Innocent I in the proposal, it was to no avail. When it became known that the rituals must be performed in public with the participation of the Senate, "no one dared."[127]

Alaric then relented. He would reduce his terms to 5,000 pounds of gold, 30,000 of silver, 4,000 silk tunics, 3,000 scarlet fleeces, and 3,000 pounds of pepper, but the Senate demurred even at this concession. An official named Palladius was delegated to assess the senators and assign an amount each should contribute, but the senators either could not or would not cooperate. Zosimus reports that ornaments were stripped from statues of the gods to furnish the required funds.[128] It appears that at least some of the money was raised, for Alaric gave a brief respite to the beleaguered Romans,[129] presumably early in 409. According to Zosimus, slaves continued to escape from the city to Alaric's camp until their number reached 40,000.[130] When Honorius also balked at Alaric's demands and did not send the hostages the Gothic chief requested, the city was blockaded and egress prevented.[131] Alaric continued to reduce his demands, without effect;[132] the denial of a generalship in the Roman army especially angered him.[133] The recalcitrance of first the Senate and then Honorius can surely be held as a contributing factor to Alaric's sack of Rome in August 410.[134]

Scholars have attempted to link events in the *Life of Melania* with the historical situation described above. Thus Gorce postulates that Serena's intervention on

behalf of Melania and Pinian (in addition to her ardent
Christian sympathies) may have prompted the Senate's
decision to execute her. With the removal of Stilicho
and Serena, whom Gorce considers the city's prime lay
champions of Christianity, a pagan leadership remained
which might have attempted a pagan restoration. He
posits that perhaps Melania's loss of her powerful pro-
tector and her fear of a pagan reaction contributed to
her desire to leave Rome.[135] John Matthews links
Alaric's demands for money to Pompeianus' attempt to
confiscate Melania's property: the sale of her property could have furnished the funds the Gothic chieftain
demanded.[136]

The most far-reaching argument linking Melania with
the events pertaining to Serena's execution and Alaric's
attack, however, is that of Alexander Demandt and Guntram Brummer.[137] According to them, Serena's intervention to help liquidate Melania's property, without
consulting the Senate, was a central reason for her
downfall;[138] it dampened the hopes of Rome's senators
who wished to lay claim to the property for their own
purposes. An economic motive was at stake.[139] The
association with Melania not only hurt Serena. The reverse was also true: Melania's link to Serena had
unpleasant consequences for the ascetic after Serena's
execution. Since it was contrary to Roman law to confiscate personal property unless a criminal charge had
been leveled against its owner,[140] some charge was
needed if Melania and Pinian's property were to be appropriated. According to Demandt and Brummer, the
charge Pompeianus probably used was the couple's association with Serena.[141] By their reckoning, the
execution of Serena and the murder of Pompeianus both
took place before the end of 408.[142]

Demandt and Brummer posit a religious as well as an economic motivation for the Senate's action against Serena. On the bases of the report that Pompeianus advocated the adoption of Etruscan rituals[143] and of Gerontius' claim that Pompeianus was "a very ardent pagan,"[144] the authors pit the "active paganism" of Pompeianus against Serena's championing of the Christian faith.[145] Thus, according to them, pagan-Christian conflict played an important role in the events of 408. Here Demandt and Brummer may be in error: Zosimus explicitly states that Pompeianus was a partisan of the "prevailing religion" (...τὴν κρατοῦσαν...δόξαν), which surely in A.D. 408 must mean Christianity, and explains that Pompeianus consulted Bishop Innocent regarding his plan for the Etruscan rituals so that he might feel "safer."[146] In general, the hostility between Christians and pagans in Rome may have been overplayed by Demandt and Brummer.

Although it is probable both that Pompeianus' plan to appropriate Melania and Pinian's property stemmed from the need to raise money for Alaric and that Melania's departure from Rome was connected with the downfall of her highly placed protectors as well as with the Gothic attack, the precise thesis of Demandt and Brummer is impossible to prove. First, our main source, Zosimus, does not present so rigorous a chronology of events for 408-409 that we can establish firm causal connections among them.[147] Second, their arguments assumes that there was a trial not just of Serena, but one (or a proposed one) for Melania[148]--and of the latter not a word appears in our sources.[149] Zosimus remarks that the Senate "unanimously decided" to execute Serena,[150] but what the process entailed is not described in fuller detail. In no material pertaining to

Melania is there any hint that actual criminal charges
were raised against her.

There remains the question of the slave uprising.
The Latin *Vita* (although not the Greek) reports that many
of Melania's slaves shared Pompeianus' view on the disposal of the property,[151] presumably meaning that they
preferred to be included with the confiscated property
than sold immediately, as Melania desired. According
to Demandt and Brummer, the slaves must have believed
that by siding with Pompeianus, they could postpone
their sale for at least a time: fear of the slave market was always present in their minds.[152] The Latin
Vita adds that many of these slaves were taken ill or
killed by God for their wicked views,[153] perhaps an
oblique reference to the famine and plague devastating
the city. Zosimus claims that Rome had become "a tomb
for the dead" and that the stench of rotting corpses
was intolerable.[154]

The uprising of Melania's slaves, however, might be
set in a larger political framework: the wholesale de-
sertion of slaves (Zosimus says 40,000 of them) to the
Goths during Alaric's attack.[155] If many of these
slaves were of barbarian extraction, as seems likely,[156]
this notice supplements Zosimus' earlier report that
after Roman soldiers massacred barbarian wives and children, barbarians in Italy raised a force of 30,000 men
for Alaric.[157] It may well be that the slave uprisings
which confronted Melania in Rome, and which she feared
would spread to her other estates, were part of the
larger slave unrest occasioned by Alaric's advance.

Finally, it would be fascinating to know--but no
sources provide the information--if Melania's uncle
Volusian was involved in the downfall of Serena and the
proposed confiscation of his niece's property. Such may

have been the case, since a Volusianus is named as
Honorius' *comes rei privatae*, master of the privy purse,
at Ravenna in the fall of A.D. 408,[158] shortly after
Stilicho's execution in August. Whether this Volusianus
was Melania's uncle, however, remains unknown. The
Vita only reports the couple's flight southward, the
next subject of our investigation.

C. North Africa and Beyond

In late 408 or 409,[1] Pinian, Melania, and Albina
left Rome, never to return. They fled first to their
estates in Sicily, a stop that is mentioned but not described in the *Vita*.[2] According to Palladius, Melania
had not sold her Sicilian or African properties at the
time her other estates were liquidated;[3] her possession
of them proved fortunate when the family escaped Rome
soon thereafter. The trio apparently joined Rufinus in
Sicily, for in the preface to his translation of
Origen's *Homilies on Numbers* on which he was then working,
Rufinus alludes to the barbarians' burning of Rhegium,
across the Strait of Messina from Sicily,[4] and to
Pinian's encouragement of his translation activities.[5]

Melania and her family intended next to cross the
strait from Sicily for a visit with Paulinus at Nola,[6]
but their plan was never realized: they were blown off
course by a storm and forced to put in at an island
where they ransomed local notables from captivity by
barbarians.[7] Nola may in fact already have been sacked
by the time the group decided to leave Sicily (Augustine
in the *City of God* reports the pious prayer uttered by
Paulinus upon the occasion of Nola's devastation).[8]
There is, in any case, no evidence that Melania saw
Nola on her flight south from Rome. Since Sicily was

also in danger of imminent attack by Alaric,[9] it was
prudent for the trio to leave for more distant shores.

    Like other aristocratic Roman refugees such as the
Anicii,[10] Melania's family decamped to their North
African estates. Upon arrival, probably in late 410,[11]
they sold their properties in Numidia, Mauretania, and
Africa Proconsularis, donating the proceeds to Christian charity,[12] and settled on their estate near
Thagaste.[13] The proper disposal of the proceeds from
the sale of their North African properties was discussed
by Augustine, Alypius of Thagaste, and Aurelius of
Carthage; their advice to found and endow monasteries
rather than grant outright gifts of money was heeded.[14]
In addition, Melania, Pinian, and Albina so enriched the
impoverished town of Thagaste that other bishops in the
province envied Alypius his wealthy benefactors.[15]

    The *Vita* here omits an interesting episode known
from the correspondence of Augustine (letters 125-126):
during the course of A.D. 411 the people of Hippo rioted
for Pinian to become their priest. The frightened
young man barely escaped forced ordination by taking a
solemn vow that he would consider Hippo his home if the
inhabitants did not press him into holy orders;[16] he
apparently also agreed not to accept ordination elsewhere.[17] Augustine's letters on the affair suggest that
Pinian was guilty of some dissimulation,[18] and that
Albina outrightly accused the residents of Hippo of
greed for Pinian's money.[19] By way of rejoinder,
Augustine rhetorically asked why the inhabitants of
Hippo would have expected to be enriched, since the trio
had not given money to the people of Thagaste (as distinguished from the church).[20] Throughout, Augustine
emphasized that the residents of Hippo loved Pinian for
his virtues, not for his wealth. But Albina hinted

that Augustine himself may have had a less than spiritual interest in Pinian's ordination. And the correspondence makes clear that when Melania protested
Augustine's role as witness to Pinian's oath, he only
grudgingly honored her wishes and left off his testifying signature.[21] Although Augustine insisted to
Albina that he wished merely to smooth ruffled
feelings,[22] he did not refrain from mentioning that
their donations were an example of Jesus' advice to make
friends with "the mammon of unrighteousness."[23] Augus-
time also asserted that if Pinian never returned to
Hippo, he would consider him guilty of perjury.[24] It
is easy to understand why Melania (or Gerontius) preferred to have this unedifying incident relegated to
oblivion.[25] Among the things we infer from Augustine's
two letters concerning this episode are that bishops
needed openly to placate wealthy laymen and that
Pinian's zeal for the religious life was perhaps less
ardent than Melania's. This point is suggested by the
Vita itself[26] and reinforced by Augustine's reference to
Pinian's "strong natural capacity for enjoying this
world."[27]

During their seven-year sojourn in North Africa,[28]
Melania's devotion to asceticism was strengthened.
There she founded her first monasteries for men and
women;[29] she intensified her fasts, lengthening their
duration to five days.[30] She slept in sackcloth,[31] and
in a box so constructed that she could neither stretch
out nor turn over.[32] She went without sleep in order to
pray more ardently,[33] studied Scripture and the writings
of the church fathers,[34] developed a strong aversion to
"heresy,"[35] bribed young people to lead lives of chastity,[36] and retreated to greater ascetic solitude.[37]

The section of the *Vita* pertaining to North Africa
is disappointingly thin in its coverage of important
events that must have impinged upon Melania's life
during her years there. Our text makes no mention of
Heraclian,[38] who as *comes Africae* held military control
over North Africa at this time as a reward for "cutting
down Stilicho with his own hand."[39] Heraclian remained
faithful to Honorius when Alaric raised the Roman city
prefect Atalus as a rival to the emperorship in A.D.
409;[40] Heraclian killed the commander of the troops
Atalus sent to relieve Heraclian of his post.[41]
Heraclian's assistance was of immense importance to
Honorius at this volatile moment in Rome's history, for
it was through Heraclian's provision of funds that
Honorius was able to strengthen his own position among
the soldiers.[42] Heraclian was able to pressure Rome's
inhabitants by blockading Africa's harbors so that
grain, oil, and other supplies could not reach the
Western capital, thus contributing to the severe
famine.[43] Yet Heraclian's loyalty was not long-lived:
when he revolted against the emperor in A.D. 413 he
rapidly met his death.[44]

The events pertaining to Heraclian may have affected Melania in two ways. First, Jerome recounts a
grim tale of Heraclian's devastations in Africa, in
particular of his attempt to lay hands on the Anician
fortune.[45] Jerome paints Heraclian as a monster, as
the king of Tartarus, who profited from forcing marri-
ages of high-born maidens to Syrian merchants.[46]
Sparing no one, he was more cruel than Alaric.[47]
Proba, grandmother of the Demetrias who vowed chastity
in A.D. 414, was constrained to bribe Heraclian to preserve the chastity of her female companions.[48] If the
Anician fortune was thus greedily eyed by Heraclian

(perhaps to raise money for Honorius, as well as for his self-aggrandizement), how did Melania's family escape a similar fate? One answer might be that they had already divested themselves of their North African property, so there was little if any left for Heraclian to covet. An alternative hypothesis, although without supporting evidence, is that the family did not escape Heraclian's ravages, and that the people of Hippo dropped their demand for Pinian's ordination when they realized that Pinian would no longer be able to enrich them or their church.[49]

Another aspect of Heraclian's revolt may have affected Melania during her stay in North Africa. The revolt became embroiled in the Donatist controversy then raging in North Africa.[50] In A.D. 410, Honorius ordered a council of Donatist and Catholic bishops to decide which party represented the "true church." Marcellinus, a friend of Augustine and of Melania's uncle, Volusian, was placed in charge of the proceedings.[51] The council met in June 411, and at its end Marcellinus ruled against the Donatists.[52] A period of Donatist repression followed.[53] When Marinus was sent from Rome to deal with the aftermath of Heraclian's revolt against the emperor in 413,[54] Marcellinus was somehow implicated, presumably by disgruntled Donatists; he was tried and summarily beheaded.[55] Only one year earlier, Augustine, Marcellinus, and Volusian, all in Africa, had exchanged letters on problematic issues of the Christian faith, and in A.D. 412-413, the first books of the *City of God*, dedicated to Marcellinus, had appeared. (The opening of books of the *City of God*, it will be recalled, reply to the queries and charges that pagans such as Volusian had raised.)[56] Melania's immediate family must have been shocked at the execution

of Volusian's highly placed friend. In the *Vita*, however, no mention is made of Heraclian, Marcellinus, or
the Donatist uprisings, even though the Latin version
suggests that many Donatist laborers resided on
Melania's estate.[57] The absence of such detail from the
Vita is yet another indication that the author probably
was not an eyewitness to events in Melania's life before
her arrival in Jerusalem.

The trio departed suddenly from Africa in 416 or
417.[58] The *Vita* implies that their trip to Jerusalem
was intended as a pilgrimage to the Holy Places,[59] and
not as a permanent relocation. They stopped en route at
Alexandria, where they were received by Bishop Cyril
and were recognized by the desert father Nestoros, who,
through his prophetic gifts, recounted to them their
troubles and cheered them with thoughts of their future
bliss.[60] Arriving in Jerusalem, they lived in the cells
for pilgrims attached to the Church of the Holy Sepulcher (the Anastasis).[61] So extensively had they dispersed their remaining wealth that they considered
enrolling themselves on the lists of the church's
poor.[62] Melania quickly resumed her former life of
study, fasting, and vigils.[63] Soon an opportunity arose
for her and Pinian to return to Egypt, a trip financed
by the sale of her Spanish property that had not been
liquidated during the barbarian onslaught.[64] In Egypt,
the couple visited and made donations to the desert
monks and nuns, pressing their largesse even upon un-
willing recipients.[65] From the desert they returned to
Alexandria, meeting there with various monks and priests
before journeying to those premier monastic settlements
at Nitria and "the Cells."[66]

When the couple returned to Jerusalem, Melania
found waiting a small cell on the Mount of Olives that

she had requested Albina have built while she was in
Egypt.[67] According to Gerontius, Melania resided in
this cell annually from Epiphany to Easter for fourteen
years.[68] The remainder of the year, we gather, she
spent in the city of Jerusalem with her mother. Only
after Albina's death did Melania abandon city life entirely.[69] Interestingly, unlike the flurry of monastery
construction which marked Melania's stay in North
Africa, she attempted no monastic foundation in Jerusalem in the early years of her sojourn there. Only
after Albina's death in 431 or 432[70] did Melania build
her first monastery, for ninety virgins, on the Mount of
Olives.[71]

D. The Mount of Olives

1. Melania's Constructions

When Melania the Younger built her monasteries on
the Mount of Olives, the site was well populated with
churches, cells, oratories, and monastic foundations.
Believed to be the spot both of Jesus' crucifixion and
his ascension (and by some misinformed Christians, of
his transfiguration[1] and proclamation of the Beatitudes
as well),[2] the mountain was heavy with associations
significant for all Christians. Church construction on
Olivet in the fourth century commemorated these events:
the Church of the Eleona, we know, was a Constantinian
foundation;[3] the Church of Gethsemane was erected in the
second half of the fourth century;[4] and the Church of
the Ascension, no longer considered a Constantinian
foundation, was probably constructed in the 380s by
Poemenia, whose patronage of the project has been recovered by twentieth-century scholarship.[5]

Monasteries and monastic cells also dotted the
mountain by the late fourth century. Melania the Elder
and Rufinus were among the first to establish monasteries there, probably in the late 370s.[6] Scholars have
posited that the remains of beautiful marbles discovered
below the Eleona, including a Corinthian capital and a
small mosaic-paved basin with a Christian inscription,
came from their foundations.[7] Rufinus testifies that
many monks inhabited the mountain;[8] Basil of Caesarea
gives a less pleasing picture of the discord rampant
among them.[9] Palladius, too, was familiar with monks
on Olivet from his three-year stay there in the 380s.[10]
At the turn of the fifth century, a convent headed by a
woman named Euphemia, presumably from Byzantium, was in
operation on the mountain.[11] Close to Melania the
Younger's time, Saint Pelagia retired to a cell on
Olivet.[12] Melania the Younger, however, appears as the
most enthusiastic builder on the Mount of Olives. Why
she decided to construct monasteries there when her
grandmother had already established two around A.D. 378-
380 has been debated[13] (and will be considered below).[14]
The younger Melania was responsible for the construction
of two monasteries, a chapel, and a martyrion on the
mountain in the decade of the 430s.

After her mother's death, Melania built a monastery
for women and enlisted Pinian to recruit about ninety
virgins for it.[15] She was especially concerned that the
nuns be strictly cloistered so that they would not risk
association with men. To this end, she had a cistern
built within the monastery.[16] The Latin *Vita* adds that
Lausus, the ex-*prepositus* of Constantinople, provided
funds upon Melania's request for the construction of a
bath inside the monastic complex, thus further protect-
ing the nuns from exposure to outsiders, especially to

men.[17] Although Melania apparently directed the affairs
of the monastery, she did not herself serve as its
superior (due to an excess of humility, according to
Gerontius), but chose another woman for the position.[18]

In the women's monastery, Melania had an oratory
with an altar built so that the Eucharist could be offered regularly for the women; services were held twice
a week. In this oratory she placed the relics of
Zechariah, Stephen, and the Forty Martyrs of Sebaste.[19]
Gerontius describes the practices of the women's monastery, including such details as the nuns' vigils,[20]
their daily and nightly offices,[21] and Melania's lectures on humility, fasting,[22] and the necessity for
obedience.[23]

After Pinian's death in late 431 or 432,[24] Melania
deposited his remains in a chapel called "the
Aposteleion" that she had constructed shortly before;[25]
Albina's remains may also have been relocated in this
chapel.[26] The Aposteleion was apparently located near
the grotto in which Christians believed that Jesus had
talked with his disciples about the eschaton;[27] indeed,
from the era of the Apocryphal Acts of John[28] the
tradition existed that this grotto was a site of Jesus'
teaching.[29]

After four years of mourning for Pinian, Melania
decided to build a monastery for men, expressly designed as a residence for those monks who would perform
the chants in the major churches on Olivet: she wished
uninterrupted psalmody to be carried out "at the place
of the Ascension of the Lord" (i.e., at the Church of
the Ascension) and "in the grotto where the Savior
talked with his holy disciples about the end of time"[30]
(i.e., presumably in the Church of the Eleona above the
grotto). The construction of the men's monastery was

subsidized by a donation of "two hundred coins" from an unidentified "Christ-loving man" and was completed within one year.[31]

Upon her return from Constantinople, Melania constructed the last of her buildings on the Mount of Olives, a martyrion located "at the place where the Lord's feet had stood,"[32] that is, at the place of the Ascension. (That you could actually *see* Jesus' footprints excited Paulinus of Nola, who presumably derived his information from Melania the Elder.)[33] To this martyrion, dedicated in the presence of the empress Eudocia,[34] Melania transferred (or brought new) relics of Saint Stephen.[35]

Melania thus emerges as a major patron of the building program on the Mount of Olives,[36] which before the Persian destruction of A.D. 614 numbered twenty-four churches plus monasteries.[37] In addition to references concerning Melania's monasteries in the already-cited works of Cyril of Scythopolis[38] and John Rufus,[39] an interesting notice given by the pilgrim Theodosius the Deacon (ca A.D. 530) mentions a women's monastery, perhaps Melania's, in which there was a sanctuary built over a cave, and cisterns. The women were so completely cloistered, Theodosius reports, that their food was brought into the monastery through a hole in the wall.[40] Presumably Melania's monasteries were destroyed in the Persian invasion.[41]

Nineteenth-and twentieth-century archeologists claim to have unearthed parts of Melania's complex. Clermont-Ganneau thought that he had identified the church of Melania's monastery for men,[42] but Rampolla objected that the three-naved church excavated could hardly be the "small martyrion" Melania built for the men's monastery.[43] Melania's monastery for women,

according to the research of Vincent and Abel, stretched
to the east and south of the Eleona sanctuary. Now in
the possession of the Carmelites and the White Fathers,
the property has been excavated and a mosaic fragment
has been found with verses inscribed from the Psalms;
Vincent and Abel posit that it may have been from one
of Melania's oratories.[44] In addition, a large cistern
was uncovered on the site that perhaps can be identified
with the cistern of the women's monastic complex mentioned in *Vita* 41.[45] Last, part of an apse recovered in
connection with excavations at the Church of the Ascension has been deemed a wall from Melania's "small
martyrion,"[46] although other scholars express hesitation
at so firm an identification.[47]

2.   Cardinal Rampolla and Melania's *Romanitas*

In his *Santa Melania Guiniore*, Rampolla made much of
the allegedly Western, indeed Roman (i.e., specific to
the city of Rome), practices that Melania imported to
Palestine and employed in her monasteries on the Mount
of Olives. His argument contravened the prevailing view
that the East, especially Egypt and Asia Minor, exerted
the prime influence on all monastic development.
      To be sure, Eastern Christianity exerted a para-
mount influence on the growth of Western asceticism, as
well as on other aspects of Christian belief and practice. Palestine, as well as Syria and Egypt, contributed greatly to the religious life of the West,
especially through those Western pilgrims and tourists
who from the fourth century on flocked to view the Holy
Places. A vast range of objects, texts, and practices
journeyed to the West through the auspices of the Latins
in Palestine. There were relics: Melania the Elder,

for example, dispensed some precious wood from the True
Cross to Paulinus of Nola, who in turn gave a piece of
his gift to Sulpicius Severus.[48] There were bones, such
as those of Stephen, which arrived at Minorca and in
North Africa not long after their *inventio* in Palestine
in 415.[49] There were translations of Greek theological
and ascetic writings, such as of Origen's *On First
Principles* and of Basil's *Rules*.[50] The liturgy of Western
churches was undoubtedly influenced by pilgrims' reports
on "how they do things in Palestine," of which Egeria's
travel diary provides the most notable example.[51] The
Veneration of the Cross and the double celebration of
the Eucharist at Christmas are two practices that Rome
probably adopted from Palestine.[52] Even the art of the
West was stimulated by the Latins' contact with Palestine: witness the apse mosaic of St. Pudenziana in
Rome, its background crowded with depictions of Jerusalem's churches.[53] There is no doubt that in these and
other ways, Westerners who had traveled to Palestine
enriched the lives of their countrymen back home.

When we turn to the contribution made by Latin-
speaking men and women to the religious life of Palestine, however, the evidence is more difficult to assess.
Certainly, Western aristocrats dispensed considerable
funds in the Holy Land for the founding of monasteries
and churches as well as for charity. It was from her
own fortune that Melania the Elder constructed monasteries for herself and Rufinus on the Mount of Olives.[54]
She also won renown by supporting some ascetics and
bishops who fled from Egypt to Diocaesarea when the
Arian emperor Valens persecuted Nicene Christians.[55]
Jerome's friend Paula expended her riches on monasteries
for men and women in Bethlehem.[56] So numerous were the
women who flocked to her convent that she divided them

into three companies,[57] and so lavish were her donations
to the monastery that, according to Jerome, she died a
pauper, leaving her daughter and successor Eustochium an
inheritance of debts.[58]

Once we leave the realm of hard cash and look for
less tangible influences of Westerners on the East, we
are rapidly stymied. There is little evidence that the
Romans in Palestine contributed much distinctively
"Western" to the religious life of the Holy Land--even
though Western customs might theoretically have proved
useful as ideological weapons in the Bethlehem contin-
gent's war against Bishop John of Jerusalem.[59] For
example, we can note some differences in observance between Paula and Jerome's monastic establishments and
those founded by Easterners. The hours of prayer differed slightly from those celebrated by the Palestinian
Church.[60] Latin, along with Greek and Syriac, was used
in the Church of the Nativity.[61] Perhaps less manual
labor was undertaken in the Western monasteries of
Palestine than was typical in Eastern ones.[62] Christmas
was celebrated on 25 December, in Roman fashion.[63]
According to Cyril of Scythopolis, a Roman woman named
Ikelia introduced the use of candles at the local
Palestinian festival from which the Feast of the Presentation in the Temple evolved.[64] But to claim on the
basis of this slight evidence that the group of Latins
founded "a small Western island"[65] at Bethlehem seems
an overstatement. Source material documenting Roman
influence on customs of the Palestinian Church is disappointingly meager. With a sense of hopefulness, then,
scholars turned to the *Life of Melania the Younger*: the
nature of the text--more detailed than the spotty
notices provided by Palladius, Jerome, and Paulinus of
Nola--inspired confidence that here we might come to a

more generous assessment of the Western contribution to
Palestinian Christianity.

The monetary contributions of Melania the Younger
to Palestinian Christianity are the easiest to gauge.
Even before she and Pinian left Rome, they had made
donations to Christians in the Holy Land.[66] Although
the size of their gift is not mentioned in the *Vita*,
Palladius supplies this particular detail: she sent
15,000 pieces of money to Palestine, the largest of her
contributions to churches in diverse regions (other
churches received only 10,000 each).[67] On their arrival
in Palestine, Melania, Pinian, and Albina promptly
turned over yet more gold to church authorities for
charitable uses.[68] Later, Melania was to build the two
monasteries, the chapel, and the martyrion already mentioned.

Less easy to document is the allegedly Western cast
that Melania lent to Jerusalem's monastic and liturgical
life. Here the evidence is clouded by two factors: our
incomplete knowledge of what would constitute a distinctively and exclusively "Roman" liturgical rite as
early as A.D. 430, and the excessive claims that Mariano
Rampolla, the discoverer and editor of the Latin *Vita*
Melaniae Junioris, makes for the "Romaninity" of his subject. Rampolla's opinions have influenced most commentators on Melania's *Life* since his monumental *Santa Melania*
Giuniore appeared in 1905.[69] To Rampolla's predisposi-
tions we shall return, but first let us survey the
allegedly Roman practices that Melania is thought to
have observed in her monasteries on Olivet.

For example, in the Latin version of the *Life* (but
not in the Greek) Melania is represented as receiving
communion every day, a practice the text claims was a
custom of the Roman Church from the time of the apostles

Peter and Paul.[70] We could of course argue on the basis
of Acts 2:46 that daily communion originated in the
Jerusalem Church, not the Roman one, but leaving aside
the testimony of Acts, the evidence regarding the fre-
quency of communion in the early church is mixed.[71] To
support his thesis that in the fourth and fifth century
daily communion was a Roman custom, Rampolla appeals to
Innocent I[72] and to Jerome,[73] yet the fact that daily
communion was observed in Western quarters other than
Rome (e.g., we have notices from Chromatius of
Aquileia[74] and from Ambrose of Milan)[75] rather weakens
the exclusiveness of Rampolla's claim. Indeed, the
practice of daily communion could be explained just as
cogently as a monastic, rather than a Roman, custom:
Rufinus[76] and John Cassian[77] mention the daily communion
of monks. Rampolla uncritically accepts the Latin *Vita's*
claim that the custom is distinctively Roman because
Peter and Paul allegedly stood at its origin. Moreover,
neither the Greek nor the Latin version suggests any of
Melania's nuns or monks followed the practice, even
though the Latin *Vita* reports that she herself did.

A second supposed testimony to the Romaninity of
Melania's practices lies in Gerontius' claim that both
she and her uncle Volusian received communion on their
deathbeds.[78] The Latin rendition of the *Life* explicitly
states that this custom accords with the practice of the
Roman Church.[79] Yet Rampolla is on shaky ground when he
argues that the rite was peculiarly Roman, for evidence
exists that it was practiced in Eastern churches even
before the time of Melania (e.g., John Chrysostom makes
notice of it).[80] The practice, to be sure, is also
well-documented by such Roman authors as Gregory the
Great,[81] almost two centuries later.

A third claim is that Melania's holding of private
masses was distinctively Roman. Here the testimony
pertaining to Melania comes from the fifth-century *Life
of Peter the Iberian*: in addition to saying mass on Sunday
at both the men's and the women's cloisters, Melania's
priest Gerontius held a private service for her every
day, "as was the custom of the Roman Church."[82] One
might reply that, whatever the custom of the Roman
Church, Melania's ability to have a daily private service was directly dependent upon the fact that she had
her own private priest. Moreover, the *Vita* provides
ample evidence that Melania was, in general, a recluse
in her approach to worship: she made her devotions at
the Church of the Holy Sepulcher when no one else was
present and left when the church opened for public service.[83] So antisocial was Melania that she periodically
shut herself in a cell and spoke to no one.[84] If the
private chapel in Melania's Roman mansion [85] is taken as
a sign that Roman Christians enjoyed private daily
masses, we think the evidence is misconstrued: Melania's
private chapel is as much a corollary of her enormous
wealth as of her piety. Counterevidence to the Roman
claim is provided by Gregory of Nazianzus: his sister
Gorgonia, living far from Rome in Cappadocia, also had
a private chapel in her home[86]--and this some years before Melania.

It is, however, Melania's liturgical practices that
Rampolla and others find most "Roman." Rampolla's argument rests on the assumption that any practices reported
in the *Vita Melaniae Junioris* differing from the customs
of the Jerusalem Church (as seen through Egeria and
Cyril of Jerusalem) are Roman. For example, the number
of Psalms recited during the night and early morning
hours at Melania's monastery differed from the customary

practice of the Jerusalem Church. According to Egeria, the lengthy night office in Jerusalem consisted of many Psalms, antiphons, prayers, and readings that were prolonged until daybreak.[87] John Cassian also reports that from Christian antiquity, twelve Psalms and two lessons had been the rule,[88] with Psalms, prayers, and Scriptural lessons continuing until dawn.[89] In Melania's monastery, by way of contrast, the night office was considerably shorter: three Psalms and three readings. The morning office, however, was extended to fifteen Psalms.[90] Gerontius explains that Melania wished the nuns to sleep enough between the night service and the morning one in order to be refreshed for the day's round of worship.[91] Here Rampolla himself does not argue that Melania's practice was distinctively Roman: following the Latin *Vita*, he explains the deviation by appealing to the delicate constitutions of the women.[92] In addition to the questionable supposition that anything different must necessarily be Roman, Rampolla also fails to acknowledge that both Egeria and Cyril customarily describe the *public* worship of the whole Jerusalem community, not private monastic practices.[93]

There is, however, some evidence that other Roman Christians followed customs similar to Melania's, which strengthens Rampolla's argument. For example, we learn from Egeria that the Jerusalem Church did not customarily recite terce, but did so only during Lent.[94] In Melania's monastery, however, terce was said daily along with the other hours and the rationale given for the practice is that the Paraclete descended upon the apostles during the third hour of the day.[95] That the daily saying of terce may in fact have been a distinctively Roman practice is suggested by references in the canons of Hippolytus,[96] materials pertaining to the

Roman widow Paula's monastery,[97] and other letters of
Jerome.[98]

Another allegedly Roman custom of Melania was
keeping solemn vigils on the feast days of martyrs.[99]
While Melania was still a girl in Rome, she participated
in such a vigil at the feast of St. Lawrence,[100] and in
Jerusalem she is represented as participating in a vigil
honoring St. Stephen's feast.[101] Jerome's mention of
vigils in his letter on the education of Laeta's daughter suggests to Rampolla that the practice was distinctively Roman.[102] We know, however, that vigils before
Sundays and Easter were an ancient practice in
Christendom, well-attested by the fourth century. Basil
of Caesarea, writing in A.D. 375, reports that vigils
were kept throughout the churches of Christendom, including the Palestinian Church.[103] The feast of St.
Lawrence that Melania observed in Rome does indeed
appear to have been of special interest to inhabitants
of that city,[104] but Gerontius does not report that
Melania maintained her observance of St. Lawrence's
feast during the years she was in Palestine.

Finally, the fact that Melania celebrated the
Nativity of Jesus on 25 December rather than on 6 January is seen by Rampolla as striking an authentically
Roman note, and here his claim of Romaninity is supported by other historians of liturgy.[105] The *Calendar
of 354* from Rome is our first evidence of that date for
the Nativity feast,[106] and Jerome provides testimony
from a few decades later that 25 December was held to
be the day of Christ's birth by Romans.[107] Thus
Melania's celebration of the Nativity on 25 December was
no innovation. To be sure, Egeria does not even mention
a celebration of the Nativity on 25 December, but re-
serves all her attention for Epiphany on 6 January. Her

silence is usually taken to mean that in the early 380s, the Nativity was not celebrated in December by Jerusalem Christians.[108] Indeed, the first reference pertaining to Jerusalem that links the Nativity to 25 December comes from Juvenal of Jerusalem,[109] bishop from 422 until after the time of Melania's death in 439. (Juvenal's attempt to change the custom of the Jerusalem Church has been termed ephemeral:[110] Justinian's epistle of A.D. 560 to the Jersualemites directing them to desist from their "error" of celebrating the Nativity on 6 January shows that Juvenal's reform was of short duration.)[111] Thus Melania's participation in a vigil at the Church of the Nativity in Bethlehem on Christmas Eve 439[112] cannot be taken as an indication that she was introducing a peculiarly Roman practice: she was simply following the custom of Jerusalem Christians during the years of Juvenal's bishopric.

The evidence, then, for a distinctively Roman cast to Melania's devotional practices is slimmer than we might have anticipated--yet the secondary literature on Melania constantly emphasizes her Romaninity. We are told, for example, that her practices are "typically Latin,"[113] and that her adoption of a liturgy like Rome's and different from Jerusalem's[114] gave a certain "autonomy" to the Roman monasteries in Palestine.[115] The overemphasis on Melania's Romaninity is directly attributable to Rampolla and the earlier scholars who followed him. More recently, Denys Gorce has also questioned the stress on the Romaninity of Melania's religious life: neither the history nor the character of Melania's monasteries, he writes, justifies attributing to her a "combative 'ultramontanism.'"[116] The "ultramontanism," it appears, belongs more to Rampolla than to Melania. Some reflections on this point are in order.

First, we should recall who Mariano Rampolla was.
He was Leo XIII's papal nuntio in Madrid in the 1880s;
later he was named a cardinal and eventually became
Leo's secretary of state.[117] Further, the discovery of
the complete Latin *Vita* was Rampolla's very own: his
exclusive claim to it, as well as the length of time he
took to edit the document and compose his extensive
commentary upon it, make understandable his desire to
have the Latin version of the *Vita* be the original.[118]
When we consider Rampolla's unquestioning trust in
the Latin version's report that Melania's devotional
practices (e.g., daily communion, the reception of
viaticum by the dying) were those of the Roman
Church[119]--in contradistinction to the total silence of
the Greek text on the origin and provenance of these
customs--and ad hominem arguments aside, we are not
surprised that Rampolla emphasizes practices of the
Roman Church to the degree that he does. Nevertheless,
on the basis of our preceding discussion, the Romaninity
of Melania's monasteries may have been considerably less
than Rampolla was prepared to believe.

Whatever Roman elements there may have been, they
vanished along with the monasteries themselves during
the destruction of Jerusalem's holy buildings in A.D.
614 at the hands of Persian troops led by Chosroes
Parviz.[120] An account from the period reports, somewhat
incredibly, that 1,207 persons were killed on the Mount
of Olives alone during the Persian onslaught, and that
62,445 died in Jerusalem as a whole.[121] Yet the
twelfth-century Byzantine writer, John Phocas, in his
Descriptio Terrae Sanctae, notes that a monastery of
Latins stood on the ruins of Melania's community:
perhaps at last the monastery had found its true Roman
orientation.[122] And in ironic contrast, on the site of

Melania's former mansion in Rome, a community of Greek-
speaking men flourished in the Monastery of St.
Erasmus.[124]

E. Constantinople and Home

Scarcely was the men's monastery on Olivet completed when Melania received news from her uncle Volusian that he was journeying to Constantinople to assist
with arrangements for the marriage of the Western
emperor Valentian III to the Eastern princess Eudoxia,
an event that took place in October 437.[1] The *Vita* reports that Melania desired to see her uncle in order to
"save his soul," that is, to rescue him from the
paganism which he still espoused.[2]

Rufius Antonius Agrypnius Volusianus was one of
Melania's more distinguished relatives. Brother of
her mother Albina,[3] Volusian in his public career had
probably served first as *comes rei privatae* at Ravenna
in A.D. 408 in the wake of the reaction to Stilicho's
execution;[4] as proconsul of Africa when he was "just
a boy," according to Rutilius Namatianus;[5] as *quaestor
sacri palati* before 412;[6] as prefect of Rome from November 417 until mid-418;[7] and as praetorian prefect in
428-429.[8]

Volusian's public offices are not, however, the
focus of attention in the *Vita Melaniae Junioris*, even
though the author impresses Volusian's importance upon
his readers (the bishop of Constantinople effects his
conversion;[9] "queen Eudoxia" herself visits him in his
last illness).[10] Rather, what concerned Melania--and
Gerontius--was the conversion of her uncle. Melania
first attempted to lure Volusian to Christianity by
suggesting that he could win the best of both worlds

through his conversion: just as he had enjoyed the
goods of this life, so by his baptism could he secure
goods for eternity.[11] Impatient at her uncle's in-
tractability, Melania threatened to "take the matter
to the emperors,"[12] i.e., attempt by imperial pressure
to wrest a conversion from Volusian. Volusian's tact-
ful response is worth quoting:

> I exhort Your Holiness not to take from me
> the gift of self-determination with which God
> has honored us from the beginning. For I am
> completely ready and long to wash away the
> stain of my many errors. But if I should do
> this by the command of the emperors, I would
> gain it as if I had come to it by force and
> would lose the reward of my free decision.[13]

Apparently Volusian's conversations with Bishop Proclus
convinced him to receive baptism on his deathbed. In
a scarcely veiled slur on Roman bishops of the day,
Volusian remarked, "If we had three men in Rome like
lord Proclus, no one there would be called a pagan."[14]
(Since in December 437, Pope Sixtus III felt obliged
to warn Proclus not to intervene in the affairs of the
Illyrian Church and to caution the Illyrian bishops
against Proclus' possible jurisdictional encroachment
upon an area that Sixtus considered within the Western
sphere, we infer that relations between the sees of
Rome and Constantinople were not at this time as warm
as they might have been.)[15] Volusian, to be sure,
died a Christian.[16]

    We are fortunate to possess, through the corre-
spondence of Augustine, Volusian, and their friend
Marcellinus, a full catalog of Volusian's scruples
regarding the Christian religion. His probing objections to central points of Christian dogma show that

Melania's attempt to lure him through the promise of
heavenly rewards was theologically naive. Yet
Melania's efforts had long been preceded by those of
Augustine. By dedicating the *City of God* to him,
Augustine probably intended to assist Marcellinus in
converting Volusian and other pagan aristocrats.[17]
Augustine's attempt, however, proved futile: Volusian
was still a pagan in 437.[18] His objections to the
Christian religion did not simply stem from a desire
to preserve the ancient traditions of Rome, but were
rooted in a more sophisticated critique of Christian
dogma.

From the letters of Volusian and Marcellinus to
Augustine (Marcellinus expanded on points that bothered
Volusian and his circle), we gather that the main difficulties were fourfold. First, Volusian found the
doctrine of the Incarnation absurd: how could the
Lord of the universe have entered a virgin's body,
been born of her in such a way that she preserved her
virginity, and become a genuine human, subject to our
needs for food and sleep, to our emotions? Had the
charge of the entire universe thus been transferred to
a creature with a paltry human body?[19] Second, the
miracles attributed to Jesus in the New Testament
seemed only "small works" for the deity to have performed;[20] pagan wonderworkers such as Apollonius of
Tyana and Apuleius wrought more spectacular deeds.[21]
Third, if God had rejected the sacrifices prescribed
in the Old Testament (as Christians taught), why did
he desire a new one in the sacrifice of Jesus? Is not
God thus represented as inconsistent?[22] Fourth, how
can the Christian teaching of "turn the other cheek,"
of nonretaliation, be reconciled with the rights and
duties of a citizen? The last point was especially

troublesome, Volusian noted, since calamities had
befallen Rome under Christian emperors.[23] (This letter was composed in A.D. 412, just two years after
Rome's sack.)

Augustine's response to these objections was predictable. His letters pose the following resolutions
to the pagan objections: the omnipresence and im-
materiality of God mean that he is not confined by his
union with a human body;[24] the greatness of Christ's
miracles, and his work in creating the world, are
superior to the tricks of pagan wonderworkers;[25] God
is changeless, but changing human conditions lead God,
in his infinite wisdom, to use varying means of education for the differing eras of human development (and
the Old Testament sacrifices were, in any case, sym-
bolic);[26] refraining from revenge is a Roman virtue
as well as a Christian one,[27] but "correction" of
evil is permitted, since Christ did not command the
soldiers he addressed to cast away their weapons.[28]
As for the calamities that had befallen the empire,
Volusian and other pagans should remember that
disasters occurred under pagan emperors as well, that
Rome was corrupt before Christ's advent (as even pagan
writers attested), and that we should more appro-
priately thank God for sending Christ to rescue us
from the corruption in which we had been wallowing
than raise bitter complaints about his injustice.[29]

It is no accident that the problems here addressed are those to which Augustine turned in his theology
of history, the *City of God*, the first books of which
appeared the year after this correspondence.[30]
Augustine dedicated the work to Marcellinus,[31] but
within the year, Marcellinus was executed--and
Volusian remained a pagan for another two dozen years.

The mixture of pagans and Christians in aristocratic
families of late antiquity has been well-documented.[32]
Volusian's case is noteworthy in that he held out for
so many decades under pressure from family members and
distinguished theologians who tried to wrest a Christian confession from him. The episode pertaining to
Volusian's conversion is thus at the center of Gerontius' description of the sojourn Melania enjoyed in
Constantinople.

Melania's adventures en route as well as her
means of travel to the Eastern capital are also of interest. Melania used the *cursus publicus* to make her
voyage;[33] arrangements with the authorities had probably been made by Volusian. Yet problems arose along
the way, according to the *Vita*, because "many" of her
entourage did not possess the passes necessary to use
the official travel service.[34] At Tripoli, the official in charge of the *cursus publicus*, Messala, was
reluctant to allow Melania's party the number of
animals they requested for the next stage of the
voyage. A minor miracle occurred to change his mind:
he was tormented by an apparition of the marytr
Leontius, who was honored with a local shrine, until
in desperation he overtook the party and begged their
forgiveness for his recalcitrance.[35]

The journey from Jerusalem to Constantinople
covers nearly 1,200 miles. Ordinarily, such a journey
would require two months, if the traveller did not
linger but stayed only one night at each of the fifty-
eight stopping places between the two cities.[36]
Melania, however, made the trip in record time: her
journey took about six weeks (forty days, the Latin
Vita precisely reports).[37] The dates and figures
given in the Greek and Latin *Vitae* are helpful in

dating Melania's trip, as well as in furnishing the
date of Volusian's death: if Volusian died on Epiphany (6 January),[38] and Melania mourned for forty days
before she left Constantinople,[39] the earliest she
could have left the Eastern capital was 15 February.
Therefore, even departing this promptly after her time
of mourning, Melania could not have reached Jerusalem
by Holy Week (as the *Vita* states she did) *if* these
events occurred in A.D. 438, for Easter that year fell
on 27 March.[40] However, if we place her trip home in
437, the traditional date given by Rampolla,[41] she
could easily have been in Jerusalem by Holy Week, even
if she left Constantinople as late as 25 February, for
Easter in 437 fell on 11 April.[42] The 437 dating also
accords better with the testimony of Greek *Vita* 56 that
she departed from Constantinople at the end of February.[43]
Although Holum argues for a 438 dating[44] on the basis
of the *Vita*'s report that, upon her return to Jerusalem, Melania built an oratory for the men's monastery "in a few days"[45] and that immediately thereafter
she heard of Eudocia's approach[46] (and we know Eudocia
visited Palestine in A.D. 438),[47] our calculation
based on the dates of Easter confirms the traditional
dating of Volusian's death and Melania's return to Jerusalem in A.D. 437.

Melania's trip home was especially arduous. The
bishops she encountered along the way proclaimed that
they had never experienced such a winter. Although the
snow was so dense that a person could not see the stars
at night,[48] Melania pressed on, keeping up her rigorous
Lenten fast the entire way.[49] The Latin *Vita* adds the
interesting note that when the animals were unable to
cross the pass at Mount Modicus, Melania descended from
her beast and trudged on foot through the snow drifts.

(The editor of the Latin *Vita* cannot refrain from
sounding his common theme: how "manly" she is!)[50]

    Melania's enthusiastic reception by bishops and
clergy en route[51] illustrates how facilities for Christian pilgrimage and travel had expanded in the course
of the fourth century, as E. D. Hunt reminds us.[52]
When we compare the lonely and difficult trek of the
Bordeaux Pilgrim in A.D. 333[53] with Melania's journey,
we cannot help but observe how often she is greeted
by local Christian notables--although the Bordeaux
Pilgrim probably had neither Melania's wealth nor her
"contacts" to make his pilgrimage exceptional in the
eyes of Christian leaders along the way.

    Describing the trip to Constantinople also gives
Gerontius an opportunity to highlight such aspects of
Melania's religiosity as her devotion to saints and
relics. Early in the *Vita* Melania celebrated the
feast of St. Lawrence in Rome. Despite the imminent
birth of a child, she kept vigil during the night in
her family's chapel and, the next morning, went with
her mother to the Church of St. Lawrence,[54] one of the
favored churches of Rome's aristocrats.[55] According to
the Latin *Vita*, Melania wanted to spend the entire
night in vigil at St. Lawrence's basilica, but her
parents did not permit her to do so.[56]

    Proceeding through the *Vita*, we learn more about
Melania's interest in saints and in relics. When she
built the oratory for the women's monastery in Jerusalem, she placed her relics of Stephen, Zechariah,
and the Forty Marytrs of Sebaste there.[57] Some of
Stephen's relics were also later deposited in the men's
monastery.[58] She used oil consecrated from the
martyr's relics to effect one of her cures.[59] And,
Gerontius reports, when Melania went to meet the

empress Eudocia on the latter's pilgrimage to Jerusalem, the martyrion of St. Phocas at Sidon was the
site of their happy reunion.[60]

Given Melania's lifelong interest in saints and
relics, we are not surprised to learn that the trip to
Constantinople provided her with occasions to honor
two other martyrs: St. Leontius at Tripoli[61] and
St. Euphemia at Chalcedon.[62]   At Tripoli, we recall,
as a result of Leontius' heavenly intervention the
official in charge of the *cursus publicus* released the
necessary animals and begged forgiveness, even returning Melania's tip.[63]   Melania took Messala's
apology as an "auspicious sign" that their journey was
in accordance with God's will.[64]

A second episode in which a martyr came to her
rescue occurred just before she entered Constantinople. We are told that Melania suffered a failure of
nerve at the thought of encountering city life again
after her years of ascetic retreat. At St. Euphemia's
shrine in Chalcedon, she received comfort from "the
victorious one" (Euphemia), who emboldened her to
face the novelty of the imperial city.[65] Melania's
devotion to the martyrs and their relics was thus manifested on her voyage as well as at other times of her
life.

The Constantinople episodes also give Gerontius
an opportunity to stress Melania's connections with
royalty and other Eastern notables, much as in earlier
chapters of the *Vita* he used the meeting of Serena with
Melania to impress his readers with the saint's importance.[66] The first of the famous people Melania encountered in Constantinople was Lausus, former
praepositus sacri cubiculi.[67] Some years earlier,
Lausus had been the recipient of Palladius' *Lausiac*

History, in which Melania was prominently featured,
and Melania had entertained its author in her home
during his mission to Rome on behalf of John Chrysostom
in A.D. 404-405.[68] According to the Latin version of
the *Vita*, Lausus was Melania's benefactor: in about
A.D. 431, he had provided funds to pay for the construction of the bath in her women's monastery.[69]
Thus, according to the Latin *Vita*, it was with Lausus
that Melania stayed while she was in Constantinople.[70]
Constantine Porphyrogenitus' *Book of Ceremonies* reports that Lausus' mansion was near the imperial
palace of Constantine,[71] and the Latin *Vita* confirms
this location: the house was "in the Forum of Augustus
Constantine."[72]

We are fortunate to have from the eleventh-century
Byzantine historian Cedrenus a list of the sculptures
in Lausus' palace. Among them was a Cnidian Aphrodite
carved by Praxiteles; an Athena of Lindos that had
been sculpted from green stone by Scyllis and Dipoenus;
a Hera of Samos carved by Lysippus and Bupalus of Chios;
and a gold and ivory Zeus sculpted by Phidias which
Pericles had given to the temple of Olympia.[73] Of interest is not just the richness of Lausus' collection,
but also that he apparently did not think his Christian devotion conflicted with collecting statues of
the pagan gods, not even (according to Cedrenus) of a
naked Aphrodite with only her hand covering her sexual
parts.[74] These statues were presumably destroyed when
Lausus' palace was burned in the great fire of A.D.
475.[75]

Also of interest in the *Vita's* notices is the
aura of devotion to John Chrysostom that lies obliquely
around the edges. One of the persons Gerontius met
on the road to Constantinople was "Tigrius, priest of

Constantinople," who gave thanks to "the holy ones."
This reference occurs not in the section of the *Vita*
pertaining to the Constantinople trip itself, but in
a passage detailing Melania and Pinian's early renun-
ciations and assistance to religious men.[76]   Tigrius
is known to us from Palladius' *Dialogue on the Life of
John Chrysostom*,[77] as well as from the histories of
Sozomen[78] and Socrates.[79]   He had been among the supporters of Chrysostom summoned to the Synod of the
Oak to answer charges; when Chrysostom was exiled,
Tigrius had been subjected to torture and banished to
Mesopotamia.[80]   That Tigrius knew of Melania's hospitality to the pro-Chrysostom delegation to Rome in
A.D. 404 is suggested by the hearty welcome and
thanks he gave her party when they encountered him
en route to Constantinople.[81]

        A second event pertaining to Chrysostom that
transpired probably within a year after Melania's
departure from Constantinople[82] was Bishop Proclus'
supervision of a splendid ceremony in January 438 in
which the bones of Chrysostom were retrieved from
exile and solemnly returned to the Eastern capital.
Members of the royal family joined in the celebration and the deposition ceremony;[83] Proclus gave an
oration on Chrysostom.[84]   The bishop of Constantinople, so praised in the *Vita* as a holy man[85] and as
the baptizer of Volusian,[86] is here also seen as a
champion of Chrysostom, whose cause had earlier been
dear to Melania's heart.

        Not only do Lausus and the devoted adherents of
Chrysostom receive special mention in the *Vita*, but
also Melania's association with the imperial family
is highlighted.   Earlier, Gerontius had stressed the
friendly relations between Serena and Melania;[87] now

he wished his audience to understand that, despite
Melania's years of renunciation, she still could
claim the attention of the royal family--indeed, her
ascetic renunciation made her all the more cherished
in their eyes. Melania is thus represented as having
extensive contact with the royal family during her
Constantinople sojourn. We have already noted
Melania's threat to broach the issue of Volusian's
paganism with the emperors,[88] who had discreetly overlooked his religious preference. Moreover, we are also
told that she benefited the "Christ-loving imperial
women" and "edified the most pious emperor Theodosius."[89]
The warm relations that here developed were cemented
in the months following. When Eudocia undertook her
pilgrimage to Jerusalem, Melania greeted her en route
in gratitude for "the extreme love the empress had
shown her in Constantinople."[90] On this occasion,
Eudocia announced that she had come to Jerusalem not
just to view the Holy Places, but also to visit her
"mother," Melania. Gerontius reports that Eudocia
found it "a glory to honor the woman who had so purely
glorified the heavenly King."[91]

In Jerusalem, Eudocia requested permission to at-
tend the deposition of relics in Melania's new martyrion.[92]
The account of this episode in the *Life of Peter the
Iberian* differs significantly from that in the *Life of
Melania the Younger*. John Rufus' version makes far more
of Eudocia's role in the deposition ceremony than does
Melania's *Life* (for Gerontius, the central episode in-
volving Eudocia was the injury to her foot).[93] In the
Life of Peter the Iberian, on the other hand, Eudocia
herself is said to be responsible for the construction
of Melania's martyrion on the Mount of Olives; she has
more precious relics to deposit at her own newly dedicated

church of St. Stephen than Melania possesses; and she
commands the presence of Cyril of Alexandria to offi-
ciate at the deposition of the relics in her own church.[94]
In John Rufus' account, Melania has clearly been up-
staged by Eudocia. For Gerontius, however, Melania remains as heroine, with Eudocia's presence adding the
luminosity of imperial prestige to Melania's already
bright saintliness. According to Gerontius, when
Eudocia returned to Constantinople, Melania escorted
her as far as Caesarea. Gerontius comments, "They were
scarcely able to be separated from one another, for they
were strongly bonded together in spiritual love."[95]
Thus the presence of Theodosius and Eudocia in the *Vita*
serves to call Melania's eminence to our attention.
Ascetic renunciation, far from diminishing the prestige
of this aristocratic heiress, had rather enhanced it.[96]
The account of the Constantinople journey and its aftermath thus serves as a central vehicle for Gerontius to
demonstrate Melania's importance in the glittering world
of imperial politics.

 Melania's voyage to Constantinople and subsequent
Palestinian reunion with Eudocia are the last major
episodes of the *Vita*. Gerontius reports three minor
miracles Melania performed,[97] relates more of her advice
to her nuns,[98] and ends his account with a long description of the illness that led to her death on 31 December,
probably A.D. 439.[99] He includes in his final chapters
Melania's celebration of Christmas and the feast of St.
Stephen in the days before she died.[100] Entrusting her
monasteries to the care of her priest,[101] Melania
breathed her last. In Gerontius' words, she was
"joyously received" by the holy angels, prophets,
apostles, and martyrs into the heavenly halls.[102]

F. Orthodoxy and Heresy

There can be no doubt that Gerontius wished to present Melania as an exemplar of sound doctrine whose
"ardor for the orthodox faith" was "hotter than fire."[1]
Yet what constituted orthodoxy in the fifth century
was not so easily ascertained in the midst of the era's
doctrinal struggles: those who won the debate were not
the only ones who thought themselves correct. Gerontius
himself well illustrates the point, for he remained convinced that as a Monophysite he upheld Christian truth.[2]

The *Vitae* of saints composed in this period, moreover, were notoriously open to doctrinal manipulation by
their authors. The *Life of Antony*, for example, is not the
simple biography of an Egyptian ascetic, but Athanasius'
amicus brief for Nicene Christianity.[3] Likewise, the
Historia Monachorum is not an innocent collection of monk-
ish lore, but "gentle propaganda" for the Origenist
cause.[4] Although Gerontius represents his heroine as a
hunter of heretics who was herself completely dissoci-
ated from heretical taint, he has perhaps slanted his
evidence, for the "historical Melania" revealed in other
sources was closely linked with heretical currents of
her time. Just as the Monophysite author deemed himself
the proclaimer of Christian truth, so he sketched
Melania in shades of high orthodoxy, despite her flirta-
tion with religious movements later deemed of dubious
rectitude.

First, let us recall who Melania the Younger was:
the granddaughter of Melania the Elder. The elder
Melania had been deeply implicated in the Origenist con-
troversy through her long and intense association with
Rufinus, prime translator of Origenist materials into
Latin; through her avid reading of Origen's works;

through her friendship with men branded as Origenists, such as Evagrius Ponticus and Palladius; and through her support of the Tall Brothers, who fled the Nitrian desert at the time of Theophilus of Alexandria's attack on Origenism in A.D. 399-400.[5] As the Origenist controversy heated up in Palestine during the course of that year, Melania the Elder took the opportunity to leave for the West.[6] What we learn from Palladius--but not from the *Vita Melaniae Junioris*--is that the grandmother returned at this time to prevent her granddaughter from being "completely ruined by evil teaching or heresy or bad living."[7] Surely Palladius had something specific in mind. We can piece the situation together from various sources.

Origenism had become a cause célèbre not only in Egypt and Palestine: Rome, too, had caught fire, with pro- and anti-Origenist factions raging.[8] The pro-Origenist group was associated with Rufinus, the anti-Origenists with Jerome's circle. Pope Anastasius, who assumed office at the end of 399, condemned Origenism[9] and his impulsion to do so came at least in part from Jerome's Roman friends. Marcella, whom Jerome praised for her public activity against Origenism, was in the front line of attack; he credits her with initiating the condemnation of Origenists, demonstrating how many had been led astray in Rome by Origenist teaching, and pointing out the dangerous passages in the Latin translation of *On First Principles*.[10] In his *Apologia ad Hieronymum*, Rufinus complained about a "certain matron" who had stirred up accusations against him by circulating false copies of his translations:[11] this must have been Marcella. E. D. Hunt has suggested, and his suggestion seems entirely correct, that Melania the Elder's hope was to save her granddaughter from falling into the

hands of the anti-Origen, pro-Jerome faction in Rome.[12]
In this goal she apparently succeeded, for the younger
Melania remained friendly with men whom Jerome considered Origenists. She sheltered Palladius in her home
when he came on a delegation to Rome in A.D. 404,[13] and
remained on excellent terms with Paulinus of Nola,[14]
whom Jerome never won for his camp.

The *Vita Melaniae* tells nothing of these incidents:
one would never guess Rufinus so loved Melania and
Pinian that he could refer to Pinian as "amantissimus
filius noster," and that he planned to translate Origen's *Homilies on Deuteronomy* for him.[15] But the *Vita* does
reveal that Melania the Younger was a special partisan
of *apatheia*, the very quality that Jerome had earlier
singled out as the hallmark of Origenist teaching.[16]
Gerontius reports that Melania strove to shape her life
to conform to angelic *apatheia*.[17] In addition, he re-
peats a story she learned from an old saint and used in
the instruction of her nuns, the point of which was that
to be a true disciple, one must become as impervious to
feeling as a statue when it is beaten.[18] In this context, it is helpful to recall that Rufinus was the
translator into Latin of Evagrius Ponticus' treatise on
apatheia.[19] We would never know from the *Vita Melaniae
Junioris*, however, that Origenism had ever figured in the
life of its heroine.

To some observers of the period, Origenist teaching
had found a dangerous successor in Pelagianism. Points
of similarity between the two theologies seemed obvious:
Pelagius' alleged teaching on the possibility of sin-
lessness, for example, could be understood as a new
version of Origenist *apatheia*.[20] That Rufinus might serve
as a bridge between the two movements is suggested by
the fact that his translation of Origen's *Commentary on*

Romans was heavily used by Pelagius.[21]   Yet the association of Melania's group with Pelagianism was not just
indirect. We know that she, Pinian, and Albina actually
met with Pelagius in Palestine in A.D. 418. They wrote
to Augustine in that year reporting that Pelagius had,
in their presence, condemned propositions labeled
"Pelagian." Perhaps Melania thought this report would
be enough to restore Pelagius to Augustine's favor; if
so, she was mistaken. Augustine replied in *De Gratia
Christi* that their attempt to rehabilitate Pelagius was
not satisfactory.[22]

     Others in Melania's circle were also friends with
Pelagius and Pelagians, for example, Paulinus of Nola.
In A.D. 417 Augustine wrote to Paulinus to express the
hope that he had terminated his association with Pela-
gius.[23]   Another of Paulinus' friends, Aemilius, bishop
of Beneventum, presided at the marriage of Julian of
Eclanum,[24] later a prime Pelagian opponent of
Augustine; to celebrate the marriage, Paulinus himself
composed an *epithalamium* urging the couple to adopt a life
of chastity.[25] We also know that Pinian's good friend
Timasius, who served as emissary between Pinian and
Augustine during the near-ordination of Pinian at
Hippo,[26] was an acknowledged disciple of Pelagius.[27]
And Melania's uncle Volusian, while he was prefect of
Rome, dragged his feet at uprooting Pelagianism from
that city.[28] Peter Brown has argued very suggestively
that Augustine's reluctance to tackle Pelagius outright
until A.D. 415 had to do with the presence in North
Africa of this highly placed group of Roman refugees.[29]
Throughout their seven years near Thagaste, they made
stunning contributions to the North African church,[30] a
good enough reason for their theological predilections
not to be too rudely handled.

A third theologically questionable association of
Melania was with the Donatists. The Latin version of
the *Vita*, though not the Greek, bluntly states that on
Melania's vast estate near Thagaste there were two
bishops in residence, one for "those of our faith" and
one for "the heretics."[31] Given the time (A.D. 410 and
thereafter) and the place (North Africa), the reference
surely is to the schismatic Donatists. That a large
property owner would tolerate the presence of a Donatist
bishop on his estate is not surprising. As Emin
Tengström has argued in *Donatisten und Katholiken*, estate
owners needed to placate their agricultural workers on
religious matters, for the workers had a propensity to
flee when repression reared its head, leaving the owners
responsible for taxes on unproductive land.[32]

Melania had already experienced a slave uprising
on her estate near Rome that had taken the intervention
of Serena and Honorius to settle. On the occasion of
that slave rebellion, the *Vita* represents Melania as
saying to Pinian,

> Perhaps the occasion calls us to see
> the empress. For if our slaves who
> are nearby have rebelled against us
> in this way, what do you think those
> outside the cities will do to us--
> I mean those in Spain, Campania,
> Sicily, Africa, Mauretania, Britain,
> and the other lands?[33]

What indeed? Apparently Melania prevented further unrest by allowing the Donatists on her North African
estate to have their own church without interference.
We know that in A.D. 409, a rumor had circulated in
North Africa that amnesty was being granted to Donatists, a rumor Augustine was quick to quell.[34] Melania

arrived in Africa shortly after the circulation of this report, and may have believed that harboring Donatists was permissible. A few years later, she would have another reason for not disturbing the Donatist sympathies of her workers: her uncle's friend Marcellinus would be executed in A.D. 413 in the aftermath of Donatist repression in North Africa.[35]

In the Greek version of the *Vita*, evidence pertaining to Donatism does not emerge--nor, for that matter, does *any* evidence that would link Melania with heresy or schism. She is orthodoxy personified, a fighter of heretics. She is careful to associate with bishops who are noted for their "doctrine."[36] She lectures her nuns on guarding "the holy and orthodox faith."[37] She resolutely attempts to convert "Samaritans, pagans, and heretics;"[38] this reference perhaps is designed to bring her activities into accord with the wording of Theodosius II's decree of January 438, *De Judaeis, Samaritanis, Haereticis, et Paganis*.[39] In fact, the most important pagan Melania converted was her uncle Volusian, probably a year before the Theodosian decree[40]--a conversion that Augustine himself years earlier had failed to obtain.

As for heretics, Gerontius reports that in Melania's zeal for orthodoxy, she attempted to convert anyone even suspected of heresy, and if she failed in her effort, she refused the person's donation for the poor.[41] When Melania journeyed to Constantinople, Gerontius depicts her there taking up the cudgels against Nestorianism; this point is not specifically mentioned in the Latin version of the *Vita*. She leads anti-Nestorian discussions among wives of senators and men noted for their learning.[42] Theodosius himself is said to have been "edified" by her religious teaching.[43]

Moreover, the high praise lavished on Bishop
Proclus of Constantinople in the *Vita*[44] takes on added
meaning when we recall his anti-Nestorian bias.
Proclus' letters and sermons testify to his high regard
for Mary as the *theotokos* and to his campaign against
Nestorianism;[45] from Proclus' perspective, the Nes-
torians were "new Jews" whose teaching reduced Christ to
a mere man.[46] Nestorius himself singled Proclus out for
special criticism as an enemy.[47] Thus Melania's anti-
Nestorian proclivities no doubt contributed to her high
regard for the anti-Nestorian bishop of Constantinople.

Pelagianism is a less prominent target in the *Vita*.
Gerontius is careful to have Melania ascribe her miracles not to her own power, but to God's agency.[48] Once
when asked to work a cure, she replied, "Since I am a
sinner, I am not capable of doing this."[49] She con-
fessed that if she ever imagined herself to be good,
she immediately recognized the thought as the Devil's
trap.[50] Gerontius also reports the empress Eudocia's
prayer testifying that God rewards us not according to
our merits, but simply through his benevolence and the
intercession of the saints.[51]

The editor of the Latin *Vita*, however, includes more
interesting detail than does the editor of the Greek
version in his report of Melania's miraculous cure of a
pregnant woman whose fetus had died within her before
birth. In the Greek *Vita*, by Melania's prayer and action
the fetus is expelled and the woman saved.[52] The Latin
editor, in addition to grimly describing the surgeon's
cutting away bits of the fetus, has Melania deliver a
speech perhaps designed to rebut the Pelagian accusation
that the doctrine of original sin implied the wickedness
of sexual intercourse and childbearing. According to
Gerontius, Melania commented to the assembled group that

because God makes human fetuses, reproduction cannot be
deemed "filthy;" only sin is "filthy" and "abominable."
Bodily parts which God creates cannot be so tainted, for
through their use were born patriarchs, prophets,
apostles, and other saints.[53] Melania admits human sin-
fulness but denies that procreation involves sin. She
did not here attribute her miraculous cure to her own
powers, but to the virtues of the saints.[54] The story
as told in the Latin *Vita* fits well into the debate between Pelagians and Augustinians over original sin,
marriage, and conception that had occurred not many
years earlier.

      Most important of all, and impossible to overlook,
the *Vita Melaniae Junioris* does not even once mention the
name of Melania the Elder.[55] There is no account of the
elder Melania's monasteries in Jerusalem, nor of her return to Rome to rescue her granddaughter from the
"heresy and evil teaching" of which Palladius speaks.[56]
Strikingly, even when Gerontius cites a passage from
the *Lausiac History* that referred to the elder Melania,
he omits this line from his citation.

      The citation appears in chapter 1 of the *Vita*:
Melania the Younger there begs Pinian to practice chastity with her. She asks that if he cannot do so because
of "the burning passion of youth," he leave her body
"free," in return for which she will give him all her
possessions. Thus will she fulfill her religious
goal.[57] In Palladius' account of this speech, Melania
claims that her ascetic motivation stems from a desire
to inherit "the zeal of my grandmother whose name I
bear."[58] Although Gerontius' use of this passage from
the *Lausiac History* served as a central point in the argument between Rampolla and Butler over the original
language of the *Vita*,[59] neither they nor others have

noted the line that the *Vita* omits, the specific reference to Melania the Elder. The omission is all the more
striking if we imagine, as both Rampolla and Butler did,
that the author of the *Vita* had the text of the *Lausiac
History* before him.[60] This omission, coupled with the
silence surrounding the elder Melania throughout the
Vita, leads us to suspect a tendentious motive. The fame
of Melania the Elder among Christians in late antiquity
was such (Paulinus claims that "volumes" were written
about her)[61] that her absence from her granddaughter's
Vita must be a deliberate move, in fact, a *damnatio
memoriae*.[62] That Gerontius may elsewhere employ this
technique is suggested by an incident reported in the
Latin *Vita*: when speaking of the city prefect who attempted to confiscate Melania and Pinian's property,
Gerontius tells his readers that he does not call to
mind the man's name: "praefectus...cuius etiam minime
nomen recordor...."[63] If his nonrecollection of the
hated prefect's name is taken as deliberate, we have a
parallel case to the omission of Melania the Elder's
name from the *Vita*.

The same castigation by silence perhaps explains
why the elder Melania's monasteries in Jerusalem receive
no mention in the *Vita*. Other explanations for the omission have indeed been posited. G. D. Gordini, for example, suggests that either the monasteries had disappeared by the time Melania the Younger sojourned in
Palestine or they had passed into the control of
"Easterners."[64] Either explanation is of course possible. Yet we know from Palladius that Melania the Elder
endowed her monasteries,[65] which would suggest that
there were funds to support them for at least some years
after her death in about A.D. 410. Second, the explanation that Melania the Younger would not have wished to

join a monastic community with "Eastern" practices assumes (with Rampolla) that Melania the Younger's monasteries were decisively "Western," a view criticized and
qualified above.[66] Conceivably the younger Melania simply wanted to have her *own* monastery, for which she
could serve as patron; yet a further motive might be
that the grandmother's association with "heresy" had
made her monasteries suspect.

One further incident in the *Vita* perhaps pertains
to Melania the Elder. In chapter 28 Gerontius relates
an event that angered his heroine. Once during the recitation of the *anaphora*, Gerontius inadvertently infuri-
ated Melania by including the name of someone who had
been suspected of heresy. The person is not named, but
is described as a foreigner to Palestine, "a certain
woman of high status" who had settled at the Holy Places
some time earlier and had finished her life there.
Melania the Younger was so angry at Gerontius' inclusion
of this name that she threatened never again to attend
the liturgy: hearing the name once was once too much
for her.[67] Could this highly born foreign woman in
Palestine who had fallen under suspicion of heresy be
Melania's own grandmother? We know of nobody else who
so fits the description.[68] The story perhaps represents
yet another attempt by Gerontius to dissociate his
heroine from heretical taint.

The thesis seems plausible that the excision of
Melania the Elder from the text was deliberate on the
author's part. The woman who Palladius claims provided
the model and inspiration for her young granddaughter's
renunciation has become a nonperson, and the only plausible reason for this appears to relate to the dogmatic
suspicions adhering to Melania the Elder's name.

The animus against Melania the Elder may also explain in part the marked antagonism running throughout the text toward her son, Valerius Publicola, who according to Gerontius posed the major obstacle to Melania the Younger's adoption of asceticism.[69] And although evidence does not permit a definitive conclusion concerning whether or not Melania the Younger had a brother,[70] Palladius' report that Melania the Elder taught such a brother and led him away to Sicily[71] leads us to ask why, if in fact there was a brother, he does not appear in the *Vita*: has he, by association with his grandmother, been removed from the text?

Yet whatever enmities had existed between Melania the Elder's monastic establishments in Jerusalem and those of Paula and Jerome in Bethlehem, they had apparently been laid to rest by Melania the Younger's time. Gerontius, to be sure, sees fit to report that the younger Paula needed her cousin Melania's urging to renounce "great vanity and the Roman way of thinking."[72] Still, the old quarrels were patched up: Melania and Pinian visited Jerome when they first arrived in Palestine;[73] and the younger Paula, granddaughter and namesake of Jerome's companion, spent Christmas Eve A.D. 439 with Melania in Bethlehem[74] and was present at her deathbed a few days later.[75]

That heretics could be the most avid of heretichunters is not unknown in Christian history: Nestorius furnishes the outstanding case in point.[76] The author of the *Vita Melaniae Junioris*, himself unorthodox, later an outcast for his ardent Monophysitism, so pictures Melania as to divorce her from all association with heretics and heretical movements. Since extratextual evidence suggests that Melania was not in truth so doctrinally pure, we may reasonably conclude that the *Vita*

Melaniae Junioris is not free of tendentious, indeed propagandistic, qualities.

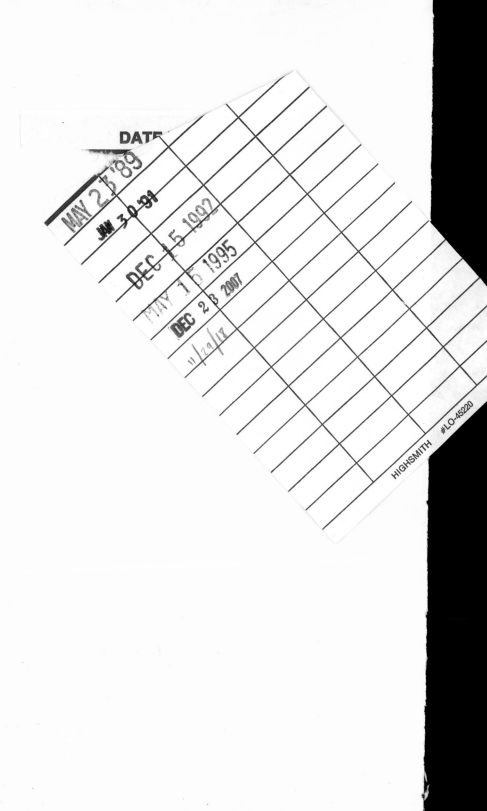

STUDIES IN WOMEN AND RELIGION

IV. THE LIFE OF MELANIA THE YOUNGER AND THE HELLENISTIC ROMANCE: A GENRE EXPLORATION

During the last century, scholars have labored to trace classical influences on early Christian literature. In this task they received much assistance from patristic authors themselves, who from the second century on stressed the accord between Christian values and the best sentiments of antiquity.[1] Steeped in ancient literature by virtue of their classical educations, church fathers such as the Cappadocians and Jerome demonstrated in their own writings that pagan classics could be adapted to serve a new Christian cause.[2]

Modern scholars, recognizing that Christian literature did not develop in isolation from pagan culture, have attempted to detail the influence of the classical genres on early Christian writing. Among the types of literature they examined was biography: did the *Lives* of Christian saints and martyrs conform to the patterns of the classical *bios*?

Yet biography was no simple genre that could be straightforwardly appropriated from pagan culture by Christian writers. Turn-of-the-century scholars, influenced by Friedrich Leo's study of Greek and Roman biographical forms,[3] distinguished two types of classical biography. The first, derived from the Peripatetic *Lives* and climaxing in Plutarch's works, was characterized by chronological organization; the second stemmed from the Alexandrian literati and found its distinctive

representative in Suetonius, who treated the hero's life
topically. Although Leo's distinction between
Plutarchian and Suetonian biographical schemes was
adopted by students of the early Christian *Vitae*, there
was little agreement on which type had decisively influenced Christian biography. Thus while Hans Mertel
pronounced the *Life of Antony* "Plutarchian" in its
arrangement,[4] other commentators who championed the
"Suetonian" elements in patristic biography noted the
topical arrangement of the hero's virtues, exhortations,
and miracles.[5] Such disagreements suggested that the
Vitae of Christian saints were not so easily assimilated
to either of Leo's types.

Arguing against both Plutarchian and Suetonian enthusiasts, Karl Holl and Richard Reitzenstein posited
that scholars might fruitfully look to the *Lives* of pagan
philosophers, especially to those produced by the
Pythagorean school, for models more readily adaptable
to Christian purposes than the biographies of generals
and statesmen.[6] Their works have now been supplemented
by such recent studies as Patricia Cox's *Biography in Late
Antiquity: A Quest for the Holy Man.*[7]

Various problems beset the demonstration of classical biographical influence on early Christian *Vitae.*
First, although discussions of "form" called needed attention to similarities between pagan and early
Christian biography, they also obscured the distinctive,
indeed the most fascinating, features of the Christian
Lives. Analogies between the pagan and Christian forms
could not be pressed too far: many of the early
Christian *Lives* lacked necessary components of the classical *bios*, including a narration of the subject's life
story. (For example, in Jerome's *Life of Paul, the First
Hermit*, ninety-seven years of Paul's life are totally

excluded from the narration!)[8] Moreover, such essen-
tial aspects of a Christian *bios* as lists of miracles
the hero performed and demons he combated were not
readily derived from the traditional schemes, although,
to be sure, the *Lives* of pagan holy men and sages
here furnish some comparisons.[9]

The second is specific to such works as the *Vita
Melaniae Junioris*: ancient biography focused on the
lives of males. Adapting the biographical format to
the lives of women proved problematic. If the *Vitae*
of statesmen, generals, and philosophers did not provide perfect models to cast *Lives* of male Christian
monastics, they present similar patterns of education
and public activities. But the essentially private
nature of most women's lives in antiquity and the virtues thought appropriate to their condition, such as
obedient devotion to a husband, were not suited to
female martyrs and ascetics. Although the *Vitae* of
early Christian women stress their overcoming of female-
ness and subsequent incoporation into a world of "male-
ness,"[10] it is still dubious whether the classical *bioi*
furnished any fitting models for these *Lives*. And if
they did not, did any other form of ancient literature,
more focused on women, suggest itself as a more suitable
model? Might not the Hellenistic romance, with its
concentration on lively heroines, provide a better
paradigm for a *Vita* like Melania's?

Similarities of content might at first consideration lead us to think so. Melania, like the romantic
heroines, is an adolescent beauty of impeccably aristocratic lineage. She battles kinfolk who would hinder
the realization of her heart's desire, flees barbarians,
suffers storms at sea, ransoms captives. She crosses
and recrosses the Mediterranean world: Rome, Sicily,

North Africa, Egypt, Palestine, Constantinople. At
first glance her story could be understood as a Hellenistic romance in which the protagonists experience (as
a Byzantine novelist put it)

> Flight, wandering, captures, rescues,
> roaring seas, robbers and prisons,
> pirates, hunger's grip....[11]

The fact that Melania was a Christian ascetic does not
immediately preclude considering her as the counterpart
of such fictional heroines as Leucippe and Callirhoe,
nor disallow an interpretation of her *Vita* as a
Christian version of the Greek novel: the travel, the
storms at sea, the ransomed captives are all present.
But we must be wary of prematurely identifying the *Vita
Melaniae Junioris* as a romance for two reasons.

First, a genre of literature cannot simply be defined by incidents occurring in the plot.[12] New Comedy,
for example, abounds in erotic complications, but we do
not for that reason label the comedies "novels." As a
relatively free literary form, the novel in its earliest
manifestations was particularly resistant to genre
classification. Ancient literary critics, not deeming
the novel worthy of discussion, failed even to give it
a species name.[13]

Second, the difference in tone and intent between
the romances and the *Life of Melania* discourages too ready
an identification. Other elements present in the *Vita
Melaniae Junioris*, are blurred by a too facile categorizing
of the *Vita* as a romance. Of these, the author's attempt to present Melania as a champion of orthodoxy and
a fighter of heresy is notable. Although the *Life of
Melania* predictably exhibits the hallmarks of both
biography and the novel, little is gained by forcing the
text into exclusive genre categories. While noting the

literary similarities between Melania's *Vita* and older
forms, we will also raise questions about the differences.

Certain affinities of the *Vita Melaniae Junioris* with
the Hellenistic novels can be rapidly summarized: (1)
the aristocratic background and extreme wealth of the
heroine; (2) her adolescent rebellion against parental
and societal authority that stand against the realization of her own life vision; (3) her association with
important personages such as empresses and emperors;
(4) the impact of dramatic events of larger political
and military history upon the heroine's life, in this
case, the barbarian invasions and the sack of Rome; (5)
an emphasis on travel and its dangers, seen especially
in the storm at sea episode when Melania leaves Sicily
and the account of her journey to and from Constantinople; (6) the heroine's association with the realm of
the extraordinary and the miraculous (Melania is able,
by God's grace, to perform cures); and (7) the religious
devotion of the heroine--in Melania's case, clearly her
all-consuming passion.

By emphasizing such romantic features as these, did
Gerontius wish readers to approach his work as a
Christianized form of the Hellenistic novel? Was Gerontius himself even familiar with such novels? These
questions cannot be definitively answered. It is not
necessary, however, to argue Gerontius' familiarity with
the novels in order to affirm the "novelistic" features
of *Vita Melaniae*: not only are they plainly present, but
the *Life of Melania* is far from the earliest Christian
work to exhibit them. Earlier writings--the Apocryphal
Acts, the Pseudo-Clementines, and the fourth-century
Lives of the holy men--were probably influenced by the
novels, and Gerontius was in all likelihood familiar

with some of this literature, since the Roman emigré
circles of ascetics in Palestine had been active in its
composition, transmission, and translation. Thus
whether or not Gerontius himself had ever perused the
adventures of Leucippe and Clitophon, or Chareas and
Callirhoe, the air on the Mount of Olives was steeped
with the perfume of Thecla, Faustinus and Faustinianus,
Antony, Paul, Malchus, and Hilarion. The romantic
heroes and heroines who yearned for each other alone as
they were swept over lands and seas, attacked by
pirates, kidnappers, and robbers, suffered shipwreck,
slavery, near or apparent death, only then to be happily
reunited at the novel's end, had been superseded before
the time of Melania and Gerontius by Christian ascetics
who maintained their purity despite the Devil's tempta-
tions and who, in the end, were reunited with their
true Bridegroom, Jesus. Any "influence" of the novels
on the *Vita Melaniae* may quite reasonably be assumed to
have been mediated through earlier Christian literature.

   Scholarship on the Greek novels or romances has
witnessed massive upheaval in the last century.[14] The
seminal work was Erwin Rohde's *Der griechische Roman und
seine Vorläufer*, published in 1876;[15] it was the
"Vorläufer" that stimulated much of the subsequent controversy. Rohde argued, with massive erudition, that
the Greek novels developed from a combination of love
stories and travel fables.[16] The specific impetus to
the development of the novels, he claimed, occurred in
the Roman rhetorical schools associated with the Second
Sophistic.[17] Indeed, a school textbook like the Elder
Seneca's *Controversiae* that proposed debate topics for
budding orators, with its casts of virgin prostitutes,
pirates' daughters yearning for respectability, and
chaste wives suspected by their husbands[18] approaches

the fictive world created by such novelists as Chariton,
Longus, Achilles Tatius, Heliodorus, and Xenophon of
Ephesus. Because Rohde tied the development of the
novels to the Second Sophistic, he dated all the novels
from A.D. second century and after, placing Chariton's
Chareas and Callirhoe last, in the late fifth or early
sixth century.[19]

The fate of Rohde's thesis provides a stunning--
and humiliating--example of how one turn of an archeol-
ogist's spade can undo the argument of a brilliant
textual scholar: papyrus fragments of early novels,
especially the *Ninus Romance*, indicate that novels must
have developed before the schools of the Second Sophistic flourished, perhaps even in the first century B.C.,[20]
and were composed only until the third or fourth century
A.D.[21] The novel that Rohde judged the latest,
Chariton's *Chareas and Callirhoe*, is now customarily dated
to the first century A.D. and thus stands as the earliest
of the complete extant novels.[22]

The discovery of Rohde's misdating, however, did
not impede the quest of those trailing the *Vorläufer*.
Since Rohde's day, scholars have hung a wildly dissimi-
lar group of ancestors on the family tree of the novel.
Among the various proposals for the novel's predecessors
are historiography,[23] local legends,[24] the Alexandrian
love elegy,[25] New Comedy,[26] nationalistic hero tales,[27]
aretalogies,[28] or a blend of epic and novelistic history.[29] Most exotic is Karl Kerényi's thesis that the
Greek novels developed from the ancient mystery cults,
especially the cult of Isis, and are veiled descriptions
of the mysteries' evocation of loss and recovery, death
and resurrection.[30] Such a bewildering variety of proposals should chasten their advocates: the search for
a rigidly defined genre for the Hellenistic novel or for

that novel's "ancestors" is probably misguided. The
novels differ considerably from each other in structure,
despite similar characters and incidents of plot.[31]
Some novels show more affinity with history, others with
pastoral poetry or with philosophy.[32] And, as Ben Edwin
Perry, taking sharp aim at Rohde's thesis, pointedly remarks, "forms" do not give birth to one another, genres
do not have genealogies.[33]

Given the quantity of scholarship after 1876 on
the Greek novels and the influence of masterworks such
as Rohde's, it was perhaps inevitable that scholars of
early Christianity would trace similarities between the
novels and such patristic writings as the Apocryphal
Acts, the Pseudo-Clementines, and the early monastic
Lives. The pioneering exploration of this question was
Ernst von Dobschütz' 1902 article, "Der Roman in der
altchristlichen Literatur;"[34] however, the fullest monograph was Rosa Söder's *Die apokryphen Apostelgeschichten und
die romanhafte Literatur der Antike*.[35] Söder argued that the
five main themes in the Apocryphal Acts (wandering;
aretalogy; teratology; religious, moral, and philosophical predilections; *eros*) were all borrowed from the
Hellenistic novel.[36] It became standard usage to refer
to the Apocryphal Acts, the Pseudo-Clementines, and the
early monastic *Lives* as "novels."[37] Even scholars, such
as Richard Reitzenstein, who downplayed the novel's influence on early Christian literature, often did so for
the wrong reasons, imagining the novels to be a type of
higher literature produced by educated circles, unlike
popular aretalogies.[38]

Indeed, many superficial connections exist between
the novels and the Apocryphal Acts, the Pseudo-
Clementines, and the *Lives* of the early hermits. For
one, women come to play a more important role in the

Christian literature, just as they do in the novels.[39]
The Apocryphal Acts would be greatly diminished if the
accounts of Thecla, Mygdonia, Xanthippe, and Drusiana
were erased from their pages. Moreover, the heroines
are almost always princesses or members of the aristocracy, although they may not at first know their true
lineages.[40] Likewise, in the Apocryphal Acts, the women
are said to be from leading families, married or engaged
to prominent men: Xanthippe is married to "a ruler of
Spain";[41] Tertia, of the Acts of Thomas, is the wife of
a king;[42] Thecla is "the first of the Iconians."[43] Just
as the beauty of the romantic heroines is compared to
that of goddesses,[44] so are the women of the Apocryphal
Acts acclaimed for their beauty,[45] which often brings
them unwanted attention from men. Thecla, for example,
wishes to chop off her hair and don male garb in order
to disguise her female attractions;[46] her beauty is
said to make her sexual renunciation and willingness
for martyrdom all the more painful to others.[47]

Likewise, incidents that mark the action of the
novels show up with predictable regularity in the
Apocryphal Acts, the Pseudo-Clementines, and the early
monk's *Lives*. Wandering and travel play a great role
in this literature. Whether by design or by accident,
the heroes and heroines are swept all over the Mediterranean world. Just as the extant Greek novels
specialize in pirates and shipwrecks, captures and en-
slavements, so do the Pseudo-Clementines[48] and Jerome's
Life of Malchus.[49]

A third set of similarities comes in the religious
complexion of the literature. In the pagan novels the
heroes and heroines are often dedicated to the service
of a deity, with Isis and Artemis particularly prominent.[50] Scholars who wish to link early Christian

literature with the Greek romance stress this theme and
indicate how easily Christians adapted the motif of
divine service to their own purposes, how effortlessly
the protagonists could be recast as Christian rather
than pagan devotees.[51] Thus strong resemblances indeed
exist between the novels and certain types of early
Christian literature. These elements, as noted above,
occur also in the *Life of Melania*: Melania is a beautiful heroine of aristocratic background, who undertakes
much travel, suffers storms at sea, encounters barbarian
kidnappers, and is devoted to a deity.

There are, however, very significant differences in
tone between the novels and early Christian literature
that have been obscured by enthusiasts who see the influence of the Greek novel behind every action of a
Thecla. The first difference pertains to sexual themes,
and the second, to the pedagogical purpose of Christian
literature.

Much has been made of the fact that the novels
stress sexual chastity:[52] the young couple often take
vows of chastity or loyalty to each other.[53] They
usually are represented, somewhat incredibly, as honoring those vows, although sold into brothels[54] or captured by pirate bands, where lustfully homosexual
pirates are as much a threat to the purity of the hero[55]
as their heterosexual counterparts are to the heroine's.[56] Two of the extant novels conclude with the
couples undergoing chastity tests, trials by ordeal, to
demonstrate their purity.[57] This feature of the novels
has been linked to early Christian literature's emphasis
on chastity,[58] suggesting that the temporary sexual re-
straint shown by the couples in the romances is equiva-
lent to Christian asceticism.

Here critics have allowed their search for similarities to lead them astray: so keen are they to note
similarity, they do not adequately register dissimi-
larity. In truth, the difference in sexual tone between
the novels and early Christian literature is extreme.
In the novels, if the couple remains chaste throughout,
it is so that the nuptial chamber will figure more
prominently at the story's end. The hero and heroine
lust after each other and avoid sexual relationship only
through considerable self-restraint.[59] In some cases,
their abstinence is not even intentional: indeed,
Leucippe and Clitophon are already bedded down when
Leucippe's mother interrupts their sexual initiation
(she has had a portending dream regarding a robber with
a naked sword).[60] In *Daphnis and Chloe*, the young shepherd
and shepherdess initially remain chaste simply because
they do not understand how to perform the sexual act,
despite close observation of their flocks.[61] The difference here between the novels and Christian literature
calls to mind Clement of Alexandria's observation that
pagan sexual morality aimed merely at the control of
sexual desire, whereas Christian teaching advocated the
extirpation of desire itself.[62] Such indeed is the gap
in sentiment between the novels and early Christian
literature.

The Apocryphal Acts, as is well known, are often
blatantly virulent in their condemnation of sexual intercourse: however "romantic" the subject matter of the
Acts, their purpose lies in the propagation of ascetic
ideals.[63] The stories pertaining to Thecla, Mygdonia,
Drusiana, and Xanthippe illustrate the difficulties
women encounter in their attempts to renounce the sexual
life. "Difficulties" is too weak a description of
events: Drusiana is shut in a sepulcher by her husband

for her refusal to acquiesce to his sexual requests;[64]
Thecla is condemned to burning and to the wild beasts.[65]
The early monastic literature also emphasizes sexual
renunciation: in Jerome's *Life of Malchus, the Captive Monk,*
the hero, captured and enslaved, plans to kill himself
on his wedding night rather than consummate the marriage
that his master has forced upon him.[66]

It is likewise with the *Life of Melania,* whose heroine counsels young people to retain their virginity and
to shun "filthy pleasures"--indeed Melania does not
merely counsel them to do so, she also bribes them.[67]
Far from lusting after Pinian, Melania, after losing
her initial struggle to convince her husband to adopt
a life of chastity,[68] tried to flee the marriage; she
was restrained only by the advice of religious authorities who reminded her of Paul's words in I Corinthians
7:16, "Wife, how do you know if you will save your husband?"[69]

Melania's asceticism was extreme in all respects:
Gerontius reports that she was "zealous to surpass
everyone in asceticism."[70] To this end, she made almost
no concessions to bodily needs or desires of any sort.
From an early age, she refused to bathe,[71] wore a rough
haircloth garment under her silk dress,[72] and spent
whole nights on her knees in vigil.[73] When her father's
death gave her the freedom to practice more rigorous
renunciations, she promptly began the complex process of
dispersing her wealth that continued to her final days,
when she sent her last fifty coins to "a certain very
holy bishop."[74] Her cheap, old clothing receives comment in several passages of the *Vita.*[75] She fasted five
days every week,[76] and would have fasted on Easter as
well if her mother had not restrained her from the
practice.[77] Even the arduous trip home from

Constantinople over snowy mountain passes did not find
Melania relaxing her strenuous Lenten fast.[78] She slept
two hours a night,[79] in sack cloth,[80] sometimes in a box
constructed so that she could neither stretch out nor
turn over;[81] during Lent she lay on a haircloth garment
that, when shaken out at Eastertide, emitted lice.[82]
Lice are not the stuff from which romances are made.

Second, early Christian literature, including the
Life of Melania, has a more extensive pedagogical purpose
than the novels. Although some of the novels contain
instructive disquisitions on religion,[83] their prime
purpose according to most scholars, the Kerényi school
excepted, was not religious instruction but entertainment.[84] It is now thought that the novel attracted a
literate but nonaristocratic audience:[85] "a latter-day
epic for Everyman."[86] The ancients themselves understood the novels as light entertainments to be enjoyed
post prandia, as Persius phrased it.[87] The fact that
Melania's daily round did not include *prandium* alerts us
that we have entered a different world.

By contrast, it is striking how much early Christian literature is devoted to instruction. Take the
Pseudo-Clementines: although the adventures of
Clement's family provide a plot around which the work
is loosely constructed, they in actuality occupy a very
small proportion of the total. The *Recognitions* and the
Homilies consist largely of lengthy sermons on such
topics as fate, providence, the Devil, and evil.[88]
Likewise, it is instructive to note that twenty-one of
the *Life of Antony's* ninety-three chapters concern not the
adventures of its hero, but strategies regarding demons.[89] And if readers could not sort out the moral
purpose of such accounts for themselves, the authors
provided assistance. Thus Jerome, concluding his tale

of Malchus, reminds the inattentive of the work's message, that *pudicitia* is never captive, that "a person devoted to Christ can die but cannot be conquered."[90] Gerontius likewise does not let the reader forget the purpose of the *Vita Melaniae*: however exciting the adventures of the heroine, they are not designed primarily for amusement. He presents his subject as the exemplar of all Christian virtues,[91] as a religious instructor and a model supporter of orthodoxy.

Even before Melania has a community of nuns to exhort, she offers instruction to Pinian, counseling him to renounce his luxurious clothing[92] and to join her in abandoning their wealth.[93] Later in the *Vita*, Melania advises her nuns on the necessity of night vigils and worship,[94] explaining the reasons for the hours of the stated daily and nightly offices.[95] She reminds the nuns that they must obey[96] and should bear "insult, reproach, and contempt" without suffering emotional disturbance.[97] The *Vita* represents Melania speaking on the topic of humility frequently: the Devil fell through arrogance,[98] she tells the nuns. They must beware of taking pride in their bodily mortifications.[99] Should pride tempt them, they must recall those who involuntarily suffer more hardships in life than they: for example, "those who lie in the marketplace naked, or only on mats, freezing in the cold."[100] To all who would listen, she explains how the ephemeral quality of life should encourage them to adopt asceticism.[101] As theologian, she preaches to the nuns on the necessity of guarding "the holy and orthodox faith without deviation,"[102] counsels her pagan uncle on the eternal bliss awaiting him if he would only convert,[103] and makes anti-Nestorian speeches at the Constantinople court.[104] Gerontius undoubtedly wished to provide Christian

instruction for his readers, using Melania as the exemplar of ascetic practice and theological orthodoxy. The
instructional content of the *Vita* is thus more pronounced than the entertainment value, the reverse of the
situation exemplified by the novels.

Since we have no evidence concerning Gerontius'
familiarity or lack of familiarity with the Greek
novels, it would be foolhardy to argue that he was
directly influenced by them. But we do know that early
Christian literature of the novelistic type here described was extremely popular in the fourth and fifth
centuries. For example, one hundred extant manuscripts
of the Pseudo-Clementines testify to the work's great
popularity and wide distribution.[105] Moreover, characters like Thecla had achieved such stature by the fourth
century that a cult had developed around her;[106] she
was represented in Christian art,[107] and her name had
become a synonym for the heroic Christian woman.[108] By
the last decades of the fourth century, the *Life of
Antony* had received not merely one but two translations
into Latin.[109]

We know even more. Not only was such literature
popular in this era and the Roman ascetics in Palestine
familiar with it, they were at the forefront in translating, transmitting, and even composing it. It was
Rufinus who introduced the Pseudo-Clementines to the
West. He brought the Greek texts with him when he returned West in 397 and completed his Latin translation
of the *Recognitions* in the early years of the fifth century.[110] Rufinus also translated a collection of monks'
lives, the *Historia Monachorum*, that provides fascinating
vignettes of the desert fathers.[111] He did not feel
impelled to translate the *Life of Antony*, he reports, because
it already existed in Latin translation.[112] Like all the

Roman group in Palestine, Rufinus had seen Egyptian
monasticism first-hand and took a lively interest in
materials pertaining to the desert fathers.[113]

As for Jerome, whether or not he had actually read
the Pseudo-Clementines, he refers to the travels of
their hero, Clement.[114] He also knew the tale of
Thecla[115] and could present her as a model of
Eustochium.[116] Before his rupture with Rufinus and
Melania the Elder, he could also style the latter a
"Thecla."[117] That Jerome, too, had visited the desert
fathers (though he did not wish to be one himself) and
was interested in their lives is evident from references
in his letters.[118] In addition we must recall that he
translated Pachomius' *Rule* and in his preface describes
the Pachomian way of life.[119] But Jerome's greatest
contribution to the "hagiographic novel"[120] is his
authorship of three ascetics' *Lives*: Paul the first
hermit (probably intended to be a correction of
Athanasius' *Life of Antony*: Paul, not Antony, was the
first),[121] Malchus, and Hilarion, the alleged founder
of Palestinian monasticism.[122]

Were women involved with such literature? We know
that the monastic leader Rufinus originally undertook
the translation of the Pseudo-Clementine *Recognitions* for
a woman, Silvia, sister of the prefect Rufinus, but she
died before the translator made headway on his assignment.[123] He also translated the *Sentences of Sextus* for
Avita, wife of his patron Apronianus and niece of
Melania the Elder.[124] And Rufinus himself testifies
that he wished some of his translations to be of works
not above women's competence to understand.[125]

Rufinus' companion, Melania the Elder, was vitally
interested in the desert fathers, whom she had visited;
she was the source for several episodes reported in the

Lausaic History.[126] She was an avid reader of theological treatises, especially of Origen's works. (Palladius says that she had read three million lines of Origen: even allowing for exaggeration, her devotion to that writer is clear.)[127] Of contemporary authors, she favored Evagrius Ponticus,[128] whom she had rescued for the ascetic life[129] and whose writings Rufinus also had translated.[130] She enjoyed reading the *Lives* of the saints, as is revealed in a letter written by Paulinus of Nola: Paulinus reports to Sulpicius Severus that on one of Melania's trips to Nola, he read to her Sulpicius' *Life of Saint Martin*, and comments that Melania was very fond of such "historical works."[121] That the lives of the famous ascetics also influenced women who remained in Rome is demonstrated by Jerome's report that hearing the tale of Antony's life led Marcella to undertake her ascetic renunciation.[132]

Melania the Younger, too, had visited the desert fathers, had made a pilgrimage to Nitria and the "Cells,"[133] and liked to read the tales of the fathers' exploits. Gerontius remarks that she read τους βίους τῶν πατέρων (in the Latin version of the *Vita, Sanctorum Vitas*).[134] She was a friend of Palladius, that collector of monastic stories who compiled the *Lausiac History*, and in Constantinople she was entertained by the recipient of the work, Lausus.[135] That ascetic women in Palestine were interested in such literature is abundantly clear from the sources.

The pieces of our argument are in place. We know that novelistic literature, such as the Apocryphal Acts, the Pseudo-Clementines, and the early *Lives* of hermits and saints, was in wide circulation in both Greek and Latin from the later fourth century onwards. We know that the men of the Roman Christian community in

Palestine wrote, translated, and transmitted such books, and that the women in their circles profited from reading these accounts, even taking them as models for their own lives. We probably need seek no further to discover why Gerontius' *Life of Melania* often sounds like a Christian romance: he was celebrating her life and virtues in a popular style of literature that Christians shared with pagans. But does this suffice to characterize Gerontius' treatise? No. We have already suggested that the Christian literature considered cannot simply be called "romance": in its exaltation of asceticism and its pedagogical intent, it is distinguished from the secular novels.

Most important, the *Vita Melaniae Junioris* is not an innocent recital of a saint's deeds and virtues, but a propagandistic treatment of a woman whose actual associations with heresy and schism were plentiful, as has been detailed above.[136] Here, of course, a central difference between the *Vita* and the novels emerges, for the latter have no "real-life" heroines whose deeds can be reconstructed from other historical sources. Gerontius has shaded his rendition of Melania's life to present her as a paragon of orthodoxy and a fighter of heretics—which she is not in other sources. This tendentious quality of the *Vita* separates it most decisively from the light entertainment offered by the Hellenistic novels. Lying beneath the standard props of the Hellenistic novel—travel, storms at sea, adolescent rebellion, ransomed captives—is literature of a quite different sort. It is inadequate to characterize the *Vita Melaniae Junioris* as a romance pure and simple: the polemic is more substantial than the pirates. Under the skin of Gerontius the novelist beat the heart of Gerontius, hammer of heretics.

NOTES

ABBREVIATIONS

AASS	*Acta Sanctorum* (Paris, 1863-1925)
AB	*Analecta Bollandiana*
Abh	Abhandlungen (followed by name of Academy, abbreviated, and by class)
ACO	*Acta Conciliorum Oecumenicorum* (Leipzig, 1922--)
AER	*American Ecclesiastical Review*
BACr	*Bulletino di Archeologia Cristiana*
BiZ	*Biblische Zeitschrift*
BullComm	*Bullettino della Commissione Archeologica Communale di Roma*
BZ	*Byzantinische Zeitschrift*
CCL	Corpus Christianorum, Series Latina (Turnholt, 1953--)
CH	*Church History*
CIL	*Corpus Inscriptionum Latinarum*
CJ	*Codex Justinianus*
CSCO	Corpus Scriptorum Christianorum Orientalium, Scriptores Syri (Louvain, 1903--)
CSEL	Corpus Scriptorum Ecclesiasticorum Latinorum (Vienna, 1866--)
CSHB	Corpus Scriptorum Historiae Byzantinae (Bonn, 1828-1897)
CT	*Codex Theodosianus*
DACL	*Dictionnaire d'Archéologie Chrétienne et de Liturgie* (Paris, 1907--)
DOP	*Dumbarton Oaks Papers*
DS	*Dictionnaire de Spiritualité Ascétique et Mystique, Doctrine et Histoire* (Paris, 1932--)
DTC	*Dictionnaire de Théologie Catholique* (Paris, 1930-1950)
GCS	Die Griechische Christliche Schriftseller der ersten drei Jahrhunderte (Leipzig, 1899--)

HE	*Historia Ecclesiastica; Historia Ecclesiae; Ecclesiastica Historia*
HTR	*Harvard Theological Review*
JHS	*Journal of Hellenic Studies*
JRS	*Journal of Roman Studies*
JThS	*Journal of Theological Studies*
Mansi	J. D. Mansi, *Sacrorum Conciliorum Nova et Amplissima Collectio* (Florence; Paris, 1759-1798)
MGH, AA	Monumenta Germaniae Historia, Auctores Antiquissimi (Berlin, 1877-1919)
NPNF	A Select Library of the Nicene and Post-Nicene Fathers. 2 series (New York, 1887-1900)
PG	Patrologia Graeca, ed. J. P. Migne (Paris, 1857-1866)
PL	Patrologia Latina, ed. J. P. Migne (Paris, 1844-1865)
PLRE	A. H. M. Jones, J. R. Martindale, and J. Morris, *The Prosopography of the Later Roman Empire*. 2 vols. (Cambridge, 1971, 1980)
PO	Patrologia Orientalis (Paris, 1906--)
RBib	*Revue Biblique*
RE	A. Pauly and G. Wissowa, *Realencyclopädie der classischen Altertumswissenschaft* (Stuttgart, 1893--)
REA	*Revue des Etudes Anciennes*
REAug	*Revue des Etudes Augustiniennes*
REB	*Revue des Etudes Byzantines*
RecAug	*Recherches Augustiniennes*
RecSR	*Recherches de Science Religieuse*
ROC	*Revue de l'Orient Chrétien*
RQ	*Römische Quartalschrift für Christliche Altertumskunde und Kirchengeschichte*
RQH	*Revue des Questions Historiques*
RSR	*Revue des Sciences Religieuses*
SB	Sitzungberichte (followed by name of Academy, abbreviated

SC   Sources Chrétiennes (Paris, 1943--)

ST   Studi e Testi (Vatican City, 1900--)

SubsHag   Subsidia Hagiographica, Société des Bollandis-
            tes (Bruxelles, 1886--)

ThRev   *Theologische Revue*

TU   Texte und Untersuchungen zur Geschichte der
            altchristlichen Literatur (Berlin, 1883--)

VChr   *Vigiliae Christianae*

ZNW   *Zeitschrift für die Neutestamentliche Wissenschaft und
            die Kunde der Älteren Kirche*

ZPalV   *Zeitschrift des Deutschen Palästina-Vereins*

TEXTS CITED BY EDITOR

Achilles Tatius. *Leucippe et Clitophon. Leucippe and Clitophon.* Ed. Ebbe Vilborg. Studia Graeca et Latina
Gothoburgensia 1. Stockholm: Almqvist & Wiksell,
1955.

Acta Apolostolorum Apocrypha. Ed. R. A. Lipsius and M. Bonnet. Leipzig: Hermann Mendelssohn, 1891-1903.

*Acta Xanthippe et Polyxenae. Apocrypha Anecdota. A Collection of
Thirteen Apocryphal Books and Fragments.* Ed. Montague
Rhodes James. Texts and Studies II.3. Cambridge:
Cambridge University Press, 1893.

Chariton. *Chareas et Callirhoe. Le Roman de Chairéas et Callirhoé.* Ed. Georges Molinié. Paris: Société d'Edition 'Les Belles Lettres,' 1979.

Corpus Iuris Civilis. Vol. I, *Institutiones.* Ed. Paulus
Krueger. *Digesta.* Ed. Theodorus Mommsen. Berlin:
Weidmann, 1893. Vol. II, *Codex Iustinianus.* Ed.
Paulus Krueger. Berlin: Weidmann, 1892. Vol.
III, *Novellae.* Ed. Rudolfus Schoell. Berlin:
Weidmann, 1895.

Evagrius Scholasticus. *Ecclesiastica Historia. The Ecclesiastical History of Evagrius with the Scholia.* Ed. J. Bidez
and L. Parmentier. London: Methuen, 1898.

Heliododrus. *Aethiopica. Les Ethiopiques (Théagène et Chariclée).* Ed. R. M. Rattenbury and T. W. Lumb. 3
vols. Paris: Société d'Edition 'Les Belles Lettres,' 1935, 1938, 1943.

Itinera Hierosolymitana et Descriptiones Terrae Sanctae. Ed. Augustus Molinier and Carolus Kohler. Geneva: J.- G. Fick, 1885.

Longus. *Daphnis et Chloe (Pastorales).* Ed. Georges Dalmeyda. 2d ed. Paris: Société d'Edition 'Les Belles Lettres,' 1960.

Palladius. *Dialogus de Vita Joannis Chrysostomi.* Ed. P. R. Coleman-Norton. Cambridge: Cambridge University Press, 1928.

_____. *Historia Lausiaca. The Lausiac History of Palladius.* Ed. Cuthbert Butler. Texts and Studies VI.1-2. Cambridge: Cambridge University Press, 1898-1904.

Socrates Scholasticus. *Ecclesiastica Historia.* Ed. Robertus Hussey. 3 vols. Oxford: Oxford University Press, 1853.

Theodosiani Libri XVI cum Constitutionibus Sirmondianis et Leges Novellae ad Theodosianum Pertinentes. Ed. Theodor Mommsen and Paul M. Meyer. Berlin: Weidmann, 1954.

Theophanes. *Chronographia.* Ed. Carolus deBoor. Hildesheim: G. Olms, 1963.

Vita Melaniae Junioris. Santa Melania Giuniore, senatrice romana: documenti contemporei e note. Ed. Mariano del Tindaro Rampolla. Roma: Tipografia Vaticana, 1905.

_____. *Vie de Sainte Mélanie.* Ed. Denys Gorce. SC 90. Paris: Editions du Cerf, 1962.

Vita Petri Hiberii. Petrus der Iberer. Ein Charakterbild zur Kirchen und Sittengeschichte des fünften Jahrhunderts. Ed. Richard Raabe. Leipzig: J. C. Hinrichs'sche Buchhandlung, 1895.

Xenophon. *Ephesiaca. Ephesiacorum Libri V. De Amoribus Anthiae et Abrocomae.* Ed. Antonius D. Papanikolaou. Leipzig: B. G. Teubner, 1973.

Zacharias Rhetor. *Historia Ecclesiatica.* Ed. E. W. Brooks. CSCO, Scriptores Syri, vols. 38-39 (=83-84) Syriac; vols. 41-42 (=87-88) Latin. Louvain: L. Durbecq, 1953.

I INTRODUCTION

[1]Augustine, *Letters*, trans. J. G. Cunningham, NPNF I: 452 n. 1.

[2]Jerome, *Ep.* 202.2 (in Augustine's correspondence; CSEL 57: 301).

[3]Augustine, *Epp.* 124 (CSEL 44: 1-2); 126.5 (CSEL 44: 11).

[4]Paulinus of Nola, *Ep.* 29.12 (CSEL 29: 258-259; an allusion to Melania the Younger); *Carmen* 21.72-83, 284-285, 836-840 (CSEL 30: 160-161, 167, 185).

[5]Palladius, *Historia Lausiaca* 61 (Butler II: 155-157). For questions regarding Palladius' reliability, see Denys Gorce, *Vie de Sainte Mélanie*, SC 90 (Paris: Editions du Cerf, 1962), pp. 8-13; Nicole Moine, "Melaniana," *RecAug* 15 (1980): 9, 25; Paulus Peeters, "Une Vie Copte de S. Jean de Lycopolis," *AB* 54 (1936): 380; Paulus Peeters, review of *Rufinus of Aquileia (345-411)*, by F. X. Murphy, *AB* 66 (1948): 327-328; for René Draguet, see below, pp. 91, 200 nn. 60, 61.

[6]Cyril of Scythopolis, *Vita S. Euthymii* 27, 45 (TU 49.2: 42, 67); *Vita S. Sabae* 30 (TU 49.2: 115); *Vita S. Theodosii* (TU 49.2: 239).

[7]John Rufus, *Plerophoria* 41 (PO 8: 92); *Vita Petri Hiberi* (Raabe, pp. 27-33 Syriac; pp. 32-37 German). See I n. 86.

[8]For references to Melania the Younger in menologies, see Albert Ehrhard, *Überlieferung und Bestand der hagiographischen und homiletischen Literatur der griechischen Kirche von den Anfängen bis zum Ende des 16. Jahrhunderts*, TU 50 (1937), 51 (1938), and 52 (1952). The following listings are noted. (1) From Cod. Vatic. Barber. gr. 318, under 31 December (TU 50: 530); also discussed TU 52: 785-786; the manuscripts came from Basilian monasteries in Italy and Sicily. (2) From the *Menologion* of Simeon Logothetes, listed for 31 December (TU 51: 472, 306). (3) The listing for "Melania the Roman" in the December *Menologion* (TU 50: 343) may refer to the

176 The Life of Melania the Younger

Notes to p. 1

elder Melania; the appellation τρισμακαρία is given
to her, an epithet the *Lausiac History* (from which this
Menologion's reference to Melania comes) accords to
Melania the Elder (*Historia Lausiaca* 46 [Butler II: 134]).
The point is overlooked by Gorce, *Vie*, pp. 17-18, who
calls this "the oldest Menologium which contains the
life of Melania." More likely, the *Menologion* confused
material on the two Melanias. Cautions on Ehrhard's
earlier research are given by Hippolyte Delehaye, "Les
Ménologes grecs," *AB* 16 (1897): 311-329; and "Le
Ménologe de Métaphraste," *AB* 17 (1898): 448-452.
Melania is also listed in the *Menologium Basilianum* II: 71-
72 (PG 117: 236), for 31 December.

⁹*Synaxarium Ecclesiae Constantinopolitanae*, ed. Hippolyte
Delehaye, *AASS* 62 (*Propylaeum ad Acta Sanctorum Novembris*).
The oldest codex of the *Synaxarium* that mentions Melania
the Younger (F=Codex Mediceo-Laurentianus, signatus San
Marco 787) is from Palestine and dates to A.D. 1050
(pp. xx-xxi); in this codex, Melania's feast day is
listed as 28 December (p. 351). She is also listed for
30 December (p. 355) in a thirteenth-century codex (Sb=
Codex Bibliothecae Nationalis Parisiensis 1571 [p. x]),
and correctly, on 31 December (p. 359) in Codex Bibliothecae Regiae Berolinensis, signatus 219 (=S); the section on Melania, fol. 121, is from the twelfth or
thirteenth century (pp. v-vii). Rampolla believed that
the *Synaxarium* notices stemmed directly from the Barberini text of Melania's *Life* (Rampolla, pp. lvi-lvii).
Gorce (*Vie*, p. 18) discounts Rampolla's claim and asserts that the *Synaxarium* is closer to the Metaphrast's
text of Melania's *Life*, without giving counterexamples
to Rampolla's rather convincing ones. For other Eastern
liturgical material on Melania, see Rampolla, *Melania*,
pp. 291-292.

¹⁰*Martyrologium Usuardi*, ed. J. B. DuSollier, rev. L.
M. Rigollot and J. Carnandet, *AASS* 26: "Sanctae Melanae
Romanae" on 31 December (p. 708). On Usuard's
Martyrology, see Jean Dubois, "Un Témoin de la vie intellectuelle à Saint-Germain-des-Près au IXe siècle: Le
Martyrologe d'Usuard," *Revue d'Histoire de l'Eglise de France*
43 (1957): 35-48. Usuard probably got his information
on Melania in Spain (see Rampolla, *Melania*, p. 289; and
Gorce, *Vie*, pp. 15-16). This detail is of interest considering the recollections of Melania in the Spanish
church calendar (see I n. 11) and the fact that the full

Latin text of Melania's *Vita* was found in Madrid and is thought to have come from Oviedo (see I n. 20).

[11]D. Marius Ferotin, *Le Liber Ordinum en usage dans l'église wisigothique et mozarabe d'espagne du cinquième au onzième siècle*, Monumenta Ecclesiae Liturgica 5 (Paris: Librairie de Firmin-Didot, 1904), pp. 494-495, with the correct feast day, 31 December, listed for Melania. The two codices are B (from A.D. 1054) and F (from A.D. 1072), but no information about Melania beyond the listing is given in them.

[12]Pietro de Natali, *Catalogus Sanctorum et Gestorum Eorum ex Diversis Voluminibus Collectus* (Venice: B. de Zanis, 1506; 1st ed., 1493), p. 214.

[13]Pietro de Natali follows *Lausiac History* 61 on details not found in the *Vita*, such as the name of the priest who helped Melania distribute her money (Paul), and her retention of some of her property to subsidize monasteries. Although Pietro de Natali used Peter Calus' work on the saints in the composition of his *Catalog*, his notice on Melania the Younger appears to be derived from a version of the *Lausiac History* (Heraclides, *Paradisus*); see Albertus Poncelet, "Le Légendier de Pierre Calo," *AB* 29 (1910): 34, 36.

[14]Also see the listing for Melania in a Georgian codex: Paulus Peeters, "De Codice Hiberico Bibliothecae Bodleianae Oxoniensis," *AB* 31 (1912): 301-318, esp. 317. The codex dates to A.D. 1038-1040 (p. 304). The possibility that there may exist an as yet undiscovered Georgian version of the *Vita Melaniae Junioris* is suggested by Gorce, *Vie*, p. 54.

[15]Simeon Logothetes, *Vita et Conversatio Sanctae Melanae Romanae* (PG 116: 753-793). For a discussion of the compiler and his dating, see Hippolyte Delehaye, "Les Ménologes grecs," p. 329; "Le Ménologe de Métaphraste," pp. 448-452; "La Vie de Saint Paul le Jeune et la chronologie de Métaphraste," *RQH* 54 (1893): 73-85; "Simeon Metaphrastes," *AER*, 3d ser., 3 (=23; 1900): 113-120.

[16]Translation probably by Laurentius Surius, first published in the 1550s under the title *Sanctorum Priscorum Patrum Vitae*; included by Lipomani in his edition of *De*

Notes to pp. 2-4

Probatis Sanctorum Historiis (Colonia Agrippina [Cologne], 1570), I: 741-753; Melania is listed under 31 January.

[17] *Martyrologium Romanum*, ed. Hippolyte Delehaye et al., *AASS* 68 (*Propylaeum ad Acta Sanctorum Decembris*), p. 610. Melania, the ninth saint listed for 31 December, is thus described: "Eodem die sanctae Melaniae iunioris, quae cum viro Piniano Roma adscedens et Ierosolymam profiscens, ipsa inter feminas Deo sacras, vir inter monachos religiosam vitam exercuit, et ambo sancto fine quieverunt."

[18] PG 116: 753-794; Rampolla's "M" text (see Rampolla, *Melania*, p. xlvii). The text, Codex 1553 of the Bibliothèque Nationale in Paris dates from the fourteenth century.

[19] Louis Sebastian Lenain de Tillemont, *Mémoires pour servir à l'histoire ecclésiastique des six premiers siècles* (Paris: Charles Robustel, 1709), XIV: 233.

[20] Rampolla, *Melania*, pp. xlv-xlvi; *Atti del IIe Congresso Internazionale di Archeologia Cristiana, 1900* (Roma: Libreria Spithöver, 1902), p. 418.

[21] *Atti del IIe Congresso*, pp. 418-419.

[22] Ibid., p. 419.

[23] Augustus Molinier and Carolus Kohler, *Itinera Hierosolymitana et Descriptiones Terrae Sanctae* (Geneva: J.-G. Fick, 1885), II: 133-142. This codex (2178 from Paris) is Rampolla's "a¹"; see Rampolla, *Melania*, p. xlvi.

[24] Chartres MS 16 of the 1840 catalog; Rampolla's "b" codex (Rampolla, *Melania*, p. xlvi); see Carolus deSmedt, "Vita Sanctae Melaniae Junioris," *AB* 8 (1889): 16.

[25] DeSmedt, "Vita," pp. 16-63.

[26] Rampolla, *Melania*, p. xlvi.

[27] Hippolyte Delehaye, "S. Melaniae Iunioris. Acta Graeca," *AB* 22 (1903): 5-50. The codex probably came

from the monastery of Grottaferrata (Rampolla, *Melania*, p. xlviii).

[28]For example, by Gorce, *Vie*, pp. 46-47.

[29]Rampolla, *Melania*, pp. xlv-xlvii; for Rampolla's manuscript tree, p. lxx.

[30]Rampolla, *Melania*, p. xlviii.

[31]Escurial codex a.I.13; noted by Guillermo Antolin, *Un Codex Regularum del Siglo IX: opúsculos desconocidos de S. Jerónimo* (Madrid: Imprenta Helenica, 1908), pp. 43-49. The *Vita Melaniae* is found on folio 125 of the codex.

[32]Gorce, *Vie*, pp. 124-271 (Greek text and French translation). Gorce notes the differences between this version and Delehaye's (see I n. 27 above).

[33]Rampolla, *Melania*, p. lxii.

[34]Ibid., pp. lxiv ff., and passim. The Latin Escurial codex dates to the tenth century, the Greek Barberini codex to the eleventh (ibid., pp. xlv, xlvii).

[35]For example, Latin *Vita* 34 contains a section pertaining to Melania's departure from Rome that belongs chronologically after chapter 19, where the editor of the Greek text has placed it. In chapter 15 of the Latin *Vita*, the editor admits some confusion in order: "Rogo ut si priora posterius et posteriora prius dixero, non sit taediosum neque meae culpae adscribas" (Rampolla, p. 11).

[36]Rampolla, *Melania*, p. lviii.

[37]Adhémar d'Alès, "Les Deux Vies de Sainte Mélanie le Jeune," *AB* 25 (1906): 448.

[38]D'Alès, "Vies," p. 413, commenting on *Vita* 15.

[39]Greek *Vita* 9 (Gorce, pp. 142, 144).

[40]Rampolla, *Melania*, p. lix.

[41]Latin *Vita* 9 (Rampolla, p. 8): "circuire omnes carceres...."

Notes to pp. 6-8

[42]Rampolla is not alone in making arbitrary judgments on the basis of content. D'Alès, for example, thinks Volusian's speech in Latin *Vita* 53 (Rampolla, p. 30), on how Melania as a child was viewed as "the pupil of the eye and the roses or lilies when they begin to bloom," is inappropriate on the lips of an elderly Roman statesman and thus not authentic ("Vies," p. 432). Yet a cherished woman's being compared to the eyes is a commonplace in Latin literature; see, for example, Catullus 3.1-5; 82.2, 4; 104.2; Plautus, *Pseudolus* 1.2.46.

[43]Latin *Vita* 41 (Rampolla, p. 24).

[44]Greek *Vita* 53 (Gorce, p. 230).

[45]Rampolla, *Melania*, p. lix.

[46]Noted by d'Alès, "Vies," p. 430; textual examples in Latin *Vita* 53, 56, 59 (Rampolla, pp. 30, 31, 34).

[47]Greek *Vita* 12 (Gorce, p. 150): "...τοῖς ἄλλοις τέκνοις..."

[48]Rampolla, *Melania*, p. lix. No other children are mentioned in the rest of the Greek *Vita*. The point is of interest in terms of Melania's inheritance and of a possible polemical bias of the *Vita*; see below, pp. 90-92.

[49]Palladius, *Historia Lausiaca* 54 (Butler II: 146): Melania the Elder's son had two children.

[50]See below, pp. 90-91, 151.

[51]Latin *Vita* 50 (Rampolla, p. 28); also in Greek *Vita* 50: "...ἡμῶν βασιλεῖ Οὐαλεντινιανῷ..." (Gorce, p. 224).

[52]Rampolla, *Melania*, p. lxviii.

[53]D'Alès, "Vies," p. 430.

[54]Rampolla, *Melania*, pp. xlvii-xlviii.

[55]D'Alès, "Vies," p. 448: the Greek flows more smoothly than the Latin; Gorce, *Vie*, p. 52: although the Greek text is written in popular language and has a

rather loose syntax, it proceeds "sans detour." It
lacks the obscurity of the Latin version, which is often
virtually unintelligible.

[56]Rampolla, *Melania*, p. lxiv.

[57]Ibid., p. lxvi.

[58]Ibid., p. lxviii.

[59]E. C. Butler, "Cardinal Rampolla's Melania the
Younger," *JThS* 7 (1906): 630-632.

[60]Ibid., p. 631.

[61]Ibid.

[62]Ibid.

[63]Greek *Vita* 20 (Gorce, p. 170).

[64]Latin *Vita* 20 (Rampolla, p. 13).

[65]Rampolla, *Melania*, p. lxvii.

[66]D'Alès, "Vies," pp. 416-417. Rampolla (*Melania*,
p. 211) posits that he was a priest or monk from Thagaste.

[67]Greek *Vita* 26 (Gorce, pp. 178, 180).

[68]Latin *Vita* 26 (Rampolla, p. 16).

[69]Ibid.

[70]*Vita Petri Hiberi* (Raabe, p. 29 Syriac; p. 34
German). Latin *Vita* 32 (Rampolla, p. 18) also refers to
Melania as working with her hands: "...opus perficeret
manibus."

[71]Greek *Vita* 26 (Gorce, p. 178).

[72]Rampolla, *Melania*, p. lxiii.

[73]D'Alès, "Vies," p. 420, affirms this as the correct way to interpret the divergence between the Greek
and Latin versions. Although Gorce translates the

passage to mean that Melania made copies of Scripture
(*Vie*, p. 178), he does not comment on the strangeness
of the Latin version's introducing shoemaking into a
discussion of Melania's intellectual activities (cf. *Vie*,
p. 93).

[74] Greek *Vita* 38 (Gorce, p. 198).

[75] Latin *Vita* 38 (Rampolla, p. 22).

[76] D'Alès, "Vies," p. 423.

[77] D'Alès, "Vies," p. 450; Gorce, *Vie*, p. 53.

[78] *Vita* prologus (Gorce, p. 124; Rampolla, p. 3).

[79] Tillemont, *Mémoires*, XIV: 233.

[80] DeSmedt, "Vita," p. 17.

[81] Cyril of Scythopolis, *Vita S. Euthymii* 45 (TU 49.2:
67); *Vita S. Theodosii* (TU 49.2: 239).

[82] Cyril of Scythopolis, *Vita S. Euthymii* 27 (TU 49.2:
42-44).

[83] Ibid., 45 (TU 49.2: 67).

[84] Cyril of Scythopolis, *Vita S. Sabae* 30 (TU 49.2:
115).

[85] John Rufus, *Plerophoria* 41 (PO 8: 92).

[86] Demonstrated by Eduard Schwartz, *Johannes Rufus, ein
monophysitischer Schriftsteller*, SB Heid. philos.-hist. Kl.
16 (Heidelberg: Carl Winter's Universitätsbuchhandlung,
1912), pp. 9-12.

[87] *Vita Petri Hiberii* (Raabe, pp. 5, 16 Syriac; pp. 15,
23-24 German). The Georgian connection of Peter's *Life*
and the fact that Melania is early mentioned in Georgian
literature bear further consideration. She was known to
a compiler of a premetaphrastic Georgian Menologion: see
Michael Tarchnišvili, *Geschichte der kirchlichen georgischen
Literatur*, ST 185 (Roma: Biblioteca Apostolica Vaticana,
1955), p. 485; and see above, I n. 14.

Notes to pp. 14-16

[88] *Vita Petri Hiberii* (Raabe, pp. 27-28 Syriac; pp. 32-33 German).

[89] Ibid. (Raabe, p. 31 Syriac; p. 35 German).

[90] Ibid.

[91] Ibid. (Raabe, p. 31 Syriac; p. 36 German).

[92] Ibid. (Raabe, p. 32 Syriac; p. 36 German).

[93] Cyril of Scythopolis, *Vita S. Euthymii* 27 (TU 49.2: 42).

[94] Rampolla, *Melania*, p. lxv. See Latin *Vita* 6 (Rampolla, p. 6): Rampolla explains how, given the church's construction, Pinian could have thrown himself *sub altare*. The view held by Rampolla and others is attacked by F. W. Deichmann, "Märtyrerbasilika, Martyrion, Memoria und Altargrab," *Mitteilungen des deutschen archaeologischen Instituts. Roemische Abteilung* 77 (1970): 146-155. (It is unlikely there was an altar above the actual grave.) See discussion and other references in Charles Pietri, *Roma Christiana. Recherches sur l'église de Rome, son organisation, sa politique, son idéologie de Miltiade à Sixte III (311-440)* (Roma: Ecole Française de Rome, 1976), pp. 39 n. 4, 526 n. 2.

[95] Rampolla, *Melania*, p. lxix.

[96] D'Alès, "Vies," pp. 407-408; Gorce, *Vie*, pp. 61-62. Examples from Latin *Vita* 12 (Rampolla, pp. 9-10): "fuissemus"; "nobis"; the author concludes, "Nos vero stupuimus in tanta piissimorum principum praestantia."

[97] D'Alès, "Vies," p. 408.

[98] Gorce, *Vie*, pp. 60-61.

[99] Latin *Vita* 15, 34 (Rampolla, pp. 11, 18).

[100] D'Alès, "Vies," pp. 407-408.

[101] Latin *Vita* 11 (Rampolla, p. 9).

[102] Noted by Gorce, *Vie*, p. 61.

Notes to pp. 16-17

[103]Gorce, *Vie*, pp. 61-62, following d'Alès, "Vies,"
p. 413. Also there is a parallel case in chapter 17:
the editor of the Greek *Vita* has Melania herself report
on the gold to be dispersed (Gorce, p. 160), while in
the Latin version, it is the biographer who recounts
essentially the same words (Rampolla, p. 12).

[104]Greek *Vita* 25 (Gorce, p. 176).

[105]Latin *Vita* 25 (Rampolla, p. 15).

[106]*Vita* 24 (Gorce, p. 176; Rampolla, p. 15).

[107]In the prologue to the *Vita*, Gerontius says that
he will rely on information others have given him, as
well as on what he has seen with his own eyes (Gorce, p.
128).

[108]For example, on the North African adventures of
Melania, see below, pp. 109-114.

[109]Franz Diekamp, review of Rampolla's *Melania*, *ThRev*
5 (1906): 245.

[110]It might be postulated that Gerontius wrote both
a Greek and a Latin version of the *Vita*, including in
each version various details he thought would interest
the different recipients. The awkwardness of the Latin
could then be understood as reflecting the fact that
Latin was not Gerontius' native tongue. Yet this hypothesis leaves unexplained both why the order of the
Latin text is confused and why there are such significant variations as those mentioned above, pp. 6-13.
The hypothesis of a Greek original appears preferable.

[111]*Vita* prologus: in Latin, "Sacerdos Dei sanctis-
sime", "Sacerdos Christi" (Rampolla, pp. 3-4); in Greek,
"ἱερεῦ ὅσιε" (twice); the author asks for the prayers
"τῆς σῆς ὁσιότητος" (Gorce, pp. 124, 126).

[112]Rampolla, *Melania*, p. lxviii.

[113]Ibid., p. 235.

[114]D'Alès, "Vies," p. 449.

Notes to pp. 17-19

[115]For example, Melania communicated daily, as was
the custom of the Roman Church from the earliest times,
(Latin *Vita* 62; Rampolla, p. 36); the bread of the
Eucharist was placed in the mouth of the dying, "as is
the Roman custom" (Latin *Vita* 68; Rampolla, p. 39).

[116]Latin *Vita* 44 (Rampolla, p. 25). The text uses
the ecclesiastical hierarchy as an example of obedience:
"Considerate et in sancte Dei Ecclesia, quomodo ipsi
episcopi sub principe episcoporum sunt...."

[117]Latin *Vita* 44 (Rampolla, p. 25): "...et princeps
episcoporum sub synodo." If this is an allusion to
Chalcedon, it surely is oblique.

[118]Marcellinus, *Chronicon*, an. 451 (MGH, AA XI: 84).
For a description of the church and the martyrion of St.
Euphemia, see Evagrius Scholasticus, *HE* II.3 (Bidez and
Parmentier, pp. 39-42).

[119]Points made by d'Alès, "Vies," p. 449. The
bishop of Rome may have been among the "holy bishops"
who presented to Serena Melania's offer to sell her the
Roman mansion being vacated; if so, the point is not
explicit (*Vita* 14 [Gorce, pp. 154, 156]).

[120]*Collectio Novariensis* 10 (ACO II.2.1: 44).

[121]See the letter in Mansi VI: 1021-1028; Liberatus,
Breviarium 10 (PL 68: 992) reports that Dioscorus wished
to use the extorted money to make loans to Alexandrian
bakers and vintners with the hope of winning popularity
by supplying good quality bread and wine at low prices.
Evagrius Scholasticus, *HE* II.18 (Bidez and Parmentier,
p. 76) also refers to the affair. See also Paul Goubert,
"Le Rôle de Sainte Pulchérie et l'eunuque Chrysaphios,"
Das Konzil von Chalkedon: Geschichte und Gegenwart, ed. A.
Grillmeier and H. Bacht, 3 vols. (Würzburg: Echter-
Verlag, 1954), I: 309-311.

[122]Mansi, VI: 1006-1011.

[123]*Vita* 34 (Gorce, p. 190).

[124]*Vita* 39 (Gorce, p. 200).

[125] *Vita* 58-59 (Gorce, p. 244).

[126] *Vita Petri Hiberii* (Raabe, p. 33 Syriac; p. 37 German).

[127] *Vita* 67 (Gorce, p. 264).

[128] *Vita* 68 (Gorce, p. 266).

[129] Simeon Logothetes, *Vita et Conversatio* 36 (PG 116: 792): a detail assumed to be incorrect by Ernest Honigmann, "Juvenal of Jerusalem," *DOP* 5 (Cambridge, Mass.: Harvard University Press, 1950), p. 228 n. 223.

[130] *Narratio de obitu Theodosii Hierosolymorum et Romani Monachi Vitae Virorum apud Monophysitas Celeberrimorum*, ed. E. W. Brooks, CSCO, Scriptores Syri, 7 and 8 (Louvain: L. Durbecq, 1955), vol. 7: 26 (Syriac); vol. 8: 18 (Latin): the Monophysite Romanus, after being released from custody, did not return to his former monastery at Tekoa because that was in Juvenal's jurisdiction; he instead went to the more hospitable area around Eleutheropolis, close to the town of Kephar Tūrban "which belonged to Eudocia." Eudocia built a "large and beautiful monastery" for Romanus. Eduard Schwartz thinks John Rufus was the author of the *De Obitu Theodosii* ("Johannes Rufus," p. 11). According to Zacharias Rhetor, Romanus was nearly chosen to be the Monophysite bishop of Jerusalem upon Juvenal's ouster, but Theodosius won the see (*HE* IV.3 [Brooks, p. 157 Syriac; p. 108 Latin]).

[131] Zacharias Rhetor, *HE* II.3 (Brooks, p. 125 Syriac; p. 87 Latin). See also Johannes Fleming, "Akten der Ephesinischen Synode vom Jahre 449, syrisch mit Georg Hoffmanns deutscher Übersetzung und seinen Anmerkungen," Abh Gött. philol.-hist. Kl., N.F., 15 (Berlin: Weidmannsche Buchhandlung, 1917), p. 6 Syriac; p. 7 German: Juvenal is listed second among the bishops, after Dioscorus. For Juvenal's role at Ephesus, see Honigmann, "Juvenal," pp. 233-237. Bishop Leo of Rome was loath to let Juvenal or others forget that Juvenal had earlier been on the side of the heretics; see Leo, *Epp.* 109.4 (PL 54: 1017-1018); and 139.1 (PL 54: 1103); and discussion in Honigmann, "Juvenal," p. 253.

[132] *Collectio Novariensis* 10 (ACO II.2.1: 44). Two years later at Chalcedon, after he had switched sides,

Juvenal alleged that the reading of a "sacred rescript"
had taken precedence over the reading of Leo's letter,
and that no one had later mentioned having Leo's letter
read (Evagrius Scholasticus, *HE* II.18 [Bidez and Parmentier, pp. 69-70]).

[133] *Vita Petri Hiberii* (Raabe, p. 52 Syriac; p. 53
German).

[134] Evagrius Scholasticus, *HE* II.18 (Bidez and Parmentier, pp. 72-73, 86-87).

[135] Zacharias Rhetor, *HE* III.3 (Brooks, p. 156 Syriac;
p. 107 Latin).

[136] Evagrius Scholasticus, *HE* II.18 (Bidez and Parmentier, p. 91); *Gesta Chalcedone* I: 282-284 (ACO II.1.1:
115).

[137] Honigmann, "Juvenal," p. 228: "Since the author
was probably Gerontius, who after 451 separated from
Juvenal's communion, this omission of Juvenal's name is
possibly a sign of Gerontius' resentment against him."

[138] On Gerontius' expressly casting someone's name
to oblivion, see below, pp. 148-151.

[139] Zacharias Rhetor, *HE* III.2 (Brooks, p. 154
Syriac; p. 106 Latin); Evagrius Scholasticus, *HE* II.5
(Bidez and Parmentier, p. 50).

[140] Zacharias Rhetor, *HE* III.2 (Brooks, p. 155
Syriac; p. 106 Latin).

[141] On Theodosius, see Evagrius Scholasticus, *HE*
II.5 (Bidez and Parmentier, p. 52); Zacharias Rhetor, *HE*
III.3-5 (Brooks, pp. 156-159 Syriac; pp. 107-109 Latin);
Vita Petri Hiberii (Raabe, pp. 53-55 Syriac; pp. 54-56
German); Cyril of Scythopolis, *Vita S. Euthymii* 27 (TU
49.2: 41-45); see Honigmann, "Juvenal," pp. 247-251 for
further discussion.

[142] *Vita Petri Hiberii* (Raabe, p. 52 Syriac; p. 53
German); Zacharias Rhetor, *HE* III.3 (Brooks, pp. 156-157
Syriac; pp. 107-108 Latin); Evagrius Scholasticus, *HE*
II.5 (Bidez and Parmentier, p. 52). According to a

letter from Emperor Marcian to Bishop Macarius and the
monks of Mount Sinai (*Ep.* 29, ACO II.1.3: 131 [=490])
and one to the Palestinian synod (*Ep.* 30, ACO II.1.3:
133 [=492]), it was Theodosius who spread the rumor that
Chalcedon had decreed that Christians should worship
"two Sons."

[143]Cyril of Scythopolis, *Vita S. Euthymii* 27 (TU 49.2:
42-44).

[144]Theophanes, *Chronographia* A.M. 5945 (deBoor I:
107); Zacharias Rhetor, *HE* III.5 (Brooks, p. 159 Syriac;
p. 109 Latin); also see Honigmann, "Juvenal," pp. 251-
252.

[145]Evagrius Scholasticus, *HE* II.5 (Bidez and Parmentier, p. 52); Zacharias Rhetor, *HE* III.4 (Brooks, p.
158 Syriac; pp. 108-109 Latin).

[146]Cyril of Scythopolis, *Vita S. Euthymii* 27, 30 (TU
49.2: 41, 47); Zacharias Rhetor, *HE* III.5 (Brooks, p.
159 Syriac; p. 109 Latin): Eudocia intervenes to spare
Peter the Iberian.

[147]Cyril of Scythopolis, *Vita S. Euthymii* 30 (TU 49.2:
47-49).

[148]*Vita* 56, 58, 59 (Gorce, pp. 238, 242, 244, 246).

[149]*Vita* prologus (Gorce, p. 124).

[150]Ibid.

[151]Latin *Vita* 62 (Rampolla, p. 36).

[152]Latin *Vita* 44 (Rampolla, p. 25).

[153]D'Alès, "Vies," p. 449.

[154]Greek *Vita* 54 (Gorce, p. 232).

[155]Only women, in the Latin version: "multae
matronae et religiosae"; "multae nobiles et inlustres
matronae" (Latin *Vita* 54; Rampolla, p. 30).

[156]Latin *Vita* 54 (Rampolla, p. 30).

[157]Greek *Vita* 56 (Gorce, p. 238).

[158]Fleming, "Akten der Ephesinischen Synode," pp. 150-155 (Syriac and German).

[159]Latin *Vita* 65 (Rampolla, p. 38).

II TRANSLATION

[1]The opening formula indicates that the worshiper asks the officiant at the service in which Melania's *Life* is read to bless him or her.

[2]Matthew 6:1-8, 16-18.

[3]Luke 12:3.

[4]Proverbs 9:9.

[5]I Corinthians 7:16.

[6]The Latin version here adds that Melania's father sent his eunuchs to make sure that she was resting in her room; Melania bribes them to report that she was asleep (Rampolla, p. 6).

[7]Probably "endangered" in a spiritual sense.

[8]Here and elsewhere used in the sense of the Devil.

[9]Psalms 45:11. This verse is commonly cited by patristic writers to encourage young women to the asce- tic life (e.g., Jerome, *Epp.* 22.1; 54.3, [CSEL 54: 143-144, 468]). In this exegesis, "the king" refers to Christ.

[10]According to Clement of Alexandria, Cilician linen was of good but not the best quality (*Paedagogus* II.10.115.2 [GCS 1: 226]).

[11]Job 31:32.

[12]Matthew 19:21.

[13]Psalms 77:10.

[14]Song of Songs 5:3.

[15]I Corinthians 11:5.

[16]I Corinthians 11:10.

[17]I Peter 1:24; cf. Isaiah 40:6-7.

[18]Matthew 5:39-41.

[19]Luke 21:2-4.

[20]*Prepositus*: a title given in the later empire to various officials. See *CT* VI.8.

[21]Matthew 25:21.

[22]Ephesians 6:12.

[23]I Corinthians 2:9.

[24]The Latin *Vita* here adds that there were 400 agricultural slaves on the estate (Rampolla, p. 13).

[25]That is, the province of Africa Proconsularis.

[26]Psalms 112:9.

[27]The Latin *Vita* reports that their property near Thagaste was larger than the town itself, had a bath, and employed many artisans who worked in gold, silver, and copper, and two bishops, "one for those of our faith and the other for the heretics" ("Dedit autem et possessionem multum praestantem reditum, quae possessio maior etiam erat civitatis ipsius, habens balneum, artifices multos, aurifices, argentarios et aerarios; et duos episcopos, unum nostrae fidei et alium haereticorum" [Rampolla, p. 14]).

[28]Luke 10:38-42.

[29]Matthew 24:42.

[30]"Philosophy" is often used by early Christian writers to mean "religious truth."

[31]I Corinthians 6:19.

[32]Matthew 5:7.

[33]Matthew 7:7.

[34]II Maccabees 7.

[35]The Latin version is chronologically confused at this point. The editor of the Latin text here inserts the story of the Roman prefect's attempt to confiscate Melania's property; the story is found in its proper position in chapter 19 of the Greek version. According to the Latin text, many of Melania and Pinian's slaves agreed with the prefect and perished "by the Providence of God." The couple are also said to have freed "many thousands of slaves." The Latin version inserts the episodes of the storm at sea and the couple's ransoming of captives, before it returns to the subject matter of Greek *Vita* 34.

[36]Romans 8:18.

[37]Acts 2:45.

[38]Meaning unknown: perhaps from Zeugitana, a Roman province in North Africa. For speculation on the name "Zeugitana", see Timothy D. Barnes, *The New Empire of Diocletian and Constantine* (Cambridge, Mass./London: Harvard University Press, 1982), p. 212.

[39]The Latin *Vita* here adds the interesting information that Lausus, the *ex praepositus sacri cubiculi* of Constantinople, paid for the construction of a bath within the monastery.

[40]Jeremiah 15:19.

[41]The Latin editor here includes an example of obedience taken from the ecclesiastical structure: in the Church, the bishops are under the prince of bishops, and he himself is under the synod ("Considerate et in sancta Dei Ecclesia, quomodo ipsi episcopi sub principe

episcoporum sunt, et princeps episcoporum sub synodo"
[Rampolla, p. 25]).

[42]Matthew 11:12.

[43]II Corinthians 9:7.

[44]Psalms 119:62, 147-148.

[45]Acts 2:4, 14.

[46]Genesis 18:1.

[47]Acts 3:1.

[48]Daniel 6:10.

[49]Matthew 20:3, 5.

[50]Luke 24:12-32.

[51]Tobit 12:7.

[52]Latin *Vita* 53 and 55 make clear that Melania
stayed with Lausus in his palace in the Forum of Augustus
Constantine (Rampolla, pp. 30, 31).

[53]Latin *Vita* 56 contains a reference to the difficulty in the crossing of Mt. Modicus, not found in the
Greek version (Rampolla, p. 32).

[54]Psalms 145:19.

[55]Latin *Vita* 57 reports that the trip took forty
days (Rampolla, p. 32).

[56]Matthew 15:27.

[57]Latin *Vita* 59: Eudocia attributes her cure to
God's benevolence toward his martyrs and Melania, not to
her own merit (Rampolla, p. 33).

[58]Latin *Vita* 61 adds that Melania also cured a man
possessed by a demon (Rampolla, p. 34).

[59]A fuller account is contained in Latin *Vita* 61 (Rampolla, pp. 34-35); see below pp. 147-148 for details.

[60]Matthew 19:21; 16:24.

[61]Latin *Vita* 62 adds the information that Melania took communion every day, as was the custom of the Roman Church from the time Peter was bishop, and the tradition was continued by Paul: "Nunquam haec cibum corporalem accepit, nisi prius corpus Domini communicasset, quod maxime propter tutelam animae percipiebat, quamquam et consuetudo Romanis sit per singulos dies communicare. Primitus enim apostolorum beatissimus Petrus episcopatum gerens, deinde beatus Paulus ibidem consummatus hanc traditionem facerunt" (Rampolla, p. 36).

[62]II Corinthians 5:2.

[63]Jeremiah 48:10.

[64]The martyrs.

[65]Matthew 25:34.

[66]Matthew 25:1-12: the parable of the ten maidens.

[67]Latin *Vita* 65 contains the story of Melania's chastisement of the sisters and of Eudocia: "Misit aliquando regina accipere aliquas ex virginibus de monasterio eius; et una ex puellis, quam ipsa beata de manu matris eius ante altare susceperat, iussa est inter alias ire. Apparet autem ei beatissima cum viris splendido vultu, et cum comminatione coepit eam increpare dicens: 'Nonne sub sanctum altare sicut ovem in holocaustum dedit te mihi mater tua, et nunc vis Constantinopolim ire? Periclitaberis modo, nisi pollicita fueris mihi quod hinc non recedas.' Tunc puella perterrita dedit verbum et dixit: 'Etsi mori me oporteat, non vadam.' Et exurgens indicavit omnibus haec. Sed et aliis sororibus in via iam euntibus apparuit et increpavit eas. Nec non et ipsa regina dixit visionem se eius vidisse, monente ne vellet eas perducere, mittensque de itinere iussit eas redire ad proprium monasterium" (Rampolla, p. 38).

[68]The epiclesis is the calling down of the Holy
Spirit upon the Eucharistic elements.

[69]Latin *Vita* 68 adds that Melania had communion on
her lips as she was dying, as was the Roman custom
(Rampolla, p. 39).

[70]I Corinthians 2:9.

III.A COMMENTARY: MELANIA'S ANCESTRY AND FAMILY

[1]For Melania the Elder's abandonment of her son and
of Rome, see Palladius, *Historia Lausiaca* 46 (Butler II:
134); and Paulinus of Nola, *Ep.* 29.9 (CSEL 29: 255-256).

[2]Palladius, *Historia Lausiaca* 61 (Butler II: 155).

[3]Paulinus of Nola, *Ep.* 29.8 (CSEL 29: 253). Jerome,
Chronicon, an. 377 (PL 27: 505-506); and Palladius, *Historia Lausiaca* 46 (Butler II: 134) call her Marcellinus'
daughter.

[4]Palladius, *Historia Lausiaca* 46 (Butler II: 134).

[5]Rampolla, *Melania*, p. 108, relates Melania the
Elder's mother to Paulinus of Nola on the basis of
Paulinus' writing about Melania, "noster sanguis pro-
pinquat" (*Ep.* 29.5 [CSEL 29: 251]); see Gorce, *Vie*,
pp. 110-111 for various interpretations of Paulinus'
wording.

[6]*PLRE* I: 592 and stemma 30 (p. 1147). See Ammianus
Marcellinus XXI.12.24 and XXIII.3.3 for Valerius Maximus;
and Rampolla, *Melania*, pp. 111-113, 117 for the Christianization of the Valerii in the fourth century. According to Palladius, Melania the Elder was "the wife of
some man of high rank, I forget which one" (*Historia
Lausiaca* 46 [Butler II: 134]).

[7]Palladius, *Historia Lausiaca* 46 (Butler II: 134).

Notes to p. 84

[8]Paulinus of Nola, *Ep.* 29.8 (CSEL 29: 254); Jerome, *Ep.* 39.5 (CSEL 54: 305).

[9]The length of time Melania the Elder spent in Jerusalem is confused by Palladius' reporting. In *Lausiac History* 46 (Butler II: 135) he says that she was there for twenty-seven years, but in chapter 54 (Butler II: 146) he reports thirty-seven years. A possible reconciliation has been suggested: perhaps the number thirty-seven also includes her Egyptian sojourn and her time in Italy upon her return from Palestine, as well as her years there (Gorce, *Vie*, p. 12). Paulinus of Nola gives her twenty-five years in Jerusalem (*Ep.* 29.6 [CSEL 29: 251]). Whether she abandoned her son to "Providence" (Paulinus) or to a curator (Palladius) does not pose a real discrepancy.

[10]See stemma 13 (the Ceionii Rufii), *PLRE* I: 1138.

[11]So listed in Photius, *Bibliotheca*, cod. 230 (PG 103: 1040). The Albinus named could possibly also be identified as Melania's great-uncle.

[12]See below, pp. 130-132.

[13]Augustine, in *Ep.* 137.20 (to Volusian; CSEL 44: 125), refers to Volusian's "pious mother" and asks that God may hear her prayers. Palladius (*Historia Lausiaca* 54 [Butler II: 147]) reports that upon her return to Rome, Melania the Elder "taught Albina"; with Gorce (*Vie*, p. 39 n. 2), we think the word indicates ascetic renunciation, not an initial conversion to Christianity, as is posited by André Chastagnol, "Le Sénateur Volusien et la conversion d'une famille de l'aristocratie romaine au Bas-Empire," *REA* 58 (1956): 250.

[14]*CIL* VI: 512; see *PLRE* I: 511.

[15]Jerome, *Ep.* 107.1 (CSEL 55: 291); thus, we deduce that the younger Paula who appears in the *Life of Melania* (40, 66, 68) was Melania's second cousin.

[16]Macrobius, *Saturnalia* I.2.15 and passim. On Albinus' building projects while governor of Numidia, see Claude Lepelley, *Les Cités de l'Afrique romaine au Bas-Empire*, 2 vols. (Paris: Etudes Augustiniennes, 1979, 1981), I: 103-104 and note 138; his name is on the

dedications of thirteen works, including the construction or restoration of a mithraeum in Cirta (II: 385)
and capitols in Lambaesis (II: 420) and Thamugadi (II:
447).

[17]*Vita* 50, 53-55 (Gorce, pp. 224, 230, 232, 234,
236, 238).

[18]The traditional dating of Melania's birth to A.D.
383 (Rampolla, *Melania*, pp. vii, 103) must be revised.
Problems of dating the events in the *Vita* are myriad;
much of the early chronology rests on the date assigned
Valerius Publicola's death. Rampolla puts his death in
A.D. 404 and Melania and Pinian's visit to Serena at
about the same time (*Melania*, pp. 101, 190), but this
date is probably wrong. The careful study of Nicole
Moine rectifies the chronology on the basis of evidence
in the letters of Paulinus and Augustine: Valerius
Publicola died in 405 or more probably A.D. 406, and the
visit to Serena took place in 407 or 408 ("Melaniana,"
pp. 53-54, 62-64). If Melania was twenty when she began her serious renunciations (*Vita* 8; Gorce, p. 140)
and this was at the time of her father's death, her
birthdate would be A.D. 385/386. Opting for a date of
A.D. 407 for Publicola's death are Pierre Courcelle,
*Les Confessions de Saint Augustin dans le tradition littéraire:
antécédents et postérité* (Paris: Etudes Augustiniennes,
1963), p. 582 n. 5; and C. P. Hammond, "The Last Ten
Years of Rufinus' Life and the Date of His Move South
from Aquileia," *JThS*, n.s., 28 (1977): 416. Moine
("Melaniana," pp. 63-64) posits that Valerius Publicola
accompanied his mother to Sicily and died there;
Courcelle (*Confessions*, p. 582 n. 5) has him die at Nola.

[19]See stemma 30 and 20 for the Valerii (*PLRE* I:
1147, 1142); Pinian's full name given by Paulinus of
Nola in *Carmen* 21.217, 220 (CSEL 30: 165).

[20]G. B. DeRossi, "La casa dei Valerii sul Celio et
il monastero di S. Erasmo," *Studi e Documenti di Storia e
Diritto* 7 (1886): 235-243; the lamp may have been either
for the father or the brother of Pinian (p. 238). Also
see Giuseppe Gatti, "Le casa celimontana dei Valerii e
il monastero di S. Erasmo," *BullComm* 30 (1902): esp. 148-
149. For pictures of the lamp and a summary of the discussion about its significance, see Giuseppe Bovini,
*Monumenti figurati paleocristiani conservati a Firenze nelle rac-
colte pubbliche e negli edifici di culto.* Monumenti di

Notes to pp. 85-86

Antichità Cristiana, 2d ser., 6 (Città del Vaticano: Pontificio Istituto di Archeologia Cristiana, 1950), pp. 8-13. For the analysis of another "Dominus legem dat" inscription, see Walter N. Schumacher, "Dominus Legem Dat," *RQ* 54 (1959): 1-39.

[21] See stemmata 20 and 30 in *PLRE* I: 1142, 1147.

[22] *Vita* 10, 12 (Gorce, pp. 144, 152).

[23] Paulinus of Nola, *Carmen* 21.220-227 (CSEL 30: 165). On the first Valerius Publicola, see Livy II.2.11; Plutarch, *Publicola*; and Ammianus Marcellinus XIV.6.11.

[24] Melania was married when she was fourteen (*Vita* 1 [Gorce, p. 130]); if she was born in about A.D. 385 (see above III.A n. 18), her marriage would have taken place about A.D. 399.

[25] *Vita* 1, 5, 6 (Gorce, pp. 132, 136). The hypothesis that the couple might have had three children is raised by the notice in Palladius (*Historia Lausiaca* 61 [Butler II: 155]) that the couple had two *sons* that died, while the *Vita* attests a daughter (*Vita* 1 [Gorce, p. 132]). The problem is addressed by Gorce, *Vie*, pp. 111-112.

[26] *Vita* 6 (Gorce, p. 136).

[27] For example, Jerome, *Epp.* 108.1, 3 (CSEL 55: 306, 308); 130.3 (CSEL 56: 177). Also see Elizabeth A. Clark, "Ascetic Renunciation and Feminine Advancement: A Paradox of Late Ancient Christianity," *Anglican Theological Review* 63 (1981): esp. 240-244.

[28] Palladius, *Historia Lausiaca* 61 (Butler II: 155).

[29] Palladius, *Historia Lausiaca* 54 (Butler II: 146).

[30] *Vita* 41, 49 (Gorce, pp. 204, 206, 220, 222).

[31] Palladius, *Historia Lausiaca* 46 (Butler II: 135-136). The site of the monasteries is unknown. Rufinus, *Apologia contra Hieronymum* II.1 (CCL 20: 92) speaks of building cells on the Mount of Olives.

[32]See below, pp. 148-151.

[33]*Vita* 6 (Gorce, p. 136).

[34]*Vita* 12 (Gorce, p. 150).

[35]Latin *Vita* 5 (Rampolla, p. 6): this point is omitted in the Greek version.

[36]Greek *Vita* 7 (Gorce, p. 138): Latin *Vita* 12 (Rampolla, p. 10).

[37]Palladius, *Historia Lausiaca* 54 (Butler II: 146).

[38]Ibid., 54 (Butler II: 146).

[39]*CIL* IX: 1591.

[40]Paulinus of Nola, *Ep.* 29.12 (CSEL 29: 260).

[41]Paulinus of Nola, *Ep.* 45.2 (CSEL 29: 381).

[42]Ibid., 45.3 (CSEL 29: 381, 382). Courcelle, *Confessions*, p. 582 n. 2, also admits puzzlement at the discrepancy between the diverging pictures of Valerius Publicola. From Paulinus' depiction, he comments, we would not think Publicola was "un farouche ennemi de l'ascéticisme."

[43]Publicola to Augustine, in Augustine, *Ep.* 46.1 (CSEL 34: 123); R. Thouvenot, "Saint Augustin et les païens d'après Epist., XLVI et XLVII," *Hommages à Jean Bayet*, eds. M. Renard and R. Schilling, Collection Latomus 70 (Bruxelles/Berchem: Latomus, 1964), p. 685. On the Arzuges, see Orosius, *Historia adversum Paganos* I.2.90 (CSEL 5: 32-33).

[44]*CIL* VI: 1684, 1685. See Gatti, "La casa celimontana," 145-146; Antonio M. Colini, *Storia e topographia del Celio nell' antichità*, Atti della Pontificia Accademia Romana di Archeologia, Memorie 7 (Roma: Tipografia Poliglotta Vaticana, 1944), pp. 253-254 (with pictures).

[45]The *Vita* assumes Valerius Publicola's presence with his family in Rome in the period directly before Melania's marriage; also see Thouvenot, "Saint Augustin," p. 683.

Notes to pp. 88-90

[46]Publicola to Augustine, in Augustine, *Ep.* 46 especially questions 2, 3, 6, 8, and 15 (CSEL 34: 124, 125, 126, 127). Given the concern with ritual purity, it is of interest that Jewish magical tables have been found near Hadrumetum: see Paul Monceaux, "Les Colonies juives dans l'Afrique romaine," *Les Cahiers de Tunisie* 18 (1970): 163-164 (=*Revue des Etudes Juives* 49 [1904]).

[47]F. Van der Meer, *Augustine the Bishop. The Life and Work of a Father of the Church*, trans. B. Battershaw and G. R. Lamb (London/New York: Sheed and Ward, 1961), p. 153.

[48]*Vita* 2 (Gorce, p. 132).

[49]Palladius, *Historia Lausiaca* 54 (Butler II: 146).

[50]Van der Meer, *Augustine*, p. 156.

[51]Thouvenot, "Saint Augustin," pp. 683-684; against Rampolla, *Melania*, p. 181; and Van der Meer, *Augustine*, p. 153, who accept the Publicola of the letter as Melania's father, Valerius Publicola. Although Madeleine Moreau has argued for the probable identification of the letter's author with Melania the Younger's father, she fails to consider the evidence from the *Vita Melania Junioris* that casts doubt on her case ("Sur un Correspondant d'Augustin: qui est donc Publicola?" *REAug* 28 [1982]: 225-238).

[52]An emphasis of John Matthews; see "The Letters of Symmachus," in *Latin Literature of the Fourth Century*, ed. J. W. Binns (London: Routledge & Kegan Paul, 1974), p. 91; and *Western Aristocracies and Imperial Court, A.D. 364-425* (Oxford: Clarendon Press, 1975), p. 195.

[53]See below, pp. 130-132.

[54]*Vita* 4-7 (Gorce, pp. 132, 134, 136, 138).

[55]Hammond, "The Last Ten Years," p. 380 n. 3.

[56]Moine, "Melaniana," p. 57.

[57]Greek *Vita* 12 (Gorce, p. 150).

[58]Palladius, *Historia Lausiaca* 54 (Butler II: 146).

Notes to pp. 90-92

[59]Ibid. (Butler II: 147): " καὶ τὸν πουπλικουλᾶ δὲ υἱὸν τὸν νεώτερον κατηχήσασα ἤγαγεν ἐπὶ τὴν Σικελίαν."

[60]For a summary of Rampolla's rejection, see Gorce, *Vie*, p. 34 n. 3; also see Moine, "Melaniana," pp. 24 n. 101, 25. For criticism of Butler's editing of the *Lausiac History*, see René Draguet, "Butleriana: Une Mauvaise Cause et son malchanceux avocat," *Le Muséon* 68 (1955): 239-258, and references therein to other articles by Draguet.

[61]The Syriac manuscripts date to ca. A.D. 500, within a century after Palladius composed the work in Greek, whereas the oldest Greek manuscripts date only to the tenth century (René Draguet, *Les Formes syriaques de la matière de l'Histoire Lausiaque*, CSCO, Scriptores Syri, I, t. 173: 6-7. [Louvain: Secrétariat du Corpus SCO, 1978].

[62]Draguet, *Les Formes*, II, t.173: 300 . The apparatus reveals, however, that other Syriac manuscripts have different readings: one includes more than one male child; one specifies "one daughter"; and still another refers to the children as "males and females," in the plural.

[63]Palladius, *Historia Lausiaca* 54 (Butler II: 146).

[64]Ibid., 54 (Butler II: 147). See III.A n. 59 above for the Greek text.

[65]Draguet, *Les Formes*, II, t.173: 302.

[66]Draguet, *Les Formes*, II, t.174: 198.

[67]Moine, "Melaniana," pp. 63-64, thinks Valerius Publicola accompanied his mother, Melania the Elder, to Sicily and died there.

[68]Gorce, *Vie*, p. 34 n. 5.

[69]Butler, *The Lausiac History* I: 3.

[70]The last event of Melania's life that Palladius reports is the beginning of her retreat from Rome and thence to Sicily and Campania, in order that she might live in greater seclusion (*Historia Lausiaca* 61 [Butler II: 157]).

[71]Moine, "Melaniana," p. 60; Pietri, *Roma Christiana*, pp. 1310, 1312.

[72]Palladius, *Dialogus* 3 (Coleman-Norton, pp. 19-20).

[73]Palladius, *Historia Lausiaca* 61 (Butler II: 157).

[74]See III.A n. 18 above.

[75]Palladius, *Historia Lausiaca* 61 (Butler II: 155): in contrast to Palladius' forgetfulness about the name of Melania the Elder's husband, whom he never knew (46; [Butler II: 134]).

[76]Were there perhaps originally two, one of whom died before Palladius' visit to Rome? This supposition might account for the phrase, "the younger son of Publicola" (*Historia Lausiaca* 54 [Butler II: 147]), which implies that there once were two sons.

III.B COMMENTARY: MELANIA'S EARLY RENUNCIATIONS

[1]Arthur Vööbus, *History of Asceticism in the Syrian Orient. A Contribution to the History of Culture in the Near East*, vol. I, *The Origin of Asceticism. Early Monasticism in Persia*, CSCO, Subsidia 14 (=184); vol. II, *Early Monasticism in Mesopotamia and Syria*, CSCO, Subsidia 17 (=197) (Louvain: Secrétariat du Corpus SCO, 1958, 1960).

[2]Evidence especially from the *Vita Antonii*: when Antony retreated to the desert in approximately A.D. 275, he met there a man who had been a hermit from his youth (chap. 3). Origins of communal monasticism in Egypt are usually traced to Pachomius in the 320s and 330s. See Derwas Chitty, *The Desert A City: An Introduction to the Study of Egyptian and Palestinian Monasticism under the Christian Empire* (Oxford: Basil Blackwell, 1966), chaps. 1 and 2; Philip Rousseau, *Ascetics, Authority, and the Church in the Age of Jerome and Cassian* (Oxford: University Press, 1978), pt. I; and idem, *Pachomius*, The Transformation of the Classical Heritage 6 (Berkeley: University of California Press, forthcoming).

202   *The Life of Melania the Younger*

Notes to pp. 93-94

[3]Jerome, *Ep.* 127.5 (CSEL 56: 149). J. N. D. Kelly suggests that Marcella probably read the *Life of Antony* and met Bishop Peter of Alexandria when he was in exile in Rome from 373 to 378 (*Jerome: His Life, Writings, and Controversies* [New York: Harper & Row, 1975], p. 92). Yet neither of these events could have led Marcella to contemplate ascetic renunciation in the 340s or 350s.

[4]Marcella died after the sack of Rome (Jerome, *Ep.* 127.14 [CSEL 56: 156]).

[5]Marcella married but was widowed after seven months. She then received a proposal, which she rejected (Jerome, *Ep.* 127.2 [CSEL 56: 146]), from Naeratius Cerealis, presumably after he had been consul in A.D. 358 (*PLRE* I: 197-198).

[6]So Jerome implies, *Ep.* 127.3-4 (CSEL 56: 147-149).

[7]Jerome, *Ep.* 127.8 (CSEL 56: 151).

[8]Damasus, *Carmen* 31 (PL 13: 406): she lived through twenty winters.

[9]Paulinus of Milan, *Vita Ambrosii* 4 (PL 14: 30); Ambrose, *De Virginibus* III.1 (PL 16: 231).

[10]Jerome, *Ep.* 24.2-3 (CSEL 54: 215).

[11]Jerome, *Ep.* 23.2 (CSEL 54: 212): Lea died in A.D. 384.

[12]Jerome, *Ep.* 108.5 (CSEL 55: 310).

[13]Moine, "Melaniana," p. 19; Gordini, "Il monachesimo romano," opts for A.D. 372 (p. 87 n. 5).

[14]Palladius, *Historia Lausiaca* 46 (Butler II: 134, 135).

[15]Augustine, *De Moribus Ecclesiae Catholicae* I.70-71 (PL 32: 1340).

[16]Jerome, *Ep.* 130.1-6 (CSEL 56: 175-182).

[17]See, for example, Jerome, *Epp.* 23.2 (CSEL 54: 212-213); 24.3-5 (CSEL 54: 215-217); 127.4-6 (CSEL 56: 148-150).

[18]Palladius, *Historia Lausiaca* 46 (Butler II: 135).
These are the earliest Western foundations in Jerusalem of which we know, dating from ca. A.D. 378-380.

[19]Jerome, *Ep.* 108.14.4; 20 (CSEL 55: 325, 334-336):
Paula's foundations date to about A.D. 390-391.

[20]*Vita* 2, 5, 6 (Gorce, pp. 132, 134, 136).

[21]*Vita* 7 (Gorce, p. 140).

[22]*Vita* 22 (Gorce, p. 172).

[23]*Vita* 41, 49 (Gorce, pp. 204, 206, 220, 222).

[24]Clark "Ascetic Renunciation," pp. 247-250; G. D.
Gordini, "Origine e sviluppo del monachesimo a Roma,"
Gregorianum 37 (1956): 248. On women's place in the
Christianization of Rome, see Anne Yarbrough, "Chris-
tianization in the Fourth Century: The Example of Roman
Women," *CH* 45 (1976): 149-165.

[25]For example, Arnaldo Momigliano, "Introduction.
Christianity and the Decline of the Roman Empire," in
*The Conflict Between Paganism and Christianity in the Fourth Cen-
tury*, ed. A. Momigliano (Oxford: Clarendon Press, 1963),
pp. 11-12: "St. Jerome was the popularizer of the
Eastern monastic ideals and found disciples among the
most aristocratic ladies of Rome." Although Jerome indeed became their intellectual mentor, he himself makes
clear that they had practiced asceticism for years be-
for his entrance to the city.

[26]*Vita* 1 (Gorce, p. 130).

[27]Ibid.

[28]*Vita* 4 (Gorce, p. 132). The verb is in the im-
perfect: ἐπειρᾶτο.

[29]*Vita* 4 (Gorce, p. 134); I Corinthians 7:16.

[30]*Vita* 5-6 (Gorce, pp. 134, 136).

[31]*Vita* 29 (Gorce, p. 182).

[32] *Vita* 2 (Gorce, p. 132).

[33] *Vita* 4 (Gorce, p. 134). For Melania's renunciation of her silk clothing, see Palladius, *Historia Lausiaca* 61 (Butler II: 156). On the value of silk in late antiquity, see André Piganiol, "Le Problème de l'or au IVe siècle," *Annales d'Histoire Sociale* 7 (1945): 52.

[34] *Vita* 5 (Gorce, p. 134).

[35] For example, *Vita* 22, 24, 31, 32, 43 (Gorce, pp. 172, 174, 176, 186, 188, 210).

[36] As in *Vita* 17 (Gorce, p. 160), when the Devil asks Melania, "What sort of place is this Kingdom of Heaven, that it can be bought with so much money?"; also see *Vita* 18 (Gorce, p. 162).

[37] On their property and income, see Stephan Beissel, "Die Hingabe eines ausserordentlich grossen Vermögens. Eine heroische Tat der Hl. Melania," *Stimmen aus Maria-Lach* 71 (1906): 477-490; Paul Allard, "Une Grande Fortune romaine au cinquième siècle," *RQH* 81 (1907): 5-30.

[38] Greek *Vita* 15 (Gorce, pp. 156, 158).

[39] Latin *Vita* 15 (Rampolla, p. 11).

[40] Rampolla, *Melania*, pp. 182-183.

[41] Beissel, "Die Hingabe," pp. 479-480.

[42] Seventy-two *solidi* equal one pound of gold. See Piganiol, "Le Problème," p. 47. Yet John Matthews calculates Melania's income to be only 1200 pounds of gold yearly (*Western Aristocracies*, p. 384 n. 5).

[43] Olympiodorus, *Frag.* 44, in Photius, *Bibliotheca* 80 (PG 103: 280).

[44] On Symmachus' property, see Otto Seeck, *Q. Aurelii Symmachi Quae Supersunt*, MGH, AA VI (Berlin: Weidmann, 1883), pp. xlv-xlvi; one of the Roman homes was on the Coelian Hill (p. xlv); Allard, "Une Grande Fortune," p. 9; Jean Rougé, "Une Emeute à Rome au IVe siècle. Ammien Marcellin, XXVII, 3-4: Essai d'interprétation," *REA* 63 (1961): 66-67.

Notes to pp. *96-98*

[45]Olympiodorus, *Frag.* 44, in Photius, *Bibliotheca* 80 (PG 103: 280).

[46]Admittedly almost two centuries later, yet even allowing for fluctuations in the value of gold, Melania's income was enormous.

[47]Paul the Deacon, *Vita S. Gregorii Magni* II.27 (PL 75: 97).

[48]John Alexander McGeachy, Jr., *Quintus Aurelius Symmachus and the Senatorial Aristocracy of the West* (Chicago: University of Chicago Libraries, 1942), p. 17: Symmachus probably was dead by A.D. 402.

[49]Symmachus, *Ep.* VII.116 (MGH, AA VI.1: 209).

[50]*PLRE* I: 702 (Pinianus I).

[51]*Vita* 14 (Gorce, pp. 154, 156).

[52]*Vita* 17 (Gorce, p. 160); Palladius, *Historia Lausiaca* 61 (Butler II: 156).

[53]*Vita* 19 (Gorce, pp. 162, 164).

[54]*Vita* 15 (Gorce, p. 158).

[55]Paulinus of Nola, *Carmen* 21.262-265 (CSEL 30: 166).

[56]Palladius, *Historia Lausiaca* 58 (Butler II: 151-152): Dorotheus kept three of the coins and sent the rest to another anchorite.

[57]Greek *Vita* 14 (Gorce, p. 154) explicitly says the house is Pinian's, while Latin *Vita* 14 (Rampolla, p. 11) simply refers to the house "they had" ("habebant") in the city of Rome.

[58]Rampolla, *Melania*, p. 173; for the inscription, see *CIL* VI.1.1532 (p. 336).

[59]DeRossi, "La casa dei Valerii," pp. 235-238; Gatti, "La casa celimontana," p. 152.

206

[60] *Vita* 14 (Gorce, p. 156). Some of the statues from the mansion were given to Serena as "tokens of friendship."

[61] *Vita* 14 (Gorce, p. 156).

[62] Gregory the Great, *Epp.* IX.67, 83 (CCL 140A: 623, 637); also mentioned in the *Liber Pontificalum*, in Stephanus III.15 (*Le Liber Pontificalis. Texte, introduction et commentaire*, ed. L. Duchesne, Bibliothèque des Ecoles Françaises d'Athènes et de Rome, 2d ser. [Paris: Ernest Tholin, 1886], I: 473).

[63] DeRossi, "La casa dei Valerii," pp. 240-242; Gatti, "La casa celimontana," pp. 149-150, 153; Rampolla, *Melania*, pp. 166-173.

[64] Colini, *Storia*, p. 258.

[65] *CIL* VI.1.1684, 1685, 1686, 1693 (pp. 364-365, 367); Colini, *Storia*, p. 254.

[66] *CIL* VI.1.1687, 1688, 1690, 1691, 1692 (pp. 366-367).

[67] Colini, *Storia* p. 254; Rampolla, *Melania*, pp. 168-169.

[68] G. B. DeRossi, "Dei primi monumenti cristiani di Ginevra, e specialmente d'una lucerna di terra cotta colle immagini dei dodici apostoli," *BACr* 5 (1867): 28; G. B. DeRossi, "Nuove scoperte nel cimitero di Priscilla per le escavazione fatte nell' a. 1887," *BACr*, 4th ser., 5 (1887): 26.

[69] DeRossi, "Le casa dei Valerii," p. 238; Colini, *Storia*, p. 258, opts for Pinian's father.

[70] Colini, *Storia*, pp. 254-255; see figure 215 for photograph.

[71] Rampolla, *Melania*, p. 170; Colini, *Storia*, pp. 255-256.

[72] Rampolla, *Melania*, pp. 176-179.

Notes to pp. 99-100

[73] *Vita* 7 (Gorce, p. 140).

[74] *Vita* 18 (Gorce, p. 162).

[75] Latin *Vita* 18 (Rampolla, p. 13); the Greek version (Gorce, p. 162) reports sixty-two houses. The Latin text could be construed to mean four hundred slaves on *each* of the sixty *villae*, giving a total of 24,000 slaves, but this figure seems exaggerated: "Habebat enim ipsa possessio sexaginta villas circa se, habentes quadringentenos servos agricultores."

[76] *Vita* 19 (Gorce, pp. 164, 166): they set sail from Sicily to go to Paulinus (in Nola); cf. Latin *Vita* 34 (Rampolla, p. 19). The Sicilian and Campanian properties are also mentioned by Palladius, *Historia Lausiaca* 61 (Butler II: 156).

[77] *Vita* 19 (Gorce, p. 164).

[78] *Vita* 11, 20 (Gorce, pp. 146, 168). They could not sell their Spanish property until later (*Vita* 37 [Gorce, p. 196]), perhaps because of the barbarian invasions in Spain in A.D. 409; see E. Demougeot, *De l'Unité à la division de l'Empire romain, 395-410. Essai sur le gouvernement impérial* (Paris: Librairie d'Amérique et d'Orient Adrien Maisonneuve, 1951), p. 454. Perhaps the sale of of Melania's property in Spain was thus connected with the Gothic surrender there in A.D. 416. See E. A. Thompson, "The Settlement of the Barbarians in Southern Gaul," *JRS* 46 (1956): 67; and idem, "The Visigoths from Fritigern to Euric," *Historia* 12 (1963): 118.

[79] Palladius, *Historia Lausiaca* 61 (Butler II: 156).

[80] Latin *Vita* 21 (Rampolla, p. 14).

[81] Olympiodorus, *Frag.* 43, in Photius, *Bibliotheca* 80 (PG 103: 277).

[82] Alexander Demandt and Guntram Brummer, "Der Prozess gegen Serena im Jahre 408 n. Chr.," *Historia* 26 (1977): 484, estimate 24,000 slaves; see III.B n. 75 above for the basis of their calculation.

[83] Latin *Vita* 34 (Rampolla, p. 19).

[84]Palladius, *Historia Lausiaca* 61 (Butler II: 156).

[85] *Vita* 10 (Gorce, pp. 144, 146).

[86]Palladius, *Historia Lausiaca* 61 (Butler II: 157);
Vita 10 (Gorce, pp. 144, 146); Elizabeth A. Clark,
"Authority and Humility: A Conflict of Values in Fourth-
Century Female Monasticism," *BZ* 76 (1983), especially
the examples of Paula (Jerome, *Ep.* 108.11, 14 [CSEL 55:
320, 325]) and of Olympias (*Vita Olympiadis* 6, 15 [SC
13 bis: 418, 440]).

[87]John Chrysostom, *Homilia 63 in Matt.* 4 (PG 58: 608).
In *Homilia 12 in Matt.* 4 (PG 57: 207), he mocks those who
have "myriads" of servants to guard their goods.

[88] *Vita* 8 (Gorce, p. 140).

[89]*CT* II.17.1 (Mommsen, pp. 102-104); *CJ* II.44(45).1-2
(Krueger, p. 114). Men could apply for the *venia aetatis*
at twenty and women at eighteen; people of senatorial
rank had to apply through the city prefect *CT* II.17.1-2
[Mommsen, p. 103]). See Demandt and Brummer, "Der Prozess," p. 488.

[90] *Iustiniani Digesta* XXVII.10.1, 3 (Mommsen I: 370);
also see Gorce, *Vie*, p. 138 n. 1.

[91] *CT* VI.2.8 (Mommsen, p. 244): all senatorial property must be listed. See Gorce, *Vie*, p. 166 n. 2 for
discussion.

[92]Olympias provides the exception. Theodosius I
did his best to prevent the alienation of her property;
he ordered the prefect of Constantinople to keep her
possessions under guard until she was thirty. See *Vita
Olympiadis* 4 (SC 13 bis: 412).

[93] *Vita* 7 (Gorce, pp. 138, 140).

[94]Allard, "Une Grande Fortune," p. 21.

[95] *Vita* 12 (Gorce, pp. 150, 152).

[96] *Vita* 10 (Gorce, pp. 144, 146).

Notes to pp. 101-103

[97] *Vita* 11 (Gorce, p. 146).

[98] On the chronology, see Moine, "Melaniana," pp. 59-63; Otto Seeck, *Regesten der Kaiser und Päpste für die Jahre 311 bis 476 n. Chr. Vorarbeit zu einer Prosopographie der christlichen Kaiserzeit* (Stuttgart: J. B. Metzlersche Verlagsbuchhandlung, 1919), pp. 306, 312-314.

[99] *Vita* 12 (Gorce, p. 148).

[100] Claudian, *Panegyricus de Sexto Consulatu Honorii Augusti*, esp. 578ff., 640ff.

[101] *Vita* 12 (Gorce, p. 150); Moine, "Melaniana," pp. 162-163.

[102] In the Latin version of *Vita* 12 (Rampolla, p. 10), Serena offers to have "them" ("eos"; "eorum") condemned and their property subjoined to the public treasury: does the author intend *all* the senatorial relatives who opposed Melania's plan?

[103] *Vita* 12 (Gorce, p. 152).

[104] *Vita* 19 (Gorce, p. 166).

[105] *CT* II.17.2 (Mommsen, p. 103).

[106] Orosius, *Historia adversum Paganos* VII.37.3-4 (CSEL 5: 537-538); Salvian, *De Gubernatione Dei* 6.82-84; 7.50, 52 (CSEL 8: 148-149, 171); Jerome, *Ep.* 123.16 (CSEL 56: 93-94); Demougeot, *De l'Unité*, pp. 521-525. Paulinus of Nola rejoices at Radagaisus' defeat in August 406 at the beginning of *Carmen* 21.1-24 (CSEL 30: 158-159). This passage is one of the sources for Melania and Pinian.

[107] Zosimus V.26 (CSHB 30: 283); Sozomen, *HE* VIII.25 (GCS 50: 383-384). On the relations of Alaric and Stilicho, see Alan Cameron, *Claudian. Poetry and Propaganda at the Court of Honorius* (Oxford: Clarendon Press, 1970), chap. 7.

[108] Zosimus V.29 (CSHB 30: 287-288); Olympiodorus, *Frag.* 5, in Photius, *Bibliotheca* 80 (PG 103: 257). On Stilicho's problems with the Senate and senatorial selfishness, see Santo Mazzarino, *Stilicone. La crisi imperiale*

dopo Teodosio, Studi Pubblicati dal R. Istituto Italiano per la Storia Antica 3 (Roma: Angelo Signorelli, 1942), chap. 6 and pp. 321, 324.

[109]Matthews, *Western Aristocracies*, p. 283.

[110]Olympiodorus, *Frag.* 9, in Photius, *Bibliotheca* 80 (PG 103: 257); Demougeot, *De l'Unité*, p. 408. Stilicho had already allowed Alaric to retreat twice, in 395 and 397 (see Cameron, *Claudian*, pp. 85-86).

[111]Zosimus V.31-32 (CSHB 30: 290-293); Orosius, *Historia adversum Paganos* VII.38.1 (CSEL 5: 542-543). On the rumor about Eucherius, Sozomen, *HE* IX.4.1 (GCS 50: 395); Demougeot, *De l'Unité*, pp. 414-415. The fears were groundless: at his death, Eucherius was still only a tribune and a notary (Cameron, *Claudian*, p. 49).

[112]Stilicho's decline in power may already have begun in the summer of 407 according to Demougeot, *De l'Unité*, p. 397.

[113]Zosimus V.32 (CSHB 30: 293).

[114]Zosimus V.33-34 (CSHB 30: 293-295); Sozomen, *HE* IX.4.1, 8 (GCS 50: 395, 396); Orosius, *Historia adversum Paganos* VII.38.5 (CSEL 5: 544). See Matthews, *Western Aristocracies*, pp. 276-278, 301; for the dating of the event, see Demougeot, *De l'Unité*, p. 427 n. 366.

[115]Zosimus V.35 (CSHB 30: 297-298).

[116]*CT* IX.40.20; 42.20, 22 (Mommsen, pp. 506, 516).

[117]Zosimus V.35, 45 (CSHB 30: 296-297, 310). See Demougeot, *De l'Unité*, pp. 427-439 on the anti-Stilicho reaction.

[118]Zosimus V.35, 37 (CSHB 30: 297, 300); Marcellinus, *Chronicon*, an. 408.1 (MGH, AA XI.1: 69). Thermantia was their second daughter to marry Stilicho; Maria had died earlier, perhaps in A.D. 404. See Stewart Irwin Oost, *Galla Placidia Augusta: A Biographical Essay* (Chicago/London: University of Chicago Press, 1968), pp. 74-75.

[119]Oost, *Galla Placidia*, pp. 83, 84-85; Demandt and Brummer, "Der Prozess," p. 481.

[120] Zosimus V.38 (CSHB 30: 301); Olympiodorus, *Frag.*
6, in Photius, *Bibliotheca* 80 (PG 103: 257).

[121] See Zosimus V.38 (CSHB 30: 301) on Serena's
stripping a necklace from a statue of the Great Mother
and putting it on her own neck; the story is designed
to show Serena's hostility to paganism. On Galla
Placidia's role, see Zosimus V.38 (CSHB 30: 301); Demandt
and Brummer, "Der Prozess," p. 481. On the Senate's
action, see Oost, *Galla Placidia*, p. 85 n. 159 and W. Ensslin, "Placidia," *RE* XX.2 (1950), cols. 1912-1913. Another
indication of Serena's Christian enthusiasm is the shrine
she built in Milan to St. Nazarius: *CIL* V.2.6250
(Mommsen, p. 687).

[122] Zosimus V.38 (CSHB 30: 301). On the story that
the Anicii opened the gates of the city to Alaric, see
Procopius, *De Bello Vandalico* III.2.27. Demougeot suggests
that Proba was suspected because she was the best-known
person living in the sixth region near where the gates
were opened (*De l'Unité*, p. 469).

[123] Zosimus V.39 (CSHB 30: 302); Sozomen, *HE* IX.6.2
(GCS 50: 397).

[124] Zosimus V.39 (CSHB 30: 303); Sozomen, *HE* IX.6.3
(GCS 50: 397); Olympiodorus, *Frag.* 4, in Photius, *Bibliotheca* 8 (PG 103: 257).

[125] Zosimus, V.40 (CSHB 30: 304).

[126] *PLRE* II: 897-898.

[127] Zosimus V.41 (CSHB 30: 305). According to Sozomen, *HE* IX.6.3 (GCS 50: 398), other pagan rituals were
proposed as well. See Pietri, *Roma Christiana*, pp. 443-
444, for discussion.

[128] Zosimus V.41 (CSHB 30: 305-306).

[129] Zosimus V.42 (CSHB 30: 307).

[130] Zosimus V.42 (CSHB 30: 307); Sozomen also reports
that slaves deserted to Alaric (*HE* IX.6.3 [GCS 50: 397-
398]).

[131]Zosimus V.44, 45 (CSHB 30: 308-311).

[132]Zosimus V.48, 50 (CSHB 30: 314-315, 315-316);
Sozomen, *HE* IX.7.5 (GCS 50: 399).

[133]Zosimus V.48, 49 (CSHB 30: 314-315).

[134]Matthews, *Western Aristocracies*, p. 286; Cameron,
Claudian, p. 157.

[135]Gorce, *Vie*, p. 165 n. 5.

[136]Matthews, *Western Aristocracies*, p. 290 n. 5.

[137]See above, III. B n. 82 for reference.

[138]Demandt and Brummer, "Der Prozess," p. 489.

[139]Ibid., p. 501.

[140]Ibid., pp. 492-493, citing *CJ* X.1.5 (Krueger,
p. 395).

[141]Demandt and Brummer, "Der Prozess," p. 493. For
the law of 24 September 408, confiscating the property
of Stilicho's "satellites," see *CT* IX.42.20 (Mommsen,
p. 516).

[142]Demandt and Brummer, "Der Prozess," pp. 494,
501. Pompeianus' death is usually assigned to February
409 (*PLRE* II: 897; Matthews, *Western Aristocracies*, p. 293
n. 2). The execution of Serena should be placed in 409,
according to Demougeot, *De l'Unité*, p. 418 n. 324.

[143]Zosimus V.41 (CSHB 30: 305); Sozomen, *HE* IX.7.4
(GCS 50: 398).

[144]*Vita* 19 (Gorce, p. 166).

[145]Demandt and Brummer, "Der Prozess," p. 496.

[146]Zosimus V.41 (CSHB 30: 305). See *PLRE* II: 897.
On the basis of Pompeianus' alleged paganism, he has
been posited as the subject of the *Carmen ad Flavianum*:
see Giacomo Manganaro, "La reazione pagana a Roma nel
408-9 D.C. e il poemetto anonimo 'Contra Paganos',"

Giornale Italiano di Filologia 13 (1960): 210-224, esp.
218ff.; challenged by Santo Mazzarino, in favor of the
elder Symmachus, in *Antico, Tardoantico ed era costantiniana*
(Bari: Dedalo Libri, 1974), I: chap. 19) and more successfully, in favor of Vettius Agorius Praetextatus,
by Lelia Ruggini, "Il paganesimo romano tra religione e
politica (384-394 D.C.): per una reinterpretazione del
Carmen contra paganos," *Atti della Accademia Nazionale dei
Lincei*, Memorie, Classe di Scienze, storiche e filolo-
giche, 8th ser., vol. 23, fasc.1 (Roma: Accademia
Nazionale dei Lincei, 1979). For a review of different
hypotheses about the poem, see John Matthews, "The Historical Setting of the 'Carmen contra paganos',"
Historia 19 (1970): 464-479.

[147]Demandt and Brummer's sequence of events: (1)
Stilicho executed, August 408; (2) Alaric enters Rome,
October 408; (3) Serena's trial and execution, while
Pompeianus was the city prefect; (4) the food riot and
Pompeianus' death, December 408; (5) Alaric's retreat
from Rome, before January 409; (6) Melania's departure
from Rome. See "Der Prozess," esp. pp. 480, 496. In
contrast (and probably wrongly), Courcelle, *Confessions*,
p. 575 n. 3, holds that Melania and Pinian fled to Nola
as early as A.D. 406 and did not return to Rome.

[148]Demandt and Brummer, "Der Prozess," p. 493.

[149]For the Senate's proceedings and Galla Placidia's
role, see Oost, *Galla Placidia*, p. 85 n. 159; Ensslin,
"Placidia," cols. 1912-1913.

[150]Zosimus V.38 (CSHB 30: 301).

[151]Latin *Vita* 34 (Rampolla, p. 19).

[152]See Demandt and Brummer, "Der Prozess," p. 491.

[153]Latin *Vita* 34 (Rampolla, p. 19).

[154]Zosimus V.39 (CSHB 30: 303).

[155]Zosimus V.42 (CSHB 30: 307).

[156]Matthews, *Western Aristocracies*, p. 289.

[157]Zosimus V.35 (CSHB 30: 298).

[158]See the law of 29 November 408, directed to a Volusianus, in *CT* V.16.31 (Mommsen, p. 236).

III.C COMMENTARY: NORTH AFRICA AND BEYOND

[1]Rampolla, *Melania*, pp. 104, 172, thinks the end of 408; Demandt and Brummer, "Der Prozess," p. 501, opt for 409 after Pompeianus' fall in December 408; Francis X. Murphy (*Rufinus of Aquileia (345-411). His Life and Works*, The Catholic University of America Studies in Medieval History, n.s., 6 (Washington, D.C.: Catholic University of America Press, 1945), p. 205, opts for October 408; Courcelle, *Confessions*, p. 575, thinks Melania and Pinian never returned to Rome after their trip to Nola in 406-407.

[2]Greek *Vita* 19 (Gorce, p. 166). Latin *Vita* 34 (Rampolla, p. 19) seems incorrect in having the trio head for Paulinus in Sicily: presumably he was in Nola.

[3]Palladius, *Historia Lausiaca* 61 (Butler II: 156).

[4]Rufinus, *Prologus in Omelias Origenis super Numeros* (CCL 20: 285). Also see Murphy, *Rufinus*, pp. 213-214; Rampolla, *Melania*, pp. 201-202.

[5]Rufinus, *Prologus in Omelias Origenis super Numeros* (CCL 20: 285): Pinian encourages Rufinus to translate Origen's *Homilies on Deuteronomy*.

[6]Greek *Vita* 19 (Gorce, p. 166). Melania, Pinian, and Albina had been in Nola in January 407 on St. Felix's anniversary (Paulinus of Nola, *Carmen* 21.216-329 (CSEL 30: 165-169). Possibly after this time, a servant of Melania and Pinian brought back to Rome a letter from Paulinus to Rufinus. The messenger of the letter is referred to as "the boy of the children we share " (Paulinus of Nola, *Ep.* 46.1 [CSEL 29: 387]). On the dating of the letter to 407 or 408, see Pierre Fabre, *Essai sur la chronologie de l'oeuvre de Saint Paulin de Nole*,

Notes to pp. 109-110

Publications de la Faculté des Lettres de l'Université de Strasbourg 109 (Paris: "Les Belles Lettres," 1948), p. 95.

[7] *Vita* 19 (Gorce, p. 168). Gorce, *Vie*, p. 169 n. 2, suggests one of the Lipari islands.

[8] Augustine, *De Civitate Dei* I.10 (CCL 47: 11-12): Paulinus prayed, in the face of the barbarian onslaught, "Lord, let me not be tortured because of gold and silver, for you know where all my riches are."

[9] Olympiodorus, *Frag.* 15, in Photius *Bibliotheca* 80 (PG 103: 261).

[10] Cf. Jerome, *Ep.* 130.4.4; 5.4; 7.7 (CSEL 56: 179, 180, 184); Augustine, *Epp.* 130, 131, 150 (CSEL 44: 40-79, 380-382).

[11] That they arrived late in A.D. 410 can be deduced from Augustine's *Epistle* 124, written probably in the spring of 411, in which he apologizes to the trio at Thagaste for not having greeted them sooner after their arrival. He claims that he had been ill during the winter and that the Hippo congregation needed his presence (*Ep.* 124.1-2 [CSEL 44: 1-2]).

[12] *Vita* 20 (Gorce, pp. 168, 170).

[13] More fully described in Latin *Vita* 21 than in Greek *Vita* 21: the estate was larger than the town itself, had many metal workers, and two bishops, one for the orthodox and one for the "heretics" (Rampolla, p. 14).

[14] *Vita* 20 (Gorce, pp. 168, 170): money gifts would quickly be depleted, while endowing monasteries would bring a lasting contribution.

[15] *Vita* 21 (Gorce, p. 172).

[16] Augustine, *Epp.* 125.3 (CSEL 44: 5); 126.1, 3, 4 (CSEL 44: 8, 9-10).

[17] Augustine, *Ep.* 126.1, 6 (CSEL 44: 8, 12).

Notes to pp. 110-111

[18]Augustine, *Ep.* 125.4 (CSEL 44: 6-7):   those who
keep only the "letter" of the promise, when they know
that the expectations of those to whom they made the vow
are different, are guilty of perjury.   Pinian has left
town, but assuming that he returns, he will not be guilty
of perjury.   May God forbid that he abandon his purpose!

[19]Augustine, *Ep.* 125.2 (CSEL 44: 3), to Alypius,
dated 411; *Ep.* 126.7 (CSEL 44: 12-13), to Albina.   According to Augustine, the people of Hippo were showing
their regard for the trio's *contempt* of wealth by wanting
Pinian as their priest (*Ep.* 126.7 [CSEL 44: 12]).   This
letter also contains the interesting notice that Augustine's personal patrimony measured only one-twentieth
the church property he now controlled as bishop of Hippo
(*Ep.* 126.7 [CSEL 44: 13]).

[20]Augustine, *Ep.* 125.2 (CSEL 44: 4), although he
acknowledges that the *church* at Thagaste benefited from
their money (*Ep.* 126.7 [CSEL 44: 12]).

[21]Augustine, *Ep.* 126.5 (CSEL 44: 11).

[22]Augustine, *Epp.* 125.2 (CSEL 44: 3); 126.9 (CSEL
44: 14).

[23]Augustine, *Ep.* 126.7 (CSEL 44: 12):   recall that
the original context of this phrase is to be found in
the parable of the dishonest steward.

[24]Augustine, *Ep.* 126.13, 14 (CSEL 44: 18).

[25]Rampolla piously attributes this omission of
events in the *Vita* to the fact that the treatise is
about Melania, not about Pinian or Albina (*Melania*, p.
205).

[26]*Vita* 1 (Gorce, pp. 130, 132):   Pinian is not enthusiastic for chastity; *Vita* 8 (Gorce, pp. 140, 142):
he has to be lured into abandoning his more elaborate
style of dress.

[27]Augustine, *Ep.* 126.7 (CSEL 44: 13; trans. J. G.
Cunningham, NPNF I.1, p. 457):   "...quanto flagrantius
in nostro Piniano amare potuerent tantam mundi istius
cupiditatem...."

Notes to pp. 111-112

[28]So *Vita* 34 (Gorce, p. 190).

[29]*Vita* 22 (Gorce. p. 172).

[30]*Vita* 22, 24, 25 (Gorce, pp. 172, 174, 176, 178).

[31]*Vita* 24 (Gorce, p. 176).

[32]*Vita* 33 (Gorce, p. 188).

[33]*Vita* 23 (Gorce, pp. 174, 176).

[34]*Vita* 23, 26 (Gorce, pp. 174, 178).

[35]*Vita* 27, 28, 29 (Gorce, pp. 180, 182, 184).

[36]*Vita* 29 (Gorce, p. 182).

[37]*Vita* 32 (Gorce, p. 188).

[38]See summary in Otto Seeck, "Heraclianus," *RE* VIII.1 (1912), cols. 405-406.

[39]Zosimus V.37 (CSHB 30: 300).

[40]Zosimus VI.7 (CSHB 30: 323-324).

[41]Zosimus VI.7, 9 (CSHB 30: 324, 325-326); Sozomen, *HE* IX.8.7 (GCS 50: 400).

[42]Zosimus VI.10 (CSHB 30: 326-327).

[43]Zosimus VI.11 (CSHB 30: 327); Sozomen, *HE* IX.7-8 (GCS 50: 400); Orosius, *Historia adversum Paganos* VII.42.10-12 (CSEL 5: 557-558). Also see Demougeot, *De l'Unité*, pp. 456, 458; Lelia Ruggini, *Economia e società nell' 'Italia Annonaria': Rapporti fra agricoltura e commercio dal IV al VI secolo d.C.*, Fondazione Guglielmo Castelli 30 (Milano: A. Giufrè, 1961), p. 173.

[44]Orosius, *Historia adversum Paganos* VII.42.14 (CSEL 5: 558); Philostorgius, *HE* XII.6 (GCS 21: 145).

[45]Jerome, *Ep.* 130.7 (CSEL 56: 184-185).

[46] Ibid.

[47] Ibid.

[48] Ibid. Jerome's anger at the events also emerges in *Dialogus contra Pelagianos* III.19 (PL 23: 616-617); *In Hiezechielem* IX.28 (CCL 75: 388).

[49] An hypothesis proposed by William H. Fremantel in *Dictionary of Christian Biography* (London: John Murray, 1887), IV: 397.

[50] See the law of 25 August 410, addressed to Heraclian as *comes Africae*, against the Donatists: *CT* XVI.5.51 (Mommsen, p. 872).

[51] *Gesta Collationis Carthaginensis* I.4 (PL II: 1260-1261); and see Peter Brown, *Augustine of Hippo. A Biography* (Berkeley/Los Angeles: University of California Press, 1969), pp. 330-334.

[52] *Gesta Collationis Carthaginensis. Sententia Cognitoris* (PL 11: 1418-1420).

[53] *CT* XVI.5.52, 54 (Mommsen, pp. 872-874); and Peter Brown, "Religious Coercion in the Later Roman Empire; The Case of North Africa," *History*, n.s., 48 (1963): 290 (= *Religion and Society in the Age of Saint Augustine* [New York: Harper & Row, 1972], pp. 310-311).

[54] Orosius, *Historia adversum Paganos* VII.42.14 (CSEL 5: 558): Orosius attributes Marcellinus' execution either to jealousy or to greed for money on Marinus' part.

[55] Orosius, *Historia adversum Paganos* VII.42.16-17 (CSEL 5: 558-559); Augustine, *Ep.*151.4-8 (CSEL 44: 384-389). Also see Philibert Martain, "Volusien. Une conversion au Ve siècle," *Revue Augustinienne* 10 (1907): 162; Madeleine Moreau, "Le Dossier Marcellinus dans la correspondance de Saint Augustin," *RecAug* 9 (1973): 93-102 (discusses Augustine's *Ep.* 151 on the death of Marcellinus). Jerome was furious at the Donatists who unleashed their vengeance on Marcellinus: *Dialogus contra Pelagianos* III.19 (PL 23: 616-617). Honorius rehabilitated Marcellinus in 414: see *CT* XVI.5.55 (Mommsen, p. 874).

Notes to pp. 113-115

[56]See below, pp. 130-132.

[57]Latin *Vita* 21 (Rampolla, p. 14), and see below, pp. 145-146.

[58]The date of their departure is not given and must be calculated from the date of their arrival. We know they were in Jerusalem by late 417 or early 418, for they write to Augustine regarding Pelagius' views and he replied in *De Gratia Christi*, dated 418. Rampolla states that the family arrived in North Africa in 410 and left for Jerusalem in 417 (*Melania*, pp. 104-105).

[59]*Vita* 34 (Gorce, p. 190).

[60]Ibid.

[61]See Charles Coüasnon, *The Church of the Holy Sepulchre in Jerusalem*, The Schweich Lectures of the British Academy, 1972 (London: Oxford University Press, 1974), p. 46, on monastic cells at the Anastasis.

[62]*Vita* 35 (Gorce, p. 194).

[63]*Vita* 36 (Gorce, pp. 194, 196).

[64]*Vita* 37 (Gorce, p. 196).

[65]*Vita* 37-38 (Gorce, pp. 196, 198).

[66]*Vita* 39 (Gorce, p. 200).

[67]*Vita* 37 (Gorce, p. 196).

[68]*Vita* 40 (Gorce, pp. 202, 204).

[69]*Vita* 41 (Gorce, p. 204).

[70]Rampolla, *Melania*, p. 105, calculates A.D. 431, apparently counting fourteen years from their arrival date in Jerusalem (417).

[71]*Vita* 41 (Gorce, pp. 204, 206).

III.D COMMENTARY: THE MOUNT OF OLIVES

[1]So believed by the Bordeaux Pilgrim (*Itinerarium Burdigalense* 595 [CSEL 39: 32]).

[2]So Jerome reports that the "simpler brothers" believed (*Commentariorum in Matteum* I [CCL 77: 24]): on Matt. 5:1.

[3]Eusebius, *Vita Constantini* III.41 (PG 20: 1101); the Bordeaux Pilgrim, *Itinerarium Burdigalense* 595 (CSEL 39: 23); Egeria, *Peregrinatio ad Loca Sancta* 33.1-2; 35 (CSEL 39: 84, 85). Also see John Wilkinson, "Christian Pilgrims in Jerusalem during the Byzantine Period," *Palestine Exploration Quarterly* 108 (1976): 84, 87; L.-H. Vincent, "L'Eléona: Sanctuaire primitif de l'Ascension," *RBib* 64 (1957): 70-71; Asher Ovadiah, *Corpus of the Byzantine Churches in the Holy Land*, Theophaneia 22 (Bonn: Peter Hanstein Verlag, 1970), pp. 82-83.

[4]Ovadiah, *Corpus*, pp. 84-85.

[5]On Poemenia, see *Vita Petri Iberii* (Raabe, p. 30 Syriac; p. 35 German); Palladius, *Historia Lausiaca* 35 (Butler II: 106); Paul Devos, "La 'Servante de Dieu' Poemenia d'après Pallade, le tradition copte et Jean Rufus," *AB* 87 (1969): 189-212. What Egeria saw in the early 380s was a "place" of the Ascension, but not a church (see Devos, "Poemenia," pp. 200, 209). Jerome mentions the cross on the Church of the Ascension in about A.D. 390, so the building was obviously constructed by this date (*In Sophoniam* I.15-16 [CCL 76A: 673]. *In Hiezechielem* III.11.23 [CCL 75: 125]). Also see Devos, "Poemenia," pp. 211-212; E. D. Hunt, *Holy Land Pilgrimages in the Later Roman Empire, A.D. 312-460* (Oxford: Clarendon Press, 1982), pp. 47-48, 162; Vincent, "L'Eléona," pp. 63, 71. The dating of the Church of the Ascension has been beset with problems pertaining to Egeria's report and thus the dating of her pilgrimage. Hugues Vincent and F.-M. Abel (*Jérusalem. Recherches de topographie, d'archéologie et d'histoire*, vol. II, *Jérusalem nouvelle* [Paris: Librairie Victor Lecoffre, 1914], fasc. 1-2, pp. 360-373, 384-385) think the church was built before A.D. 378 and was seen by Egeria, called by her the "Imbomon." J. G. Davies, "The Peregrinatio Egeriae

Notes to pp. 115-116

and the Ascension," *VChr* 8 (1954): 95-96, also thinks the
church was built by A.D. 378, and since he dates Egeria's
pilgrimage to the 390s, he holds that she saw it (pp.
93, 99). But Egeria's pilgrimage now seems firmly dated
to A.D. 383-385 by Paul Devos, "La Date du voyage
d'Egérie," *AB* 85 (1967): 165-194. Thus we discard the
view of older scholars that the Church of the Ascension
was a Constantinian foundation (e.g., Fernand Cabrol,
Les Eglises de Jérusalem. La Discipline et la liturgie au IVe
siècle. Etude sur la Peregrinatio Silviae [Paris/Poitiers:
Librairie Religieuse H. Oudin, 1895], p. 22). Paulinus
of Nola's information on the Church of the Ascension
was presumably derived from Melania the Elder when she
returned West in A.D. 399-400, bringing him a piece of
the True Cross (Paulinus of Nola, *Ep.* 31.1, 4 [CSEL 29:
268, 271]).

[6]Murphy (*Rufinus*, p. 37) has Melania the Elder
leave Rome probably in November 372; she makes a visit
to Egypt before she arrives in Palestine; Eduard Schwartz
("Palladiana," p. 167) has Melania the Elder in Palestine
in A.D. 374.

[7]Vincent and Abel, *Jérusalem* II, fasc. 1-2, p. 389.

[8]Rufinus, *Apologia contra Hieronymum* II.11 (CCL 20: 92).

[9]Basil of Caesarea, *Ep.* 258.2 (PG 32: 950).

[10]Palladius, *Historia Lausiaca* 44 (Butler II: 131).

[11]Sylvester J. Saller, "The Tombstone Inscription
in the Church of Mary's Tomb at Gethsemane," in Virgilio
C. Corbo, ed., *Richerche Archeologiche al Monte degli Ulivi*,
Pubblicazioni dello Studium Biblicum Franciscanum 16
(Jerusalem: Tipografia dei Padri Francescani, 1965),
pp. 77-79.

[12]John the Deacon, *Vita S. Pelagiae* 12, 14 (PL 73:
669, 670). The *Vita* of this reformed actress was found
interspersed with that of Melania in a Latin manuscript
of the *Vita Melaniae Junioris* coming from Chartres (see
above, p. 3).

[13]For example, Gordini ("Il monachesimo romano,"
p. 90) thinks that Melania the Elder's monastic

Notes to pp. 116-117

foundations had either "disappeared or passed into the hands of the Easterners."

[14]See below, pp. 148-150.

[15] *Vita* 41 (Gorce, p. 206). The fact that some of the women were from "places of ill-repute," perhaps houses of prostitution, does not inspire confidence in their alleged virginity.

[16]Ibid.

[17]Latin *Vita* 41 (Rampolla, p. 24).

[18] *Vita* 41 (Gorce, p. 206).

[19] *Vita* 48 (Gorce, p. 218).

[20] *Vita* 42 (Gorce, p. 208).

[21] *Vita* 46-47 (Gorce, pp. 214-216), with Biblical citations that give a rationale for the day's stated hours of worship.

[22] *Vita* 43, 45 (Gorce, pp. 210, 214).

[23] *Vita* 44 (Gorce, pp. 210, 212). Melania's example of obedience: the emperor does not command without seeking the counsel of the Senate--precisely what was *not* done in Honorius' dispensation regarding the sale of Melania's property; see pp. 36-37, 101-102 above.

[24]Pinian's death occurred eight years before Melania's: *Vita* 49 (Gorce, p. 220).

[25] *Vita* 49 (Gorce, p. 220). Vincent and Abel (*Jérusalem* II, fasc. 1-2, p. 387) posit that the Aposteleion was annexed to the women's monastery, thus near the grotto of the Eleona.

[26]Latin *Vita* 49 (Rampolla, p. 27). Greek *Vita* 41 (Gorce, p. 204) simply reports that Albina's remains were carried to the Mount of Olives, with no mention of a specific burial spot. But Greek *Vita* 49 (Gorce, p. 222) adds the information that Melania wished the bones of her mother, as well as those of Pinian, to find rest through the monks' chanting, and one site of their

chanting was in the Aposteleion next to the church at the grotto.

[27] *Vita* 49 (Gorce, pp. 220, 222).

[28] *Acta Iohannis* 97-105 (Bonnet II.1: 199-203); Eusebius, *Demonstratio Evangelica* VI.18.23 (GCS 23: 278).

[29] Apparently the grotto was also considered to be the site of the Last Supper, for according to Egeria, this is where pilgrims went on Holy Thursday (*Peregrinatio ad Loca Sancta* 49 [CSEL 39: 101]); suggested by Vincent and Abel, *Jérusalem* II, fasc. 1-2, pp. 383-384.

[30] *Vita* 49 (Gorce, pp. 220, 222).

[31] *Vita* 49 (Gorce, p. 222).

[32] *Vita* 57 (Gorce, p. 240); Rampolla, *Melania*, p. 281. According to *Vita Petri Hiberii* (Raabe, p. 28 Syriac; p. 33 German), the monasteries of Melania and Pinian were near the Church of the Holy Ascension.

[33] Paulinus, *Ep.* 31.4 (CSEL 29: 271); Sulpicius Severus, *Chronica* II.33.7-8 (CSEL 1: 87).

[34] *Vita* 58-59 (Gorce, p. 244).

[35] *Vita* 64 (Gorce, pp. 254, 256). According to the *Vita Petri Hiberii* (Raabe, p. 33 Syriac; p. 37 German), the relics Melania deposited in her new martyrion were those of the Persian martyrs and the Forty Martyrs of Sebaste.

[36] See Vincent and Abel, *Jérusalem* II, fasc. 1-2, bk. 3, for a description of the various sanctuaries on the Mount of Olives, including Melania's. See Palladius, *Historia Lausiaca* 43 (Butler II: 130) for oratories on the mount of the Ascension.

[37] Theodosius the Deacon, *De Situ Terrae Sanctae* 6 (CSEL 39: 140).

[38] Cyril of Scythopolis, *Vita S. Euthymii* 27, 45 (TU 49.2: 42, 67); *Vita S. Sabae* 29 (TU 49.2: 115); *Vita S. Theodosii* (TU 49.2: 239).

Notes to pp. 118-120

[39] *Vita Petri Hiberii* (Raabe, pp. 28, 31, 33 Syriac; pp. 33, 35-36, 37 German).

[40] Theodosius the Deacon, *De Situ Terrae Sanctae* 10-11 (CSEL 39: 143).

[41] John Phocas, *Descriptio Terrae Sanctae* 15 (PG 133: 945): a monastery of Latin monks is said to have been built on the foundations of the old monastery of Melania.

[42] Ch. Clermont-Ganneau, "Deux Nouvelles Inscriptions grecques du Mont des Oliviers," *Recueil d'Archéologie Orientale* 5 (1903): 163-164; "Fiches et Notules," *Recueil d'Archéologie Orientale* 5 (1903): 181; for original plan of the church, see M.-J. Lagrange and P.-M. Séjourné, "Chronique de Jérusalem," *RBib* 4 (1895): 92-93, 437-439.

[43] Rampolla, *Melania*, p. 285. The inscription that led researchers to posit that the remains were from Melania's monastery for men, however, was not found in the three-naved church, but in a "mortuary chapel" (Lagrange, "Chronique," p. 92) attached to it. The inscription is in Greek: if it *did* pertain to Melania's monastery, we would imagine that the latter was in the hands of Easterners. But nothing in the inscription suggests a link with Melania. The inscription reads, in translation, "For the refreshment of the priest Eusebius, of the deacon Theodosius, of Eugenius, of Elpidius, of Euphratius, of Agathonicus, monks."

[44] Vincent and Abel, *Jérusalem* II, fasc. 1-2, p. 389.

[45] Ibid.

[46] J. T. Milik, "Notes d'épigraphie et de topographie palestiniennes," *RBib* 67 (1960): 558-559, fig. 2.

[47] Virgilio Corbo, "Scavo archeologico a ridosso della basilica dell'Ascensione," pt. 2 of Corbo, *Richerche Archeologiche*, p. 110 n. 1; for Corbo's summary on Melania's buildings on the Mount of Olives, see pp. 105-110, 148-149.

[48] Paulinus of Nola, *Ep.* 31.3 (CSEL 29: 268).

Notes to pp. 120-121

[49]"Revelatio Sancti Stephani," ed. S. Vanderlinden *REB* 4 (1946): 179.

[50]Both by Rufinus: see G. W. Butterworth, *Origen, On First Principles* (New York: Harper & Row, 1966), pp. xxxi-xli. Rufinus' translation of Basil's *Rules* was undertaken for the Italian monastery of Pinetum (see *Prologus in Regulam Sancti Basilii* [CCL 20: 241]).

[51]For example, having readings that suited the events commemorated on a particular day; see Hunt, *Holy Land Pilgrimages*, p. 121.

[52]Anton Baumstark, *Comparative Liturgy*, rev. B. Botte, trans. F. L. Cross (Westminster, Md.: Newman Press, 1958), pp. 41, 142-143, 155-156.

[53]Hunt, *Holy Land Pilgrimages*, p. 17; Vincent and Abel, *Jérusalem* II, fasc. 1-2, p. 371.

[54]Palladius, *Historia Lausiaca* 46, 54 (Butler II: 135-136, 147-148); Paulinus of Nola, *Ep.* 29.10 (CSEL 29: 257).

[55]Palladius, *Historia Lausiaca* 46 (Butler II: 134-135); Paulinus of Nola, *Ep.* 29.11 (CSEL 29: 257-258).

[56]Jerome, *Ep.* 108.14 (CSEL 55: 325).

[57]Jerome, *Ep.* 108.20 (CSEL 55: 335).

[58]Jerome, *Ep.* 108.30 (CSEL 55: 348-349).

[59]See Jerome, *Contra Joannem Hierosolymitanum* (PL 23: 371-412).

[60]Jerome, *Epp.* 22.35 (CSEL 54: 198); 108.20 (CSEL 55: 335).

[61]Jerome, *Epp.* 108.29 (CSEL 55: 348); cf. 147.4 (CSEL 56: 319); *Homilia in Psalmos 143* (CCL 78: 313).

[62]Clark, "Ascetic Renunciation," pp. 246-247, 250-251.

[63]Jerome, *Homilia de Nativitate Domini* (CCL 78: 527); Baumstark, *Comparative Liturgy*, pp. 153-154.

[64]Cyril of Scythopolis, *Vita S. Theodosii* (TU 49.2: 236); Baumstark, *Comparative Liturgy*, p. 150.

[65]Gordini, "Il monachesimo romano," p. 94; Germain Morin, "Les Monuments de la prédication de Saint Jerome," *Revue d'Histoire et de Littérature Religieuses* 1 (1896): 413-414.

[66]*Vita* 19 (Gorce, p. 162).

[67]Palladius, *Historia Lausiaca* 61 (Butler II: 156).

[68]*Vita* 35 (Gorce, p. 194).

[69]See p. 174 above for complete biographical information.

[70]Latin *Vita* 62 (Rampolla, p. 36).

[71]See, for example, John Chrysostom, *Homilia in Epistolam ad Hebraeos* 17.3 (PG 63: 131): the offering is made every day; 17.7 (PG 63: 131), but some take it only once a year; *Homilia in Epistolam ad Ephesios* III (PG 62: 28): some take the Eucharist only at Epiphany or Easter; Ambrose, *De Sacramentis* V.4.25 (PL 16: 471): we should take the Eucharist daily, not once a year as Easterners do; Augustine, *De Sermone Domini in Monte* 2.7.25-26 (CCL 35: 114-115): we have daily reception, but the East does not; Eusebius of Caesarea, *Demonstratio Evangelica* I.10 (PG 22: 88): there is daily reception of the Lord's body and blood; also see references in III.D nn. 72-78 following.

[72]Innocent I, *Ep.* 25.4.7 (PL 20: 555-556).

[73]Jerome, *Epp.* 48.15 (CSEL 54: 377); 71.6 (CSEL 55: 6).

[74]Chromatius of Aquileia, *Tractatus XIV in Evangelium Mattaei* 5 (PL 20: 361).

[75]Ambrose, *De Sacramentis* V.25 (PL 16: 471); *Expositio in Psalmum 118*, Sermo Octavus 48 (PL 15: 1383-1384). Also see Gorce, *Vie*, p. 108: neither daily communion nor

Notes to pp. 123-125

viaticum at death was an exclusively Roman custom; daily communion was also practiced in the Eastern church.

[76]Rufinus, *Historia Monachorum* 7 (PL 21: 418): "Communionem Dominicam perciperent circa horam diei nonam...."

[77]John Cassian, *Collationes* VII.30.2 (CSEL 13: 208).

[78]*Vita* 55, 67 (Gorce, pp. 236, 264).

[79]Latin *Vita* 68 (Rampolla, p. 39).

[80]John Chrysostom, *De Sacerdotio* VI.4 (PG 48: 681).

[81]Gregory the Great, *Dialogorum* 4.35; 2.37 (PL 77: 376-377; PL 66: 202).

[82]*Vita Petri Hiberii* (Raabe, p. 31 Syriac; p. 36 German).

[83]*Vita* 36 (Gorce, pp. 194, 196).

[84]*Vita* 32 (Gorce, p. 188).

[85]Latin *Vita* 5 (Rampolla, p. 6).

[86]Gregory of Nazianzus, *Oratio* VIII: *In Laudem Sororis Suae Gorgoniae* 18 (PG 35: 809).

[87]Egeria, *Peregrinatio ad Loca Sancta* 24.12 (CSEL 39: 74).

[88]John Cassian, *De Coenobiorum Institutis* II.4 (PL 49: 83).

[89]Ibid. II.13; III.5 (PL 49: 104, 134).

[90]*Vita* 47 (Gorce, p. 216).

[91]*Vita* 46 (Gorce, p. 214).

[92]Rampolla, *Melania*, pp. 264-265; Latin *Vita* 46 (Rampolla, p. 26).

[93]Seen, for example, in Cyril of Jerusalem, *Catecheses* 19-23 (PG 33: 1065-1128).

[94]Egeria, *Peregrinatio ad Loca Sancta* 27.4; cf. 24.2-3 (CSEL 39: 78, 71).

[95] *Vita* 47 (Gorce, p. 216).

[96]Hippolytus, *Constitutiones Apostolicae* VIII.34 (PG 1: 1136).

[97]Jerome, *Ep.* 108.20.2 (CSEL 55: 335).

[98]Jerome, *Epp.* 107.9.3 (CSEL 55: 300); 22.37.1 (CSEL 54: 201); 130.15.1 (CSEL 56: 195).

[99]Rampolla, *Melania,* pp. 266-268.

[100] *Vita* 5 (Gorce, p. 6).

[101] *Vita* 64 (Gorce, pp. 254, 256).

[102]Jerome, *Ep.* 107.9.2 (CSEL 55: 300); Rampolla, *Melania,* p. 266.

[103]Basil of Caesarea, *Ep.* II.207.3 (PG 32: 764).

[104]Pietri, *Roma Christiana,* pp. 37-40, 135, 140, 321 n. 2, 621 n. 5, 659, 1637. See Leo the Great, *Sermo* 85.4 (PL 54: 437): Rome has equal glory with Jerusalem because of the luster of Saint Lawrence.

[105]Rampolla, *Melania,* pp. 268-270; Baumstark, *Comparative Liturgy,* pp. 153ff.

[106] *Chronographus Anni CCCLIIII* XII (MGH, AA IX: 71): "VIII Kal. Ian, natus Christus in Betleem Iudeae."

[107]Jerome, *Homilia de Nativitate Domini* (CCL 78: 527-529).

[108]Egeria, *Peregrinatio ad Loca Sancta* 9.1 (CSEL 39: 49); cf. *Armenian Lectionary* 71, where the only Feast listed for 25 December, in the Jerusalem and Paris manuscripts, is the Feast of James and David (the Erevan manuscript places their feast on 24 December); see Athanase Renoux, "Le Codex arménien Jérusalem 121. II. Edition comparée du texte et de deux autres manuscrits. Introduction, textes, traduction et notes," PO 36 (1971): 366-367. Renoux acknowledges a fourth-century origin

of some of the material in the *Armenian Lectionary*, but A.D. 415-417 were the decisive years in which the *Lectionary* received its form.

[109]According to Pseudo-Basil of Seleucia, it was Juvenal who began the celebration of Christ's birth: *Oratio* 42 (PG 85: 469); also see Hunt, *Holy Land Pilgrimages*, p. 111 n. 18; Georg Kretschmar, "Festkalendar und Memorialstätten Jerusalems in altkirchlicher Zeit," *ZPalV* 87 (1971): 177 (the relative positioning of Christmas and Epiphany can be seen as weapons of warfare in the Christological battle over the human and divine natures of Jesus).

[110]Baumstark, *Comparative Liturgy*, p. 155.

[111]Justinian's letter to the Jerusalemites is translated from the Georgian version by M. van Esbroeck, "La Lettre de l'empereur Justinian sur l'Annonciation et la Nöel en 561," *AB* 86 (1968): 351-371, esp. letter on pp. 356-362; section IV.12 of the letter concerns our theme. See *AB* 87 (1969): 442-444 for a correction of the letter's date.

[112]*Vita* 63 (Gorce, p. 254).

[113]Gordini, "Il monachesimo romano," p. 102.

[114]Georges Goyau, *Sainte Mélanie* (Paris: Lecoffre, 1952), p. 163; cited with approval by Vincent and Abel, *Jérusalem* II, fasc. 1-2, p. 386.

[115]Gordini, "Il monachesimo romano," p. 105.

[116]Gorce, *Vie*, p. 107.

[117]See, for example, *Lessico Universale Italiano* (Roma: Istituto della Enciclopedia Italiana, 1977), XVIII: 398; *Who's Who 1905* (London: A. & C. Black, 1905), p. 1326.

[118]Rampolla, *Melania*, pp. lvii-lxiii.

[119]See above, pp. 14-15, 22, 122-127.

[120]Coüasnon, *The Church of the Holy Sepulchre*, p. 17; C. Couret, "La Prise de Jérusalem par les Perses en 614," *ROC* 2 (1897): 125-164.

[121]The account of "a monk of St. Sabas," printed in Courcet, "La Prise," p. 163.

[122]John Phocas, *Descriptio Terrae Sanctae* 15 (PG 133: 945).

[123]DeRossi, "La casa dei Valerii," p. 242; Gatti, "La casa celimontana," p. 153.

III.E COMMENTARY: CONSTANTINOPLE AND HOME

[1]*Vita* 50 (Gorce, p. 224); Marcellinus, *Chronicon*, an. 437 (MGH, AA XI: 79).

[2]*Vita* 50 (Gorce, p. 224). Whether Melania's trip dates from the end of 436 to early 437, or one year later, is somewhat problematic. See pp. 133-134 below.

[3]*PLRE* I: 1142 (stemma 20); II: 1184. Their mother was a Christian: see above, p. 84.

[4]*CT* V.16.31 (Mommsen, p. 236); Matthews, *Western Aristocracies*, pp. 285-286, 353.

[5]Rutilius Namatianus, *De Reditu Suo* I.167-176. Rutilius left home in October 417 and heard about Volusian's appointment as prefect of Rome en route; for the date of this poem, see Alan Cameron, "Rutilius Namatianus, St. Augustine, and the Date of the *De Reditu*," *JRS* 57 (1967): 39. The traditional view held that Volusian was proconsul of Africa in A.D. 411-412, when he corresponded with Augustine; this dating is too late (see André Chastagnol, *Les Fastes de la préfecture de Rome au Bas-Empire*, Etudes Prosopographiques II [Paris: Nouvelles Editions Latines, 1962], pp. 267-277). Volusian must have been in Carthage for private reasons then. Matthews dates Volusian's proconsulship of Africa before A.D. 410 (*Western Aristocracies*, p. 286 n. 1).

[6]*PLRE* II: 1184; Matthews, *Western Aristocracies*, p. 286.

Notes to pp. 129-131

[7]*PLRE* II: 1185; Chastagnol, *Fastes*, p. 278; Chastagnol, "Le Sénateur Volusien," pp. 241-245.

[8]Chastagnol, *Fastes*, p. 278; *PLRE* II: 1185.

[9]*Vita* 53 (Gorce, p. 232).

[10]Latin *Vita* 55 (Rampolla, p. 31): or Eudocia? The names of Eudocia and Eudoxia are confused in the text (e.g., in Latin *Vita* 58 [Rampolla, p. 33], Melania hears that *Eudoxia* is en route to Jerusalem). If Volusian's death took place in January 438, Eudoxia would already have been in Thessalonica with Valentinian; see Marcellinus, *Chronicon*, an. 437 (MGH, AA XI: 79).

[11]*Vita* 53 (Gorce, p. 230).

[12]*Vita* 53 (Gorce, p. 232).

[13]Ibid.

[14]Ibid. Sixtus III was bishop of Rome from 432 to 440.

[15]Sixtus III, *Epp.* 9, 10 (PL 50: 612-618). Franz X. Bauer, *Proklos von Konstantinopel. Ein Beitrag zur Kirchen- und Dogmengeschichte des 5. Jahrhunderts.* Veröffentlichungen aus dem Kirchenhistorischen Seminar München, IV Reihe, Nr. 8 (München: J. J. Lentnerschen Buchhandlung, 1919), p. 110, insists that Sixtus' epistle to Proclus was "very friendly" and that Proclus, a peace-loving soul, needed no further reminder.

[16]*Vita* 55 (Gorce, p. 236).

[17]See, for example, Henry Bettenson, *Augustine, Concerning the City of God Against the Pagans* (New York: Penguin Books, 1976), p. 5 n. 1; Chastagnol, "Le Sénateur Volusien," pp. 247-248.

[18]Chastagnol, *Fastes*, p. 279, posits that it was Melania and Albina who enlisted Augustine's support in the attempted conversion of Volusian. Chastagnol also proposes that the *Poema Ultimum* was written for Volusian ("Le Sénateur Volusien," pp. 252-253); here he follows Rampolla, *Melania*, pp. 130-133.

[19]Volusian to Augustine, in Augustine, *Ep.* 135.2 (CSEL 44: 91-92). The topic of Mary's virginity apparently remained problematic; Augustine returns to it in a letter to Marcellinus, *Ep.* 143.12 (CSEL 44: 262).

[20]Volusian to Augustine, in Augustine, *Ep.* 135.2 (CSEL 44: 92).

[21]Marcellinus to Augustine, in Augustine, *Ep.* 136.1 (CSEL 44: 94).

[22]Marcellinus to Augustine, in Augustine, *Ep.* 136.2 (CSEL 44: 95).

[23]Ibid.

[24]Augustine, *Ep.* 137.2.4-3.12 (CSEL 44: 100-114).

[25]Augustine, *Epp.* 137.2.4; 4.14 (CSEL 44: 101, 116-117); 138.4.18 (CSEL 44: 145).

[26]Augustine, *Ep.* 138.1.2-8 (CSEL 44: 127-133).

[27]Augustine, *Ep.* 138.2.9-10 (CSEL 44: 134-135).

[28]Augustine, *Ep.* 138.2.14-15 (CSEL 44: 139-141).

[29]Augustine, *Ep.* 138.3.16-17 (CSEL 44: 142-145).

[30]Bettenson, Introduction, *Augustine, City of God,* pp. xv-xvi.

[31]Augustine, prefatio, *De Civitate Dei* (CCL 47: 1).

[32]Chastagnol, "Le Sénateur Volusien," pp. 241-253; Yarbrough, "Christianization," pp. 149-165; Peter Brown, "Aspects of the Christianization of the Roman Aristocracy," *JRS* 51 (1961): 1-11 (= *Religion and Society,* pp. 161-182).

[33]*Vita* 52 (Gorce, p. 226). On the *cursus publicus,* see Otto Seeck, "Cursus Publicus," *RE* IV (1901), cols. 1846-1863; Bernhard Kötting, *Peregrinatio Religiosa. Wallfahrten in der Antike und das Pilgerwesen in der alten Kirche,* Forschungen zur Volkskunde 33-35 (Münster Westf.: no pub., 1950), pp. 344-345; Lionel Casson, *Travel in the*

Notes to pp. 133-134

Ancient World (London: George Allen and Unwin, 1974),
pp. 182-190; Denys Gorce, *Les Voyages, l'hospitalité et le
port des lettres dans le monde chrétien des IVᵉ et Vᵉ siècles*
(Wépion-sur-Meuse: Monastère du Mont-Vierge; Paris:
Librairie Auguste Picard, 1925), pp. 41-60.

[34]See *CT* VIII.5.35 (Mommsen, pp. 384-385) on
penalties for large groups (such as Melania's entourage)
using the *cursus publicus*. The fact that sixty-six chapters of *CT* VIII.5 are devoted to the *cursus publicus*
indicates the problems the government experienced with
the system.

[35]*Vita* 52 (Gorce, pp. 226, 228). Casson (*Travel*,
p. 185, no source cited) claims that the larger stations
had as many as forty horses or mules in readiness.

[36]It took the Bordeaux Pilgrim two months: *Itinerarium Burdigalense* 571-589 (CSEL 39: 13-21); also see Hunt,
Holy Land Pilgrimages, pp. 56, 73.

[37]Latin *Vita* 57 (Rampolla, p. 32). The text is
misread as "forty-four days" by some commentators, but
should be construed as forty: "Pervenimus igitur
Hierosolymam post dies quadraginta et quatuor ante diem
passionis Domini...."

[38]Greek *Vita* 55 (Gorce, p. 236).

[39]Greek *Vita* 56 (Gorce, p. 238); Latin *Vita* 56
(Rampolla, p. 31).

[40]V. Grumel, *Traité d'études byzantines. I: La Chronologie*
(Paris: Presses Universitaires de France, 1958), p. 268.

[41]Rampolla, *Melania*, pp. 104-105.

[42]Grumel, *Chronologie*, p. 268. Casson (*Travel*, p. 315)
estimates that Melania must have traveled about twenty-
six miles a day, although he assumes the trip took
forty-four days. Kötting (*Peregrinatio*, p 345) estimates
about the same (forty kilometers per day).

[43]Greek *Vita* 56 (Gorce, p. 238):   "...ἐν τῷ τέλει
τοῦ Φεβρουαρίου μηνὸς ἐξήλθομεν ἐκεῖθεν."

[44]Kenneth Holum, *Theodosian Empresses: Women and Imperial Dominion in Late Antiquity* (Berkeley: University of California Press, 1982), p. 183 n. 39.

[45] *Vita* 57 (Gorce, p. 240).

[46] *Vita* 58 (Gorce, p. 240).

[47]Marcellinus, *Chronicon*, an. 439.2 (MGH, AA XI: 80): she returns from Jerusalem.

[48]Latin *Vita* 56 (Rampolla, p. 32).

[49] *Vita* 56 (Gorce, p. 238).

[50]Latin *Vita* 56 (Rampolla, p. 32); also see Latin *Vita* prologus, 39 (Rampolla, pp. 3, 22). Mount Modicus is probably Mount Magaba in Galatia, near Ancyra; see *RE* XIV (1928), col. 287, s.v. "Magaba."

[51] *Vita* 51, 56 (Gorce, pp. 224, 226, 238, 240).

[52]Hunt, *Holy Land Pilgrimages*, pp. 65-66: the Galatian and Cappadocian bishops mentioned in the *Vita* might well be those at sees established by Basil of Caesarea, such as at Sasima and Podanos.

[53] *Itinerarium Burdigalense* (CSEL 39: 3-33): noticeably absent are greetings and receptions by local bishops en route.

[54] *Vita* 5 (Gorce, pp. 134, 136). Melania's sleepless night on her knees may have hastened the premature birth of her child.

[55]Pietri, *Roma Christiana*, pp. 37-40, 525-526, on Lawrence's basilica. The Romans turned (in vain) to Lawrence for help during Alaric's attack: Augustine, *Sermo* 296.5 (PL 38: 1353).

[56]Latin *Vita* 5 (Rampolla, pp. 5-6). It is on this occasion that Melania's father sent his eunuchs to spy upon her; she bribed them to say that she was in her room sleeping, not keeping vigil in the oratory.

[57] *Vita* 48 (Gorce, p. 218). On the Forty Martyrs, see Hippolyte Delehaye, "The Forty Martyrs of Sebaste," *American Catholic Quarterly Review* 24 (1899): 161-171.

[58] *Vita* 64 (Gorce, pp. 256, 258).

[59] *Vita* 60 (Gorce, p. 248).

[60] *Vita* 58 (Gorce, p. 242). See Carolus Van de Vorst and Paulus Peeters, "Saint Phocas," *AB* 30 (1911): 252-295. The *Vita Petri Hiberii* (Raabe, pp. 100-103 Syriac; pp. 106-109 German) tells of the discovery of Phocas' relics near Sidon.

[61] *Vita* 52 (Gorce, p. 226). The bones of Leontius are known to the author of the *Vita Petri Hiberii* (Raabe, pp. 103-104 Syriac; pp. 110-111 German); to Antonius Martyr, *Itinerarium* 1 (CSEL 39: 159); and to Severus of Antioch (Zacharias, *Vita Severi* [PO II: 79, 92]).

[62] *Vita* 53 (Gorce, p. 228). Both Phocas and Euphemia are the subjects of panegyrics by Asterius of Amasea (PG 40: 300-313, 333-337). Egeria also stops at Euphemia's shrine at Chalcedon (*Peregrinatio ad Loca Sancta* 23.7 [CSEL 39: 70]). See Evagrius Scholasticus, *HE* II.3 (Bidez and Parmentier, pp. 39-42), for a description of the Basilica of St. Euphemia at Chalcedon. For the legend of St. Euphemia, see Francois Halkin, ed., *Euphémie de Chalcédoine. Légendes byzantines*, SubsHag 41 (Bruxelles: Société des Bollandistes, 1965), pp. 9-33.

[63] *Vita* 52 (Gorce, p. 228).

[64] Ibid.

[65] *Vita* 53 (Gorce, p. 228). According to Evagrius Scholasticus, *HE* II.3 (Bidez and Parmentier, p. 41), Euphemia's bones still oozed blood.

[66] *Vita* 12 (Gorce, p. 148, 150, 152).

[67] *Vita* 53 (Gorce, p. 230). The Latin *Vita* 41 (Rampolla, p. 24) makes clear that Lausus was a former *prepositus* and *Vita* 53 (Rampolla, p. 30), that he had died before the Latin *Vita* was composed ("ad beatae

memoriae Lausum"). Rampolla, who favors an early date
for the Latin Vita's composition, thus has Lausus dead
by A.D. 440-442 (Melania, p. 235).

[68]See above, p. 92.

[69]Latin Vita 41 (Rampolla, p. 24); also see Rampolla, Melania, p. 235.

[70]Latin Vita 53, 55 (Rampolla, pp. 30, 31): in
Latin Vita 53, Lausus "hospitaverat" Melania; according
to Vita 55, she was staying in the Forum of Augustus
Constantine, where we know Lausus' palace was. Rampolla
argues that the author of the Latin Vita had a better
knowledge of Constantinople than did the Greek editor;
thus, for Rampolla we are given another clue to the
primacy of the Latin text (Melania, pp. 231, 234-236,
lix). Rampolla thinks Volusian stayed at the Domus
Augustae Eudociae in the Xth region of Constantinople
(Melania, p. 231).

[71]Constantine Porphyrogenitus, De Caerimoniis Aulae
Byzantinae I.64; II.1 (CSHB 9: 285, 518-520).

[72]Latin Vita 55 (Rampolla, p. 31): the messenger
comes here to report to Melania that Volusian has been
baptized.

[73]George Cedrenos, Historiarum Compendium (CSHB 34:
564). See the interesting commentary by Cyril Mango,
"Antique Statuary and the Byzantine Beholder," DOP 17
(1963): 55-75, esp. 58.

[74]George Cedrenos, Historiarum Compendium (CSHB 34:
564). Compare Lausus' acceptance of such statues with
the attitudes revealed in Mark the Deacon's Vita Porphyri
59-61 (Teubner, pp. 49-51), where a statue of naked
Aphrodite meets its doom at the hands of Christians.

[75]George Cedrenos, Historiarum Compendium (CSHB 34:
616); John Zonaras, Epitomae Historiarum XIV 2.22-24 (CSHB
46: 130-131).

[76]Vita 19 (Gorce, Vie, p. 164).

[77]Palladius, Dialogus 28, 71 (Coleman-Norton, pp.
48, 127-128).

[78]Sozomen, *HE* VIII.17.7; 24.8 (GCS 50: 372, 382).

[79]Socrates Scholasticus, *HE* VI.15 (Hussey II: 705).

[80]Ibid.; Sozomen, *HE* VIII.24.8 (GCS 50: 382); Palladius, *Dialogus* 71 (Coleman-Norton, pp. 127-128).

[81]Pietri, *Roma Christiana*, pp. 1313, 1319.

[82]See above, p. 134 for dating.

[83]Socrates Scholasticus, *HE* VII.45 (Hussey II: 833-834).

[84]Proclus, *Oratio* 20 (PG 65: 827-834).

[85]*Vita* 53 (Gorce, p. 232).

[86]Latin *Vita* 55 (Rampolla, p. 31).

[87]*Vita* 12 (Gorce, pp. 148, 150, 152).

[88]*Vita* 53 (Gorce, p. 232).

[89]*Vita* 56 (Gorce, p. 238).

[90]*Vita* 58 (Gorce, p. 242).

[91]Ibid.

[92]*Vita* 58-59 (Gorce, p. 244).

[93]*Vita* 59 (Gorce, pp. 244, 246).

[94]*Vita Petri Hiberii* (Raabe, p. 37 Syriac; pp. 32-33 German). For a fuller discussion, see Elizabeth A. Clark, "Claims on the Bones of Saint Stephen: The Partisans of Melania and Eudocia," *CH* 51 (1982): 141-156.

[95]*Vita* 59 (Gorce, pp. 244, 246).

[96]Clark, "Ascetic Renunciation," pp. 243-244, 257.

[97]*Vita* 60-61 (Gorce, pp. 246, 248, 250). In Latin *Vita* 60-61 (Rampolla, pp. 34-35), four miracles are reported instead of three.

[98] *Vita* 62 (Gorce, pp. 250, 252).

[99] *Vita* 63-70 (Gorce, pp. 252, 254, 256, 258, 260, 262, 264, 266, 268, 270).

[100] *Vita* 63-64 (Gorce, pp. 254, 256, 258, 260).

[101] *Vita* 65, 68 (Gorce, pp. 262, 266).

[102] *Vita* 70 (Gorce, p. 270).

III.F COMMENTARY: ORTHODOXY AND HERESY

[1] Greek *Vita* prologus (Gorce, p. 126); the editor of the Latin *Vita* claims in the prologue that Melania affirmed "the unity of the Trinity" (Rampolla, p. 4).

[2] See above, pp. 13-15.

[3] Robert C. Gregg and Dennis E. Groh, *Early Arianism: A View of Salvation* (Philadelphia: Fortress Press, 1981), chap. 4.

[4] Hammond, "The Last Ten Years," pp. 395, 397; Jerome, *Ep.* 133.3 (CSEL 56: 246).

[5] See E. D. Hunt, "Palladius of Helenopolis: A Party and Its Supporters in the Church of the Late Fourth Century," *JThS*, n.s., 24 (1973): 472-473; E. Schwartz, "Palladiana," *ZNW* 37 (1937): 169-174; Charles Pietri, "Esquisse de conclusion: l'aristocratie chrétienne entre Jean de Constantinople et Augustin d'Hippone," *Jean Chrysostome et Augustin: Actes du Colloque de Chantilly* 22-24 September 1974, ed. Charles Kannengiesser, Théologie Historique 35 (Paris: Editions Beauchesne, 1975), pp. 294, 300; Antoine Guillaumont, *Les 'Kephalaia Gnostica' d'Evagre le Pontique et l'histoire de l'Origénisme chez les Grecs et chez les Syriens*, Patristica Sorbonensia 5 (Paris: Editions du Seuil, 1962), pp. 47, 57, 64; Maurice Villain, "Rufin d'Aquilée--La Querelle autour d'Origéne," *RecSR* 27 (1937): 5-37, 165-195;

Murphy, *Rufinus*, pp. 126-131. For primary source material on Theophilus' attack on the Tall Brothers and their flight, see Sozomen, *HE* VIII.12-13 (GCS 50: 364-367) and Palladius, *Dialogus* 6-7 (Coleman-Norton, pp. 37-42). On Melania's reading of Origen, see Palladius, *Historia Lausiaca* 55 (Butler II: 149)--a passage now thought to pertain to her.

[6]Melania the Elder returned West in the last weeks of 399 or early in 400; see Moine, "Melaniana," p. 27. For the Tall Brothers' flight from Palestine to Constantinople, see the letter of Theophilus in Jerome, *Ep.* 90.2 (CSEL 55: 144); Schwartz, "Palladiana," p. 174; Hunt, "Palladius," p. 473.

[7]Palladius, *Historia Lausiaca* 54 (Butler II: 146).

[8]For discussion, see Pietri, *Roma Christiana*, pp. 435, 448-450.

[9]Anastasius, *Epistola ad Simplicianum Mediolanensem* 1-2 (PL 22: 772-774).

[10]Jerome, *Ep.* 127.9-10 (CSEL 56: 152-153); Murphy, *Rufinus*, pp. 126-127.

[11]Rufinus, *Apologium contra Hieronymum* I.19 (CCL 20: 53); Murphy, *Rufinus*, pp. 129-131, 134; Hammond, "The Last Ten Years," p. 385.

[12]Hunt, "Palladius," pp. 477-478.

[13]Palladius, *Historia Lausiaca* 61 (Butler II: 157); and see above, p. 92.

[14]Paulinus of Nola, *Ep.* 29.12 (CSEL 29: 258-259); *Carmen* 21.198-307, 836-840 (CSEL 30: 164-168, 185). Recall that Melania was on her way to see Paulinus on her flight from Rome when she was blown off course (*Vita* 19 [Gorce, p. 166]).

[15]Rufinus, *Prologus in Omelias Origenis super Numeros* (CCL 20: 285).

[16]Jerome, *Ep.* 133.3 (CSEL 56: 246); this point is stressed by Guillaumont, *Les 'Kephalaia Gnostica'*, p. 67.

[17]*Vita* 70 (Gorce, p. 270).

[18] *Vita* 44 (Gorce, p. 212); for suggestions as to possible sources for the story, see Rampolla, *Melania*, p. 233 n. 30.

[19] Jerome, *Ep.* 133.3 (CSEL 56: 246). According to Guillaumont, the reference is to Evagrius' *Practicos* (*Les 'Kephalaia Gnostica*,' p. 67).

[20] For a discussion of the evidence, see Robert F. Evans, *Pelagius: Inquiries and Reappraisals* (New York: Seabury Press, 1968), pp. 17, 20-23.

[21] Evans, *Pelagius*, p. 19; Rufinus' translation of Origen's *Commentariorum in Epistolam B: Pauli ad Romanos* is in PG 14: 833-1292.

[22] Augustine, *De Gratia Christi* I.1-2 (PL 44: 359-361); also see Hammond, "The Last Ten Years," p. 422.

[23] Augustine, *Ep.* 186.1.1, 3; 12.39 (CSEL 57: 45, 47, 78).

[24] On Aemilius and the wedding, see P. G. Walsh, *The Poems of Paulinus of Nola*, Ancient Christian Writers 40 (New York/Ramsey, N.J.: Newman Press, 1975), pp. 399 n. 1, 402 n. 47. Aemilius was among the bishops sent to Constantinople from the West in late 405 or early 406 to address the matter of John Chrysostom's exile (Palladius, *Dialogus* 4 [Coleman-Norton, p. 22]); thus Aemilius is another link between Melania's circle and Chrysostom. See Rampolla, *Melania*, pp. 194-195; Pietri, *Roma Christiana*, pp. 1321-1322, 1324n.; Peter Brown, "The Patrons of Pelagius," *JThS*, n.s., 21 (1970): 60-62 (= *Religion and Society*, pp. 214-215).

[25] Paulinus of Nola, *Carmen* 25.231-236 (CSEL 30: 245).

[26] Augustine, *Ep.* 126.6 (CSEL 44: 12).

[27] Ibid.; *De Natura et Gratia* I.1 (PL 44: 247); Pietri, "Esquisse," pp. 302-303.

[28] *Decretum Constantinii Imperatoris et Edictum* (PL 45: 1750-1751; PL 56: 499-500).

[29] Brown, "Patrons of Pelagius," p. 65 (=*Religion and Society*, pp. 217-218).

[30] *Vita* 20-22 (Gorce, pp. 168, 170, 172).

[31] Latin *Vita* 21 (Rampolla, p. 14). That a Donatist bishop is meant is also assumed by Allard, "Une Grande Fortune," p. 11; Goyau, *Sainte Mélanie*, p. 9; Henri LeClercq, "Mélanie la Jeune (Sainte)," *DACL* XI: 213.

[32] Emin Tengström, *Donatisten und Katholiken. Soziale, wirtschaftliche und politische Aspekte einer nordafrikanischen Kirchenspaltung* (Göteborg: Elanders Boktryckerei Aktiebolag, 1964), pp. 135-138.

[33] *Vita* 11 (Gorce, p. 146).

[34] Augustine, *Ep.* 105.2.6 (CSEL 34: 599).

[35] See above, pp. 113-114.

[36] *Vita* 36 (Gorce, p. 194).

[37] *Vita* 43 (Gorce, p. 210).

[38] *Vita* 29 (Gorce, p. 184). Although Jews are well-documented in North Africa during the Common Era, Samaritans are not explicitly mentioned. See Jean-Baptiste Frey, *Corpus Inscriptionum Iudaicarum. II: Asie-Afrique*, Sussidi allo Studio delle Antichità Cristiane 3 (Città del Vaticano: Pontificio Istituto di Archeologia Cristiana, 1952), 349-353; Monceaux, "Les Colonies juives," pp. 159-184; Jean-Marie Lassère, *Ubique Populus. Peuplement et mouvements de population dans l'Afrique romaine de la chute de Carthage à la fin de la dynastie des Sévères (146 a.C.-235 p.C.)* (Paris: Editions du Centre National de la Recherche Scientifique, 1977), pp. 413-426.

[39] *Novella* 3 (Mommsen II: 7-11).

[40] *Vita* 53 (Gorce, p. 232); see above, p. 134, for dating.

[41] *Vita* 27 (Gorce, p. 180).

[42] *Vita* 54 (Gorce, p. 232).

[43] *Vita* 56 (Gorce, p. 238).

[44] *Vita* 53 (Gorce, p. 232); see above, pp. 65-66, 138.

Notes to pp. 147-148

[45]See Proclus' sermon, "De Laudibus S. Mariae" (PG 65: 680-692) and his "Letter to the Armenians" (*Ep.* 2 [PG 65: 856-873]).

[46]Proclus, *Ep.* 2.13-14 (PG 65: 869, 872).

[47]In a sermon translated by Marius Mercator (*Collectio Palatina* 23 [*ACO* I.5: 44]), Nestorius, after speaking of the disturbances religious disagreement had brought to the city, reminds his audience that Paul (in Titus 1:9) writes that a bishop must adhere to true doctrine, so that he can move his hearers and refute objectors-- but Paul did not mean that a bishop has the right to wound those who disagreed with him (as Nestorius thus implies Proclus did).

[48] *Vita* 60, 61 (Gorce, pp. 246, 248, 250).

[49] *Vita* 60 (Gorce, p. 248).

[50] *Vita* 62 (Gorce, p. 250).

[51]Latin *Vita* 59 (Rampolla, p. 33).

[52]Greek *Vita* 61 (Gorce, pp. 248, 250).

[53]Latin *Vita* 61 (Rampolla, p. 34): "Nihil enim foedum aut immundum Deus fecit in homine, sed omnia membra consequentia creavit: solum enim peccatum immundum est et abominabile; nam membra immunda esse non possunt quae Dominus creavit, unde nati sunt patriarchae, prophetae et apostoli et ceteri sancti."

[54]In both Greek and Latin *Vitae* 61 (Gorce, p. 250; Rampolla, p. 35).

[55]Notes also by Gorce, *Vie*, pp. 180-181 n. 3; and Moine, "Mélanie la Jeune (Sainte)," *DS* X: 960.

[56]Palladius, *Historia Lausiaca* 54 (Butler II: 146); see above, pp. 85-86.

[57] *Vita* 1 (Gorce, pp. 130, 132).

[58]Palladius, *Historia Lausiaca* 61 (Butler II: 155).

[59]See above, pp. 9-10.

Notes to pp. 149-151

[60]Rampolla, *Melania*, pp. lxvii-lxviii; Butler, "Cardinal Rampolla's Melania," p. 631.

[61]Paulinus of Nola, *Ep.* 29.6 (CSEL 29: 251).

[62]Gorce, agrees: *Vie*, p. 35.

[63]Latin *Vita* 34 (Rampolla, p. 18).

[64]Gordini, "Il monachesimo romano," p. 90.

[65]Palladius, *Historia Lausiaca* 54 (Butler II: 148): money was left to provide for the monastery.

[66]See above, pp. 122-128.

[67]*Vita* 28 (Gorce, pp. 180, 182).

[68]This independently proposed hypothesis is supported by Moine, "Melaniana," pp. 73-74. This interpretation depends on understanding the phrase that the woman was "in communion with us, the orthodox" ("...κοινωνοῦσα μεθ᾽ἡμῶν τῶν ὀρθοδόξον ..." [*Vita* 28; Gorce, p. 182]) to mean not that she was participating in services with Melania and Gerontius on Olivet, but merely that she considered herself part of the orthodox communion. Conceivably, it could alternately mean that she had earlier communed with Melania the Younger (if the woman were Melania the Elder, possibly during her sojourn in the West in A.D. 400 and the years following). The Latin version (Rampolla, p. 16) reads: "Communicabat autem et nobiscum, fictam fidens habens," which sounds as if the woman were taking the Eucharist in the company of Melania.

[69]*Vita* 6, 12 (Gorce, pp. 136, 138, 150).

[70]See above, pp. 7, 90-92.

[71]Palladius, *Historia Lausiaca* 54 (Butler II: 147).

[72]*Vita* 40 (Gorce, p. 204). The younger Paula was the subject of Jerome's famous *Epistle* 107 (CSEL 55: 290-305) on bringing up a Christian daughter.

[73]Jerome, *Ep.* 143.2 (CSEL 56: 293).

Notes to pp. 151-153

[74] *Vita* 63 (Gorce, p. 254).

[75] *Vita* 68 (Gorce, p. 264).

[76]Nestorius' famous words, as reported in Socrates Scholasticus, *HE* VII.29 (Hussey II: 799): "Δός μοι, φησίν, ὦ Βασιλεῦ, καθαρὰν τὴν γῆν τῶν αἱρετικῶν, κἀγώ σοι τὸν οὐρανὸν ἀντιδώσω."

IV THE LIFE OF MELANIA THE YOUNGER AND THE HELLENISTIC ROMANCE: A GENRE EXPLORATION

[1]A sampling of the vast literature on the theme: L. W. Barnard, *Justin Martyr: His Life and Thought* (Cambridge: Cambridge University Press, 1967), chap. 3; Werner Jaeger, *Early Christianity and Greek Paideia* (Cambridge, Mass.: Belknap Press of Harvard University Press, 1961); Henry Chadwick, *Early Christian Thought and the Classical Tradition: Studies in Justin, Clement, and Origen* (New York: Oxford University Press, 1966); R. Arnou, "Platonism des Pères," *DTC* 12 (1935), cols. 2258-2392; Charles Bigg, *The Christian Platonists of Alexandria* (Oxford: Clarendon Press, 1913); Pierre Camelot, "Les Idées de Clément d'Alexandrie sur l'utilisation des sciences et de littérature profane," *RecSR* 21 (1931): 38-66; idem, "Clément d'Alexandrie et l'utilisation de la philosophie grecque," *RecSR* 21 (1931): 541-569; Robert P. Casey, "Clement of Alexandria and the Beginnings of Christian Platonism," *HTR* 18 (1925): 39-101; Eugène de Faye, *Clément d'Alexandrie: Etude sur les rapports du Christianisme et de philosophie grecque au IIe siècle* (Paris: Ernest Leroux, 1906); Michel Spanneut, *Le Stoïcisme des pères de l'église de Clément de Rome à Clément d'Alexandrie* (Paris: Editions du Seuil, 1957); Salvatore R. C. Lilla, *Clement of Alexandria: A Study in Christian Platonism and Gnosticism* (Oxford: Oxford University Press, 1971); Elizabeth A. Clark, *Clement's Use of Aristotle: The Aristotelian Contribution to Clement of Alexandria's Refutation of Gnosticism*, Texts and Studies in Religion 1 (New York/Toronto: Edwin Mellen Press, 1977); Hal Koch, *Pronoia und Paideusis. Studien über Origenes und sein Verhältnis zum Platonismus* (Berlin/Leipzig: W. deGruyter &

Co., 1932); Johannes Stelzenberger, *Die Beziehungen der frühchristlichen Sittenlehre zur Ethik der Stoa* (München: 1933); Eugène de Faye, *Origène: sa vie, son oeuvre, sa pensée, Vol. II: L'Ambiance philosophique, Vol. III: La Doctrine*. Bibliothèque de l'Ecole de Haute Etudes, sciences religieuses 43, 44 (Paris: Ernest Leroux, 1927-1928); Robert Joly, *Christianisme et philosophie: études sur Justin et les apologistes grecs du deuxième siècle* (Bruxelles: Editions de l'Université de Bruxelles, 1973); Henri Crouzel, *Origène et la philosophie* (Paris: Aubin, 1962); John M. Rist, *Eros and Psyche: Studies in Plato, Plotinus, and Origen* (Toronto: University of Toronto Press, 1964).

[2]For discussion of the theme, see, for example, Pierre Courcelle, *Les Lettres grecques en occident de Macrobe à Cassiodore* (Paris: E. de Boccard, 1948); Harald Hagendahl, *Latin Fathers and the Classics. A Study on the Apologists, Jerome, and Other Christian Writers*, Studia Graeca et Latina Gothoburgensia 6 (Göteborg: Elanders Boktr. Aktiebolag, 1958); David S. Wiesen, *St. Jerome as a Satirist* (Ithaca: Cornell University Press, 1964); Edwin A. Quain, "St. Jerome as a Humanist," in *A Monument to Saint Jerome: Essays on Some Aspects of His Life, Works and Influence*, ed. Francis X. Murphy (New York: Sheed & Ward, 1952), pp. 203-232; John Nicholas Hritzu, *The Style of the Letters of St. Jerome*, The Catholic University of America Patristic Studies 60 (Washington, D.C.: The Catholic University of America Press, 1939); Herbert Kech, *Hagiographie als christliche Unterhaltungsliteratur: Studien zum Phänomen des Erbaulichen anhand der Mönchsviten des Hl. Hieronymus* (Göppingen: A. Kümmerle, 1977); Jean Daniélou, *Platonisme et théologie mystique: essai sur la doctrine spirituelle de saint Grégoire de Nysse* (Paris: Aubier, 1944); Robert C. Gregg, *Consolation Philosophy: Greek and Christian Paideia in Basil and the Two Gregories*, Patristic Monograph Series 3 (Cambridge, Mass.: Philadelphia Patristic Foundation, 1975); *Gregor von Nyssa und die Philosophie: zweites internationales Kolloquium über Gregor von Nyssa*, Freckenhorst bei Münster, 18-23 September 1972, ed. H. Dörrie, M. Altenburger, and U. Schramm (Leiden: Brill, 1976); Agnes Clare Way, *The Language and Style of the Letters of St. Basil*, The Catholic University of America Patristic Studies 13 (Washington, D.C.: The Catholic University of America Press, 1927); Rosemary R. Ruether, *Gregory of Nazianzus, Rhetor and Philosopher* (Oxford: Clarendon Press, 1969); John M. Rist, "Basil's 'Neoplatonism': Its Background and Nature," and George L. Kustas, "Saint Basil and the Rhetorical Tradition," in

Notes to pp. 153-155

Basil of Caesarea: Christian, Humanist, Ascetic: A 1600th Anniversary Symposium, pt. 1, ed. Paul J. Fedwick (Toronto: Pontifical Institute of Mediaeval Studies, 1981), pp. 137-220, 221-279; George A. Kennedy, *A History of Rhetoric. Vol. III: Greek Rhetoric Under Christian Emperors* (Princeton: Princeton University Press, 1983), chap. 4.

[3]Friedrich Leo, *Die griechisch-römische Biographie nach ihrer literarischen Form* (Leipzig: B. G. Teubner, 1901; rpt. Hildesheim: Georg Olms Verlagsbuchhandlung, 1956); critique of Leo's thesis in Wolf Steidle, *Sueton und die antike Biographie,* Zetamata 1 (München: Verlag C. H. Beck, 1951), pp. 126-177.

[4]Hans Mertel, *Die biographische Form der griechischen Heiligenlegenden* (München: C. Wolf & Sohn, 1909), pp. 16-17.

[5]Martin Schanze, Carl Hosius, and Gustav Krüger, *Geschichte der römischer Literatur* III.3 (München: C. H. Beck'sche Verlagsbuchhandlung, 1922), p. 65; Alfred Kappelmacher, "Sulpicius Severus," *RE* IV.A (1931): col. 869.

[6]Karl Holl, "Die schriftstellerische Form des griechischen Heiligenlebens," *Neue Jahrbücher für das klassische Altertum* 29 (1912): 406-427, esp. 421ff.; Richard Reitzenstein, "Des Athanasius Werk über das Leben des Antonius," *SB* Heid. philos.-hist. Kl. 5 (1914), pp. 3-68, esp. 30ff.

[7]Patricia Cox, *Biography in Late Antiquity: A Quest for the Holy Man,* The Transformation of the Classical Heritage 5 (Berkeley: University of California Press, 1983).

[8]As noted by Manfred Fuhrmann, "Die Mönchsgeschichten des Hieronymus. Formexperimente in erzählender Literatur," *Christianisme et formes littéraires de l'antiquité tardive en Occident,* ed. Alan Cameron et al., Entretiens sur l'Antiquité Classique 23 (Geneva: Fondation Hardt, 1977), p. 97.

[9]Even Mertel, *Die biographische Form,* p. 18, conceded that there were numerous aspects of the *Vita Antonii* that did not fit a "Plutarchian" scheme. On the difficulties of fitting miracle stories to a classical form, see Georg Luck, "Die Form der Suetonischen Biographie und die frühen Heiligenviten," in *Mullus. Festschrift Theodor*

Klausner, Jahrbuch für Antike und Christentum Ergänzungs-
band 1 (Münster-West.: Aschendorffsche Verlagsbuchhandlung, 1964), p. 237. For the Christians' nonuse of
written documents in the compilation of their *Lives*, see
Luck, "Die Form," p. 235. See Cox, *Biography*, pp. 17-44,
for a discussion of types of "holy man" biographies.

[10]For example, Latin *Vita* 56 (Rampolla, p. 32);
Greek *Vita* 39 (Gorce, p. 202). See Clark, *Jerome*, pp.
56-57 for other references and discussion.

[11]Nicetas Eugenianus, *Drosillae et Chariclis* (*Nicetae
Eugeniani Narrationem Amatoriam et Constantini Manassis Fragmenta*),
ed. J. F. Boissanade [Lugdunum Batavorum (Leyden):
J. Luchtmans, 1819]); S. Gaselee's translation of the
prefatory poem to Longus' *Daphnis and Chloe* appears in *The
Love Romances of Parthenius and Other Fragments*, trans. Stephen
Gaselee, Loeb Classical Library (London: William
Heinemann; Cambridge, Mass.: Harvard University Press,
1935), pp. 410-411. Since it is standard practice in
the secondary literature to use the terms "novel" and
"romance" interchangeably, we shall follow that conven-
tion throughout this section.

[12]Ben Edwin Perry, *The Ancient Romances: A Literary-
Historical Account of Their Origins*, Sather Classical Lectures
37 (Berkeley: University of California Press, 1967),
p. 19.

[13]Ibid., pp. 4-5, 29; E. Schwartz, "Unzeitgemässe
Beobachtungen zu den Clementinen," *ZNW* 31 (1932): 178;
Franz Altheim, *Literatur und Gesellschaft im ausgehenden
Altertum* (Halle/Salle: Max Niemeyer Verlag, 1948), I:
18; Tomas Hägg, *The Novel in Antiquity* (Berkeley/Los
Angeles: University of California Press, 1983), pp. 3-
4.

[14]Otto Mazal, "Der griechische und byzantinische
Roman in der Forschung von 1945 bis 1960," *Jahrbuch der
österreichischen byzantinischen Gesellschaft* 11/12 (1962/1963):
9: few other aspects of ancient literary history have
been so affected by revolutions in scholarship as the
novel. Papyrus finds in recent years have brought to
light fragments of other novels. See Albert Henrichs,
ed., *Die Phoinikika des Lollianus. Fragmente eines neuen
griechischen Roman*, Papyrologische Texte und Abhandlungen
14 (Bonn: Rudolf Habelt Verlag, 1972); and M. W.

Haslam, ed., "Narrative about Tinouphis in Prosimetrum," in *Papyri Greek and Egyptian Edited in Various Hands in Honour of Eric Gardner Turner*, Egypt Exploration Society, Graeco-Roman Memoirs 68 (London: Egypt Exploration Society, 1981), pp. 35-45. For discussion of the *Phoinikika*, see also C. P. Jones, "Apuleius' *Metamorphoses* and Lollianus' *Phoinikika*," *Phoenix* 34 (1980): 243-254, and Jack Winkler, "Lollianus and the Desperadoes," *JHS* 100 (1980): 155-181.

[15]Erwin Rohde, *Der griechische Roman und seine Vorläufer* (Leipzig: Breitkopf und Hartel, 1876).

[16]Ibid., pts. I and II.

[17]Ibid., pt. III.

[18]The Elder Seneca, *Controversiae* I.2; I.6; II.7. (Annaeus Seneca, *Oratorum et Rhetorum. Sententiae Divisiones. Colores*, ed. Adolphus Kiessling [1872; rpt., Stuttgart: B. G. Teubner, 1967], pp. 80-93, 112-119, 224-229).

[19]Rohde, *Der griechische Roman*, p. 489.

[20]For accounts of the papyrus finds and their significance, see Bruno Lavagnini, *Studi sul romanzo greco* (Messina/Firenze: Casa Editrice G. D'Anna, 1950), pp. 10-11, 72-81; Perry, *The Ancient Romances*, pp. 6, 153; Otto Weinreich, "Nachwort," in Heliodorus, *Aithiopika. Die Abenteur der schönen Chariklea. Ein griechischer Liebesroman*, ed. Rudolf Reymer (Zürich: Artemis-Verlag, 1950), pp. 327-328; Martin Braun, *History and Romance in Graeco-Oriental History* (Oxford: Basil Blackwell, 1938), chap. 1. See IV n. 14 above for references to two recent discoveries.

[21]Weinreich, "Nachwort," pp. 328-336; Perry, *The Ancient Romances*, pp. 5-6, suggests Christian influence for the novel's decline; R. M. Rattenbury, "Chastity and Chastity Ordeals in the Ancient Greek Romances," *Proceedings of the Leeds Philosophical and Literary Society* 1 (1926): 60, 71, posits that the "unnaturally high moral standard" and "inhuman morality" of the Greek romance may have contributed to its decline.

[22]Perry, *The Ancient Romances*, p. 96; Weinreich, "Nachwort," p. 330; Chariton von Aphrodisias, *Kallirhoe*, ed. Karl Plepelits, Bibliothek der griechischen Literatur 6 (Stuttgart: Anton Hiersemann, 1976), pp. 4-8.

Notes to pp. 159-160

[23]Eduard Schwartz, *Fünf Vorträge über den griechischen Roman. Das Romanhafte in der erzählenden Literatur der Griechen*, 2d ed. (Berlin: Walter de Gruyter, 1943), chaps. 2-4, and p. 156.

[24]Lavagnini, *Studi*, pp. 20-50.

[25]Giuseppe Giangrande, "On the Origins of the Greek Romance: The Birth of a Literary Form," *Eranos* 60 (1962): 148-156.

[26]Moses Hadas, trans., *Three Greek Romances* (Indianapolis: Bobbs-Merrill, 1964), p. viii.

[27]Braun, *History*, chap. 1.

[28]Moses Hadas and Morton Smith, *Heroes and Gods. Spiritual Biographies in Antiquity* (New York: Harper & Row, 1965), p. 86.

[29]Otto Weinreich, *Der griechische Liebesroman* (Zürich: Artemis-Verlag, 1962), pp. 25, 30.

[30]Karl Kerényi, *Die griechisch-orientalische Romanliteratur in religionsgeschichtlicher Beleuchtung* (Tubingen: J. C. B. Mohr [Paul Siebeck], 1927), esp. chap. 2 and pp. 231ff. Kerényi's thesis is developed by Reinhold Merkelbach, *Roman und Mysterium in der Antike* (München/Berlin: C. H. Beck, 1962); and Remy Petri, *Über den Roman des Chariton*, Beiträge zur klassischen Philologie 11 (Meisenheim am Glan: Verlag Anton Hain, 1963), esp. pp. 8-17, 57, 64; and Altheim, *Literatur*, I: 30-31. For a ritualistic interpretation of the *Phoinikika*, see Henrichs, *Die Phoinikika*, pp. 28-79; challenged by Winkler, "Lollianus," pp. 155-166. For a summary of Merkelbach's position, see Hägg, *Novel*, pp. 101-104.

[31]Tomas Hägg, *Narrative Technique in Ancient Greek Romances. Studies of Chariton, Xenophon Ephesius, and Achilles Tatius*, Skrifter Utgivna av Svenska Institutet i Athen, 8°, 8 (Stockholm: Svenska Institutet i Athen, 1971), p. 13.

[32]Aristide Calderini, *Caritone di Afrodisia, Le Avventure di Cherea e Calliroe* (Torino: Fratelli Bocca, 1913), pp. 191ff. For a summary of the options, see Hägg, *Novel*, pp. 109-124.

Notes to p. 160

[33]Perry, *The Ancient Romances*, pp. 10-15, 20. For a
qualification of this assessment as regards the Latin
novels, see P. G. Walsh, *The Roman Novel. The 'Satyricon' of
Petronius and the 'Metamorphoses' of Apuleius* (Cambridge:
Cambridge University Press, 1970), p. 4.

[34]Ernst von Dobschütz, "Der Roman in der altchristlichen Literatur," *Deutsche Rundschau* 111 (1902): 87-106.

[35]Rosa Söder, *Die apokryphen Apostelgeschichten und die
romanhafte Literatur der Antike*, Würzburger Studien zur
Altertumswissenschaft 3 (Stuttgart: W. Kohlhammer,
1932).

[36]Ibid., pp. 3-4, and chap. 2.

[37]Of the dozens of such references, the following
represent a small sample: Johannes Geffcken, *Christliche
Apokryphen*, Religionsgeschichtliche Volksbücher für die
deutsche christliche Gegenwart, I.15 (Tübingen: J. C.
B. Mohr [Paul Siebeck], 1908), pp. 26-37; Schwartz,
"Unzeitgemässe Beobachtungen," pp. 178-187; Otmar
Schiffel von Fleschenberg, *Entwicklungsgeschichte des
griechischen Romanes im Altertum* (Halle a.S.:   Max Niemeyer,
1913), pp. 95-96; L. Radermacher, *Hippolytos und Thekla.
Studien zur Geschichte von Legende und Kultus*, SB Wien, philos.-
hist. Kl. 182.3 (Vienna: Alfred Hölder, 1916), pp. 83-
92; Paul Wendland, *Die urchristlichen Literaturformen*
(Tübingen: J. C. B. Mohr [Paul Siebeck], 1912), pp.
269-276; Werner Heintze, *Der Klemensroman und seine
griechischen Quellen*, TU 40.2 (Leipzig: J. C. Hinrichs,
1914): 130-138; Martin Blumenthal, *Formen und Motive in den
apokryphen Apostelgeschichten*, TU 48.1 (Leipzig: J. C.
Hinrichs, 1933): pts. 12 and 26; Rudolf Helm, *Der antike
Roman* (Berlin: Wissenschaftliche Editionsgesellschaft,
1948), pp. 53-61; René Aigrain, *L'Hagiographie: ses
sources, ses méthodes, son histoire* (Paris: Bloud & Gay,
1953), pp. 148-149, 160; Fuhrmann, "Die Mönchsgeschichten," pp. 50, 57, 64, 66, 85; Elizabeth Hazelton Haight,
More Essays on the Greek Romances (New York: Longmans,
Green & Co., 1945), chaps. 2 and 3; Kerényi, *Die
griechisch-orientalische Romanliteratur*, chap. 4; Hägg, *Novel*,
pp. 154-165. For a fuller bibliography on the "Christian novel," see Mazal, "Der griechische und
byzantinische Roman," pp. 69-86.

[38]Richard Reitzenstein, *Hellenistische Wundererzählung*
(Leipzig: B. G. Teubner, 1906), pp. 84, 97.

[39]The new emphasis on female protagonists has been
linked to the rising position of women in the Roman Em-
pire at this period (Haight, *More Essays*, p. 57). It has
also been suggested that women were a prime audience for
both the pagan and Christian works: Perry, *The Ancient
Romances*, p. 98; Hägg, *Novel*, pp. 95-96, 162; Carlos
Miralles, "*Eros* as *nosos* in the Greek Novel," in *Erotica
Antiqua: Acta of the International Conference on the Ancient
Novel*, Bangor, Wales, 12-17 July 1976, ed. B. P. Reardon
(Bangor: n.p., 1977), pp. 20-21; Stevan L. Davies, *The
Revolt of the Widows: The Social World of the Apocryphal Acts*
(Carbondale, Ill.: Southern Illinois University Press,
1980), chap. 4, and p. 86.

[40]As they fail to do in Longus, *Daphnis et Chloe*
IV.21, 35 (Dalmeyda, pp. 94, 103-104) and in Heliodorus,
Aethiopica X.14-16 (R. M. Rattenbury and T. W. Lumb
III: 92-98). Alfred von Gutschmid, "Die Königsnamen
in den apokryphen Apostelgeschichte. Ein Beitrag zur
Kenntnis des geschichtlichen Romans," *Rheinisches Museum*
19 (1964): 161-183, 380-401, argues that the Apocryphal
Acts tend to represent their characters as in contact
with highly placed people.

[41]*Acta Xanthippae et Polyxenae* 1-2 (James, pp. 58-59).

[42]*Acta Thomae* XI.134 (Lipsius and Bonnet II.2:
240).

[43]*Acta Pauli et Theclae* 26 (Lipsius and Bonnet I:
254).

[44]Chariton, *Chareas et Callirhoe* I.1.2 (Molinié, p.
50); Xenophon, *Ephesiaca* I.2.7 (Papanikolaou, p. 3);
Heliodorus, *Aethiopica* I.2.1 (Rattenbury and Lumb I: 4).

[45]*Acta Xanthippae et Polyxenae* 22 (James, p. 73); *Acta
Thomae* IX.88, 115 (Lipsius and Bonnet II.2: 203, 225-226);
Acta Pauli et Theclae 29 (Lipsius and Bonnet I: 257).

[46]*Acta Pauli et Theclae* 25, 40 (Lipsius and Bonnet I:
253, 266).

[47]For example, Thecla in *Acta Pauli et Theclae* 29 (Lipsius and Bonnet I: 256-257). Even Paul thinks of Thecla's beauty rather than her piety; see the discussion in Davies, *The Revolt*, pp. 59-60.

[48] *Homiliae* XII.16; XIII.7 (GCS 42: 181-182, 196-197); *Recognitiones* VII.15-16; VII.32; IX.36 (GCS 51: 203-204, 212, 321).

[49]Jerome, *Vita Malchi* 4-5 (PL 23: 56-57).

[50]Xenophon, *Ephesiaca* V.13.2-4 (Papanikolaou, p. 69); Heliodorus, *Aethiopica* I.22.2; II.25; II.33.4; III.11 (Rattenbury and Lumb I: 33, 79-80, 92, 112-114); Achilles Tatius, *Clitophon et Leucippe* IV.1.4; VII.13.2 (Vilborg, pp. 70, 137).

[51]For example, Merkelbach, *Roman*, pp. 172-177: the Clementines are derived from an Isis novel.

[52]Söder, *Die apokryphen Apostelgeschichten*, pp. 115-116; Rattenbury, "Chastity," pp. 59-71; Kerényi, *Die griechisch-orientalische Romanliteratur*, pp. 217-218; Walsh, *The Roman Novel*, p. 188; E. Feuillatre, *Etudes sur les 'Ethiopiques' d'Héliodore. Contribution à la connaissance du roman grec*, Publications de la Faculté des Lettres et Sciences Humaines de Poitiers 2 (Paris: Presses Universitaires de France, 1966), p. 146; B. F. Reardon, *Courants littéraires grecs de II*e *et III*e *siècles après J.-C.*, Annales littéraires de l'Université de Nantes 3 (Paris: Société d'Edition 'Les Belles Lettres,' 1971), pp. 400-401. For typical passages on chastity in the novels, see, e.g., Achilles Tatius, *Clitophon et Leucippe* IV.1; V.18-20 (Vilborg, pp. 70-71, 101-103); Heliodorus, *Aethiopica* II.4.3-4; II.33.4-5; III.17.3-5; IV.8.7; V.4.4-5 (Rattenbury and Lumb I: 51-52, 92, 120-121; II: 16, 42-43); Xenophon, *Ephesiaca* V.14 (Papanikolaou, p. 70).

[53]Heliodorus, *Aethiopica* IV.18.5 (Rattenbury and Lumb II: 30); Xenophon, *Ephesiaca* I.11.3-6 (Papanikolaou, pp. 12-13); Longus, *Daphnis et Chloe* II.39 (Dalmeyda, pp. 52-53); also see Rattenbury, "Chastity," pp. 59-71.

[54]Xenophon, *Ephesiaca* V.5.7-8; V.14.1 (Papanikolaou, pp. 59, 70).

[55]Xenophon, *Ephesiaca* V.14.7-15.6 (Papanikolaou, pp. 16-17).

[56]Xenophon, *Ephesiaca* I.15.4; I.16.7 (Papanikolaou, 17, 18); Heliodorus, *Aethiopica* I.22; V.20 (Rattenbury and Lumb I: 33-35; II: 62-64); Achilles Tatius, *Clitophon et Leucippe* VI.21.3 (Vilborg, pp. 124-125).

[57]Heliodorus, *Aethiopica* X.7.7-9.1 (Rattenbury and Lumb III: 83-85); Achilles Tatius, *Clitophon et Leucippe* VIII.13-14 (Vilborg, pp. 156-157); also see Rattenbury, "Chastity," pp. 64-70.

[58]For example, Söder, *Die apokryphen Apostelgeschichten*, pp. 115-116; Dobshütz, "Der Roman," p. 101. Perhaps the stress on chastity led later generations of Christians to posit a Christian connection with the novels; see Heinrich Dörrie, "Die griechischen Romane und das Christentum," *Philologus* 93 (1938): 274-275; and Rattenbury and Lumb, "Introduction," I: vii-xiii, for evidence.

[59]Achilles Tatius, *Clitophon et Leucippe* V.15-16 (Vilborg, pp. 98-100); Heliodorus, *Aethiopica* IV.18.5; V.4.4-5 (Rattenbury and Lumb II: 30, 42-43); Longus, *Daphnis et Chloe* III.20.1-2 (Dalmeyda, p. 67); also see Rattenbury, "Chastity," pp. 62-63.

[60]Achilles Tatius, *Clitophon et Leucippe* II.23 (Vilborg, pp. 38-39).

[61]Longus, *Daphnis et Chloe* II.9-11; III.13-14 (Dalmeyda, pp. 33-35, 62-63).

[62]Clement of Alexandria, *Stromateis* III.7.57.1 (GCS 52: 222).

[63]Perry, *The Ancient Romances*, pp. 30-31.

[64]*Acta Johannis* 63 (Lipsius and Bonnet II.1: 181-182).

[65]*Acta Pauli et Theclae* 21-22 (Lipsius and Bonnet I: 249-251).

[66]Jerome, *Vita Malchi* 6 (PL 23: 58-59).

[67]*Vita* 29 (Gorce, p. 182).

[68] *Vita* 1, 3 (Gorce, pp. 130, 132).

[69] *Vita* 4 (Gorce, pp. 132, 134).

[70] *Vita* 22 (Gorce, p. 174).

[71] *Vita* 2 (Gorce, p. 132).

[72] *Vita* 4 (Gorce, p. 134).

[73] *Vita* 5 (Gorce, p. 134).

[74] *Vita* 30 (Gorce, p. 184).

[75] *Vita* prologus, 8, 12 (Gorce, pp. 126, 140, 142, 148).

[76] *Vita* 22 (Gorce, p. 174).

[77] *Vita* 25 (Gorce, pp. 176, 178).

[78] *Vita* 56 (Gorce, p. 238).

[79] *Vita* 23 (Gorce, p. 174).

[80] *Vita* 24 (Gorce, p. 176).

[81] *Vita* 32 (Gorce, p. 188).

[82] *Vita* 40 (Gorce, p. 204).

[83]Heliodorus, *Aethiopica* III.1-3; X.39 (Rattenbury and Lumb I: 97-102; III: 124-125).

[84]Perry, *The Ancient Romances*, p. 31; Rattenbury and Lumb, "Introduction," I: xx; Walsh, *The Roman Novel*, pp. 3-4; Hadas and Smith, *Heroes*, p. 86; Hans-Georg Beck, "Marginalien zum byzantinischen Roman," *Kyklos, Festschrift R. Keydall*, ed. H.-G. Beck et al. (Berlin/New York: Walter de Gruyter, 1978), p. 119: Byzantine physicians recommended the novels for erotic stimulation.

[85]Walsh, *The Roman Novel*, pp. 2-3; Perry, *The Ancient Romances*, p. 88; Reardon, *Courants*, pp. 25, 323; Chariton, *Kallirhoe* (Plepelits, p. vii); Rattenbury and Lumb, "Introduction," I: xx; B. E. Perry, "Chariton and His Romance from a Literary-Historical Point of View," *American Journal of Philology* 51 (1930): 93, 98.

[86]Perry, *The Ancient Romances*, p. 48. The fact that marriage is considered an appropriate end for the novels shows they represent an unheroic world: see Hadas, *Three Greek Romances*, p. xii; B. P. Reardon, "The Greek Novel," *Phoenix* 23 (1969): 296.

[87]Persius, *Saturae* I.134: "post prandia Callirhoen do" (*A. Persi Flacci Saturarum Liber*, ed. W. V. Clausen [Oxford: Clarendon Press, 1956], p. 10).

[88]For example, *Homiliae* XIX.1-23 (GCS 42: 253-266); *Recognitiones* III.21-26; VIII.7-34, 39-57 (GCS 51: 112-116, 220-238, 241-253).

[89]Athanasius, *Vita Antonii* 22-34 (PG 26: 876-908).

[90]Jerome, *Vita Malchi* 10 (PL 23: 62).

[91]*Vita* prologus (Gorce, p. 126).

[92]*Vita* 8 (Gorce, pp. 140, 142).

[93]*Vita* 15 (Gorce, p. 158).

[94]*Vita* 23, 42, 46 (Gorce, pp. 176, 206, 208, 214).

[95]*Vita* 47 (Gorce, p. 216).

[96]*Vita* 44 (Gorce, pp. 210, 212).

[97]Ibid. (Gorce, p. 212).

[98]*Vita* 43 (Gorce, p. 210).

[99]Ibid.

[100]*Vita* 62 (Gorce, p. 250).

[101]*Vita* 29 (Gorce, pp. 182, 184).

[102]*Vita* 43 (Gorce, p. 210).

[103]*Vita* 53 (Gorce, pp. 230, 232).

[104]*Vita* 54 (Gorce, pp. 232, 234).

[105] J. Irmscher, "Introduction to the Pseudo-
Clementines," in *New Testament Apocrypha*, eds. Edgar Hennecke and Wilhelm Scheemelcher, English edition (Philadelphia: Westminster Press, 1964) II: 555.

[106] Radermacher, *Hippolytos*, p. 68; Gilbert Dagron,
ed. and trans., *Vie et miracles de Sainte Thècle: texte grec,
traduction et commentaire*, SubsHag 62 (Bruxelles: Société
des Bollandistes, 1978), p. 33, and chaps. 3, 5, 6.
See also Carl Holzhey, *Die Thekla-Akten. Ihre Verbreitung
und Beurteilung in der Kirche*, Veröffentlichungen aus dem
kirchenhistorischen Seminar-München II.7 (München: J.
J. Lentner, 1905), pp. 31, 50-74.

[107] Ulrich Fabricius, *Die Legende im Bild des Jahrtausends
der Kirche. Der Einfluss der Apokryphen und Pseudepigraphen auf
die altchristliche und byzantinische Kunst* (Kassel: J. C.
Onken Verlag, 1956), pp. 109-112; Holzhey, *Die Thekla-
Akten*, p. 100.

[108] See below, p. 108, for Jerome's use of Thecla's
name. Also see *Acta Pauli: Übersetzung, Untersuchungen und
koptischer Text*, ed. Carl Schmidt, 2d ed. (Leipzig: J. C.
Hinrichs, 1905), pp. 147-151; Richard A. Lipsius, *Die
apokryphen Apostelgeschichten und Apostellegenden* (Braunschweig:
C. A. Schwetschke und Sohn, 1887), II.1: 424-428.

[109] Gerard Garitte, *Un Témoin important du texte de la
Vie de S. Antoine par S. Athanase. La Version latine inédite des
Archives du Chapitre de S. Pierre à Rome*, Etudes de Philologie,
d'Archéologie et d'Histoire Anciennes 3 (Bruxelles:
Palais des Académies; Rome: Academia Belgica, 1939),
pp. 1-7; the *Life of Antony* was soon translated into Cop-
tic, Armenian, Syriac, Arabic, Ethiopian, and Georgian
(p. 1); H. W. F. M. Hoppenbrouwers, *La Plus Ancienne Version latine de la Vie de S. Antoine par S. Athanase* (Utrecht:
Dekker & Van de Vegt, 1960), p. xiii. Also see Jerome,
Vita Pauli 1 (PL 23: 18): the *Life of Antony* exists in
both Greek and Latin versions.

[110] Schwartz, "Unzeitgemässe Beobachtungen," pp.
165-166; Murphy, *Rufinus*, p. 113. Paulinus of Nola also
dabbled with translating the Pseudo-Clementine literature, but the project apparently came to nothing. He
appealed to Rufinus for help with the Greek (Paulinus of
Nola, *Ep.* 46.2 [CSEL 29: 387-388]).

[111]André-Jean Festugière, ed., *Historia Monachorum in Aegypto*. SubsHag 53 (Bruxelles: Société des Bollandistes, 1971). For an update on older arguments regarding the *Historia Monachorum*, see A.-J. Festugière, "Le Problem littéraire de l'Historia Monachorum," *Hermes* 83 (1955): esp. 257-258.

[112]Rufinus, *HE* X.8 (GCS 9.2: 971).

[113]Jerome, *Ep.* 3.1-2 (CSEL 54: 13-14); Rufinus, *Apologia contra Hieronymum* II.15 (CCL 20: 94-95).

[114]Jerome, *Adversus Jovinianum* I.26 (PL 23: 257); *Commentarius in Epistolam S. Pauli ad Galatas* I.1.18 (PL 26: 354). Also see Schwartz, "Unzeitgemässe Beobachtungen," pp. 160-161; John Chapman, "On the Date of the Clementines," *ZNW* 9 (1908): 32.

[115]Jerome, *De Viris Illustribus* 7 (PL 23: 651). See Schmidt, *Acta Pauli*, pp. xix-xxi, corrected by W. Schneemelcher, "The Acts of Paul," in *New Testament Apocrypha* II: 324-325.

[116]Jerome, *Ep.* 22.41 (CSEL 54: 209).

[117]Jerome, *Chronicum*, an. 374 (GCS 47: 247).

[118]Jerome, *Epp.* 22.33, 36 (CSEL 54: 195-196, 200-201); 58.5 (CSEL 54: 533-535); 108.14 (CSEL 55: 324-325); 125.11 (CSEL 56: 131); 147.5 (CSEL 56: 321). For Jerome's own struggle in the desert, see *Ep.* 22.7 (CSEL 54: 152-154).

[119]Amand Boon, ed., *Pachomiana Latina*, Bibliothèque de la Revue d'Histoire Ecclésiastique 7 (Louvain: Bureaux de la Revue, 1932), pp. 3-74.

[120]The phrase is Hippolyte Delehaye's: "roman hagiographique" (*Les Légendes hagiographiques*, 2d ed. [Bruxelles: Bureaux de la Société des Bollandistes, 1906], p. 4); adopted by Hägg, *Novel*, pp. 164-165.

[121]Fuhrmann, "Die Mönchsgeschichten, pp. 74-75; Rousseau, *Ascetics*, pp. 132, 144. Also see Jerome on the *Life of Antony*: *Epp.* 57.6; 22.36 (CSEL 54: 511, 200).

[122]For parallels between the *Vita Hilarionis* and the *Vita Probi* I.1-2, see Alan Cameron, "Paganism and Literature in Late Fourth Century Rome," in *Christianisme*, p. 14; and Fuhrman, "Die Mönchsgeschichten," pp. 52-53.

[123]Rufinus, *Prologus in Clementis Recognitiones* (CSEL 20: 281); Murphy, *Rufinus*, p. 200 n. 59. There are sixty-seven manuscripts listed for Rufinus' translation of the Pseudo-Clementine material; see Albert Siegmund, *Die Überlieferung der griechischen christlichen Literatur in der lateinschen Kirche bis zum zwölften Jahrhundert*, Abh Bayerischen Benediktiner-Akademie 51 (München-Pasing: Filser-Verlag, 1949), pp. 59-61. On Silvia, see E. D. Hunt, "St. Silvia of Aquitaine: The Role of a Theodosian Pilgrim in the Society of East and West," *JThS*, n.s., 23 (1972): 351-373, esp. 367.

[124]Rufinus, *Praefatio in Sexti Sententias* (CCL 20: 259); Murphy, *Rufinus*, pp. 119-121.

[125]Rufinus, *Praefatio in Omelias Sancti Basili* (CCL 20: 237); *Prologus in Explanationem Origenis super Psalmos XXXVI-XXXVIII* (CCL 20: 251).

[126]Palladius, *Historia Lausiaca* 5, 9, 10, 18, 38 (Butler II: 21-22, 29-32, 47-58, 116-123), for materials contributed by Melania the Elder.

[127]Palladius, *Historia Lausiaca* 55 (Butler II: 149).

[128]On Evagrius Ponticus' letters to Melania the Elder, see Wilhelm Frankenberg, *Euagrius Ponticus*. Abh Gött., philog.-hist. Kl., n.f. 13.2 (Berlin: Weidmann, 1912; text of *Epistula ad Melanium*, pp. 610-619); and the discussion of the letters (text in Syriac, original Greek lost) in J. Muyldermans, ed. and trans., *Evagriana Syriaca: textes inédites de British Museum et de la Vaticane*, Bibliothèque du Muséon 31 (Louvain: Publications Universitaires/Institut Orientaliste, 1952), pp. 76-78. Also see Jerome, *Ep.* 133.3 (CSEL 56: 246).

[129]Palladius, *Historia Lausiaca* 38 (Butler II: 119-120).

[130]Jerome, *Ep.* 133.3 (CSEL 56: 246): for other translations Rufinus made of Evagrius Ponticus' works,

Notes to pp. 169-170

see Courcelle, *Les Lettres grecques*, pp. 130, 215 n. 2.

[131]Paulinus of Nola, *Ep.* 29.14 (CSEL 29: 261: "talium historiarum"). That Paulinus was the first to bring Sulpicius Severus' *Life of Martin* to Rome is attested by Sulpicius, *Dialogus* I.23 (CSEL 1: 176).

[132]Jerome, *Ep.* 127.5 (CSEL 56: 149).

[133]*Vita* 37-39 (Gorce, pp. 196, 198, 200, 202).

[134]*Vita* 23 (Gorce, p. 174; Rampolla, p. 15).

[135]Palladius, *Historia Lausiaca* 61 (Butler II: 157); *Vita* 53 (Gorce, p. 230).

[136]See above, pp. 141-152.

BIBLIOGRAPHY

I. PRIMARY SOURCES

Achilles Tatius. *Leucippe et Clitophon. Leucippe and Clito-phon.* Ed. Ebbe Vilborg. Studia Graeca et Latina Gothoburgensia 1. Stockholm: Almqvist & Wiksell, 1955.

Acta Apolostolorum Apocrypha. Ed. R. A. Lipsius and M. Bonnet. Leipzig: Hermann Mendelssohn, 1891-1903.

_____. *New Testament Apocrypha.* Eds. Edgar Hennecke and Wilhelm Schneemelcher; English trans. and ed. R. McL. Wilson. Vol. 2. Philadelphia: Westminster Press, 1965.

Acta Pauli: Übersetzung, Üntersuchungen und koptischer Text. Ed. Carl Schmidt. 2d ed. Leipzig: J. C. Hinrichs, 1905.

Acta Pauli et Theclae. Passio S. Theclae Virginis. Die lateinische Übersetzung der Acta Pauli et Theclae. Ed. Oscar von Gebhardt. TU 22.2 (=n.s., 7.2). Leipzig: J. C. Hinrichs, 1902.

Acta Xanthippe et Polyxenae. Apocrypha Anecdota. A Collection of Thirteen Apocryphal Books and Fragments. Ed. Montague Rhodes James. Texts and Studies II.3. Cambridge: Cambridge University Press, 1893.

Ammianus Marcellinus. *Ammianus Marcellinus.* English trans. John C. Rolfe. 3 vols. Loeb Classical Library. Cambridge, Mass.: Harvard University Press; London: William Heinemann Ltd., 1935-1939.

Antonius Martyr. *Itinerarium. In Itinera Hierosolymitana Saeculi IIII-VIII.* Ed. Paul Geyer. CSEL 39. Prague/Vienna: F. Tempsky; Leipzig: G. Freytag, 1898.

Athanasius. *Vita Antonii.* PG 26 (1887): cols. 835-976.

_____. *The Life of Antony and the Letter to Marcellinus.* Trans. Robert C. Gregg. The Classics of Western Spirituality. New York/Ramsey, N.J./Toronto: Paulist Press, 1980.

_____. *The Life of Saint Antony*. Trans. Robert T. Meyer. Ancient Christian Writers 10. Westminster, Md.: Newman Press, 1950.

_____. *La Plus Ancienne Version latine de la Vie de S. Antoine par S. Athanase*. Ed. H. W. F. M. Hoppenbrouwers. Utrecht: Dekker & Van de Vegt, 1960.

Augustine. *Concerning the City of God Against the Pagans*. Ed. and trans. Henry Bettenson. New York: Penguin Books, 1976.

_____. *Epistolae*. Ed. Al. Goldbacher. CSEL 34, 44, 57, 58. Prague/Vienna/Leipzig: F. Tempsky, 1895, 1904, 1911, 1932.

_____. *Letters*. In *The Confessions and Letters of St. Augustine*, trans. J. G. Cunningham. NPNF, ser. 1, vol. 1.

Callinicos. *Vita Hypatii. Vie d' Hypatios. Introduction, texte, traduction et notes*. Ed. G. J. M. Bartelink. SC 177. Paris: Les Editions du Cerf, 1971.

Chariton. *Caritone di Afrodisia, Le Avventure di Cherea e Calliroe*. Ed. Aristide Calderini. Torino: Fratelli Bocca, 1913.

_____. *Chareas et Callirhoe. Le Roman de Chairéas et Callirhoé*. Ed. Georges Molinié. Paris: Société d'Edition 'Les Belles Lettres, 1979.

_____. *Chariton von Aphrodisias. Kallirhoe*. Ed. Karl Plepelits. Bibliothek der griechischen Literatur 6. Stuttgart: Anton Hiersemann, 1976.

Chronographus Anni CCCLIIII. Ed. Theodor Mommsen. Chronica Minora I. MGH, AA IX. Berlin: Weidmann, 1892.

Claudian. *Claudian, With an English Translation*. Trans. Maurice Platnauer. 2 vols. Loeb Classical Library. London: William Heinemann; New York: G. P. Putman's Sons, 1922.

"Le Codex arménien Jérusalem 121. II. Edition comparée du texte et de deux autres manuscrits. Introduction, textes, traduction et notes." Ed. Athanase Renoux. PO 36 (1971): 144-388.

Collectio Novariensis de Re Eutychis. Ed. Eduard Schwartz.
  ACO II.2.1. Berlin/Leipzig: Walter de Gruyter
  & Co., 1932.

Collectio Palatina. Ed. Eduard Schwartz. *ACO* I.5.
  Berlin/Leipzig: Walter de Gruyter & Co., 1924-26.

Corpus Inscriptionum Iudaicarum. II: Asie-Afrique. Ed. Jean-
  Baptiste Frey. Sussidi allo Studio delle Antichità
  Cristiane 3. Città del Vaticano: Pontificio
  Istituto di Archeologia Cristiana, 1952.

Corpus Inscriptionum Latinarum. Eds. E. Borman et al. Berlin: G. Reimarus, 1876-1885.

Corpus Iuris Civilis. Vol. I, *Institutiones*. Ed. Paulus
  Krueger. *Digesta*. Ed. Theodorus Mommsen. Berlin:
  Weidmann, 1893. Vol. II, *Codex Iustinianus*. Ed.
  Paulus Krueger. Berlin: Weidmann, 1892. Vol.
  III, *Novellae*. Ed. Rudolfus Schoell. Berlin:
  Weidmann, 1895.

Cyril of Scythopolis. *Kyrillos von Skythopolis*. Ed. Eduard
  Schwartz. TU 49: 2. Leipzig: J. C. Hinrichs
  Verlag, 1939.

Early Christianity Biographies. Trans. Roy J. Deferrari et
  al. The Fathers of the Church 15. New York:
  Fathers of the Church, 1952.

Egeria. *Peregrinatio ad Loca Sancta*. In *Itinera Hierosolymitana Saeculi IIII-VIII*, ed. Paul Geyer. CSEL 39.
  Prague/Vienna: F. Tempsky; Leipzig: G. Freytag,
  1898.

_____. *Diary of a Pilgrimage*.
  Trans. George E. Gingras. Ancient Christian Writers
  38. New York/Ramsey, N.J.: Newman Press, 1970.

_____. *Egeria's Travels*. Trans.
  John Wilkinson. London: S. P. C. K., 1971.

_____. *Ethérie. Journal de
  voyage. Texte latin, introduction et traduction*. Trans.
  Hélène Pétré. Sources Chrétiennes 21. Paris: Les
  Editions du Cerf, 1948.

Euphémie de Chalcédoine. Légendes byzantines. Ed. Francois
Halkin. SubsHag 41. Bruxelles: Société des
Bollandistes, 1965.

Evagrius Ponticus. *Evagriana Syriaca: textes inédites de
British Museum et de la Vaticane.* Ed. and trans. J.
Muyldermans. Bibliothèque du Muséon 31. Louvain:
Publications Universitaires/Institut Orientaliste,
1952.

Evagrius Scholasticus. *Ecclesiastica Historia. The Ecclesiastical History of Evagrius with the Scholia.* Ed. J. Bidez
and L. Parmentier. London: Methuen, 1898.

Gesta Chalcedone. Ed. Eduard Schwartz. *ACO* II.1.1.
Berlin/Leipzig: Walter de Gruyter & Co., 1933.

Gregory of Nazianzus. *Oratio* VIII: *In Laudem Sororis Suae-
Gorgoniae.* PG 35 (1886): cols. 789-818.

Haslam, M. W., ed. "Narrative about Tinouphis in
Prosimetrum." In *Papyri Greek and Egyptian Edited in
Various Hands in Honour of Eric Gardner Turner.* Egypt
Exploration Society, Graeco-Roman Memoirs 68.
London: Egypt Exploration Society, 1981.

Heliodorus. *Aethiopica. Les Ethiopiques (Théagène et
Chariclée).* Ed. R. M. Rattenbury and T. W. Lumb. 3
vols. Paris: Société d'Edition 'Les Belles Lettres, 1935, 1938, 1943.

_____. *Heliodor. Aithiopika. Die Abenteur der schönen
Chariklea. Ein griechischer Liebesroman.* Ed. Rudolf
Reymer. Zürich: Artemis-Verlag, 1950.

Historia Monachorum in Aegypto. Edition critique du texte grec.
Ed. André-Jean Festugière, SubsHag 53. Bruxelles:
Société des Bollandistes, 1971.

_____. PL 21 (1878): cols. 391-462.

Itinera Hierosolymitana et Descriptiones Terrae Sanctae. Ed.
Augustus Molinier and Carolus Kohler. Geneva:
J.-G. Fick, 1885.

Itinerarium Burdigalense. In *Itinera Hierosolymitana Saeculi
IIII-VIII.* Ed. Paul Geyer. CSEL 39. Prague/Vienna:
F. Tempsky; Leipzig: G. Freytag, 1898.

Jerome. *Contra Joannem Hierosolymitanum*. PL 23 (1883):
     cols. 371-412.

_____. *Contra Rufinum*. PL 23 (1883): cols. 415-514.

_____. *Epistolae*. Ed. Isidorus Hilberg. CSEL 54, 55,
     56. Vienna: F. Tempsky; Leipzig: G. Freytag,
     1910, 1912.

_____. (Eusebius') *Chronicon*. PL (1866): cols. 11-508.

_____. *Homilia de Nativitate Dei*. In *S. Hieronymi Presbyteri
     Opera*. Part II, *Opera Homiletica*, ed. Germain Morin.
     2d ed. CCL 78. Brepols: Turnholt, 1958.

_____. *Vita Hilarionis Eremitae*. PL 23 (1883): cols. 29-
     54.

_____. *Vita Malchi Monachi Captivi*. PL 23 (1883): cols.
     55-62.

_____. *Vita Pauli Primi Eremitae*. PL 23 (1883): cols.
     17-30.

John Phocas. *Descriptio Terrae Sanctae*. PG 133 (1864):
     cols. 927-962.

John Rufus. *Plerophoria. Plérophories. Témoignages et révéla-
     tions contre le Concile de Chalcédoine. Version syriaque et
     traduction française*. Ed., trans. F. Nau. PO 8 (1912):
     11-183.

*Liber Pontificalum. Le Liber Pontificalis. Texte, introduction
     et commentaire*. Ed. L. Duchesne. 3 vols. Biblio-
     thèque des Ecoles Françaises d'Athènes et de Rome.
     2d ser. Paris: Ernest Tholin, 1886.

Lipomani, Aloysius. *De Probatis Sanctorum Historiis*. Colonia
     Agrippina [Cologne]: 1570.

Lollianus. *Die Phoinikika des Lollianus. Fragmente eines neuen
     griechischen Roman*. Ed. Albert Henrichs. Papyrolo-
     gische Texte und Abhandlungen 14. Bonn: Rudolf
     Habelt Verlag, 1972.

Longus. *Daphnis et Chloe (Pastorales)*. Ed. Georges Dalmeyda.
     2d ed. Paris: Société d'Edition 'Les Belles Let-
     tres,' 1960.

The Love Romances of Parthenius and Other Fragments. Trans. Stephen Gaselee. Loeb Classical Library. London: William Heinemann; Cambridge, Mass.: Harvard University Press, 1935.

Marcellinus. *Chronicon*. Ed. Theodor Mommsen. Chronica Minora II. MGH, AA XI. Berlin: Weidmann, 1894.

Martyrologium Romanum. Ed. Hippolyte Delehaye et al. *AASS* 68. *Propylaeum ad Acta Sanctorum Decembris*. Bruxelles: Société des Bollandistes, 1940.

Martyrologium Usuardi Monachi. Ed. J. B. DuSollier; rev. L. M. Rigollot and J. Carnandet. *AASS* 26. Paris/Rome: Victor Palmé, 1866.

Menologium Basilianum. PG 117 (1894): cols. 19-614.

Narratio de Obitu Theodosii Hierosolymorum et Romani Monachi. In *Vitae Virorum apud Monophysitas Celeberrimorum*. Vol. I. Ed. E. W. Brooks. CSCO, Scriptores Syri, vols. 7 and 8. Louvain: L. Durbecq, 1977.

Natali, Pietro de. *Catalogus Sanctorum et Gestorum Eorum ex Diversis Voluminibus Collectus*. Venice: B. de Zanis, 1506.

Nicetas Eugenianus. *Drosillae et Chariclis. Nicetae Eugeniani Narrationem Amatoriam et Constantini Manassis Fragmenta*. Ed. J. F. Boissanade. Lugdunum Batavorum (Leyden): J. Luchtmans, 1819.

Origen. *On First Principles*. Ed. G. W. Butterworth. New York: Harper & Row, 1966.

Orosius. *Historia adversum Paganos*. Ed. Karl Zangemeister. CSEL 5. Vienna: C. Geroldi Filium, 1882.

Pachomiana Latina. Ed. Amand Boon. Bibliothèque de la Revue d'Histoire Ecclésiastique 7. Louvain: Bureaux de la Revue, 1932.

Palladius. *Dialogus de Vita Joannis Chrysostomi*. Ed. P. R. Coleman-Norton. Cambridge: Cambridge University Press, 1982.

_____. *Historia Lausiaca. The Lausiac History of Palladius.* Ed. Cuthbert Butler. Texts and Studies VI.1-2. Cambridge: Cambridge University Press, 1898-1904.

_____. *The Lausiac History.* Trans. Robert T. Meyer. Ancient Christian Writers 34. New York/Ramsey, N.J.: Newman Press, 1964.

_____. *Les Formes syriaques de la matière de l'Histoire Lausiaque.* Ed. René Draguet. 2 vols. in 4 (=t. 169-170, 173-174). CSCO, Scriptores Syri. Louvain: Secrétariat du Corpus SCO, 1978.

Paulinus of Milan. *Vita Sancti Ambrosii.* PL 14 (1882): cols. 29-50.

Paulinus of Nola (Pontius Meropius Paulinus). *Carmina.* Ed. Wilhelm von Hartel. CSEL 30. Prague/Vienna: F. Tempsky; Leipzig: G. Freytag, 1894.

_____. *The Poems of Paulinus of Nola.* Ed. P. G. Walsh. Ancient Christian Writers 40. New York/Ramsey, N.J.: Newman Press, 1975.

_____. *Epistolae.* Ed. Wilhelm von Hartel. CSEL 29. Prague/Vienna: F. Tempsky; Leipzig: G. Freytag, 1894.

_____. *The Letters of Paulinus of Nola.* Trans. P. G. Walsh. 2 vols. Ancient Christian Writers 35-36. New York/Ramsey, N.J.: Newman Press, 1966, 1967.

Photius. *Bibliotheca.* PG 103 (1900): cols. 41-1588.

Plutarch. "Publicola." In *Plutarch's Lives.* English trans. Bernadotte Perrin. Vol. I. Loeb Classical Library. London: William Heinemann; New York: G. P. Putnam's Sons, 1914.

Pontius. *Vita Cypriani. Ponzio. Vita e martirio di San Cipriano. Introduzione, testo critico, versione e note.* Ed. Michele Pellegrino. Alba: Edizione Paoline, 1955.

Proclus of Constantinople. *Opera Omnia.* PG 65 (1864):
    cols. 679-888.

The Prosopography of the Later Roman Empire. Vol. I, A.D. 260-395.
    Eds. A. H. M. Jones, J. R. Martindale, and J. Mor-
    ris. *Vol. II, A.D. 395-527.* Ed. J. R. Martindale.
    Cambridge: Cambridge University Press, 1971, 1980.

Pseudo-Clement. *Homiliae.* In *Die Pseudoklementinen*, Vol. I,
    Homilien, ed. Bernhard Rehm. GCS 42. Berlin:
    Akademie-Verlag; Leipzig: J. C. Hinrichs Verlag,
    1953.

——————————. *Recognitiones.* In *Die Pseudoklementinen*,
    Vol. II, *Rekognitionen*, ed. Bernhard Rehm. GCS 51.
    Berlin: Akademie-Verlag, 1965.

"Revelatio Sancti Stephani." Ed. S. Vanderlinden. *REB*
    4 (1946): 178-217.

*Rituale Armenorum, Being the Administration of the Sacraments and
    the Breviary Rites of the Armenian Church, Together With the
    Greek Rites of Baptism and Epiphany.* Ed. F. C. Conybeare;
    trans. A. J. Maclean. Oxford: Clarendon Press,
    1905.

Rufinus of Aquileia. *Tyranni Rufini Opera.* Ed. Manlio
    Simonetti. CCL 20. Turnholt: Brepols, 1961.

Salvian. *De Gubernatione Dei.* In *Opera Omnia*, ed. Franz
    Pauly. CSEL 8. Vienna: C. Geroldi Filium, 1883.

Seneca, Annaeus. *Oratorum et Rhetorum. Sententiae Divisiones.
    Colores.* Ed. Adolphus Kiessling. 1872. Reprint.
    Stuttgart: B. G. Teubner, 1967.

Severus, Sulpicius. *Vita Martini. Vie de Saint Martin. In-
    troduction, texte, et traduction.* Trans. Jacques Fon-
    taine. 3 vols. SC 133. Paris: Les Editions du
    Cerf, 1967.

Simeon Logothetes. *Vita et Conversatio Sanctae Melanae
    Romanae.* PG 116 (1891): cols. 753-793.

Socrates Scholasticus. *Ecclesiastica Historia.* Ed. Rober-
    tus Hussey. 3 vols. Oxford: Oxford University
    Press, 1853.

Sozomen. *Historia Ecclesiastica. Kirchengeschichte.* Ed.
    Joseph Bidez. GCS 50. Berlin: Akademie Verlag,
    1960.

Symmachus. *Q. Aurelii Symmachi Quae Supersunt.* Ed. Otto
    Seeck. MGH, AA VI. Berlin: Weidmann, 1883.

Synaxarium Ecclesiae Constantinopolitanae. Ed. Hippolyte Dele-
    haye. *AASS* 62. *Propylaeum ad Acta Sanctorum Novembris.*
    Bruxelles: Société des Bollandistes, 1902.

*Theodosiani Libri XVI cum Constitutionibus Sirmondianis et Leges
    Novellae ad Theodosianum Pertinentes.* Ed. Theodor
    Mommsen and Paul M. Meyer. Berlin: Weidmann, 1954.

Theodosius the Deacon. *De Situ Terrae Sanctae.* In *Itinera
    Hierosolymitana Saeculi IIII-VIII*, ed. Paul Geyer. CSEL
    39. Prague/Vienna: F. Tempsky; Leipzig: G.
    Freytag, 1898.

Theophanes. *Chronographia.* Ed. Carolus deBoor. Hilde-
    sheim: G. Olms, 1963.

Three Greek Romances. Trans. Moses Hadas. Indianapolis:
    Bobbs-Merrill, 1964.

*Vita Melaniae Junioris. Santa Melania Giuniore, senatrice romana:
    documenti contemporei e note.* Ed. Mariano del Tindaro
    Rampolla. Roma: Tipografia Vaticana, 1905 (Greek
    and Latin texts).

_____. *Vie de Sainte Mélanie.* Ed. Denys
    Gorce. SC 90. Paris: Editions du Cerf, 1962
    (Greek text).

_____. *Das Leben der Heiligen Melania von
    Gerontius.* Trans. St. Krottenthaler. In *Griechische
    Liturgien.* Trans. Remigius Storf. Bibliothek der
    Kirchenväter 5. Kempten/München: Jos. Köselschen
    Buchhandlung, 1912.

_____. *Gerontius's Sanctae Melaniae Junioris Vita
    (The Life of Saint Melania the Younger): A Translation with
    Introduction, Notes, and Commentary.* Theodore C.
    Papaloizos. Unpublished Ph.D. dissertation. The
    Catholic University of America, 1977.

Vita Petri Hiberii. Petrus der Iberer. Ein Charakterbild zur Kirchen-und Sittengeschichte des fünften Jahrhunderts. Ed. Richard Raabe. Leipzig: J. C. Hinrichs'sche Buchhandlung, 1895.

Vita Theclae. Vie et miracles de Sainte Thècle: texte grec, traduction et commentaire. Ed. and trans. Gilbert Dagron. SubsHag 62. Bruxelles: Société des Bollandistes, 1978.

Xenophon. *Ephesiaca. Ephesiacorum Libri V. De Amoribus Anthiae et Abrocomae.* Ed. Antonius D. Papanikolaou. Leipzig: B. G. Teubner, 1973.

Zacharias Rhetor. *Historia Ecclesiatica.* Ed. E. W. Brooks. CSCO. Scriptores Syri, vols. 38-39 (=83-84) Syriac; vols. 41-42 (=87-88) Latin. Louvain: L. Durbecq, 1953.

Zosimus. Ed. Immanuel Bekker. CSHB 30. Bonn: Ed. Weber, 1837.

II. SECONDARY SOURCES

Aigrain, René. *L'Hagiographie: ses sources, ses méthodes, son histoire.* Paris: Bloud & Gay, 1953.

Allard, Paul. "Une Grande Fortune romaine au cinquième siècle." *RQH* 81 (1907): 5-30.

Altheim, Franz. *Literatur und Gesellschaft im ausgehenden Altertum.* 2 vols. Halle/Salle: Max Niemeyer Verlag, 1948.

Antolin, Guillermo. *Un Codex Regularum del Siglo IX: opúsculos desconocidos de S. Jerónimo: historia, estudio y description.* Madrid: Imprenta Helenica, 1908.

Arnheim, M. T. W. *The Senatorial Aristocracy in the Later Roman Empire.* Oxford: Clarendon Press, 1972.

Atti del IIe Congresso Internazionale di Archeologia Cristiana, 1900. Roma: Libreria Spithöver, 1902.

Barnes, Timothy D. *The New Empire of Diocletian and Constantine.* Cambridge, Mass./London: Harvard University Press, 1982.

Bartelink, G. J. M. "Quelques Observations sur la bio-
    graphie chrétienne greco-latine." *Orpheus* 7 (1960):
    45-50.

Bauer, Franz X. *Proklos von Konstantinopel. Ein Beitrag zur
    Kirchen-und Dogmengeschichte des 5. Jahrhunderts.* Veröf-
    fentlichungen aus dem Kirchenhistorischen Seminar
    München, IV Reihe, Nr. 8. München: J. J.
    Lentnerschen Buchhandlung, 1919.

Baumstark, Anton. *Comparative Liturgy.* Rev. B. Botte;
    trans. F. L. Cross. Westminster, Md.: Newman
    Press, 1958.

Beck, Hans-Georg. "Marginalien zum byzantinischen
    Roman." In *Kyklos, Festschrift R. Keydall,* ed. H.-G.
    Beck et al. Berlin/New York: Walter de Gruyter,
    1978.

Beissel, Stephan. "Die Hingabe eines ausserordentlich
    grossen Vermögens. Eine heroische Tat der Hl.
    Melania." *Stimmen aus Maria-Lach* 71 (1906): 477-490.

Blumenthal, Martin. *Formen und Motive in den apokryphen
    Apostelgeschichten.* TU 48.1. Leipzig: J. C. Hin-
    richs, 1933.

Bernard, Botte. *Les Origines de la Noël et de l'Epiphanie.
    Etude historique.* Textes et Etudes Liturgiques 1.
    Louvain: Abbaye du Mont César, 1932.

Bouyer, Louis. *La Vie de S. Antoine. Essai sur la spiritualité
    du monachisme primitif.* 2d ed. Spiritualité Orientale
    22. Bégrolles en Mauges: Abbaye de Bellefontaine,
    1977.

Bovini, Giuseppe. *Monumenti figurati paleocristiani conservati
    a Firenze nelle raccolte publiche e negli edifici di culto.*
    Monumenti di Antichità Cristiana, 2d ser., 6.
    Città del Vaticano: Pontificio Istituto di Arche-
    ologia Cristiana, 1950.

Braun, Martin. *History and Romance in Graeco-Oriental History.*
    Oxford: Basil Blackwell, 1938.

Brown, Peter. "Aspects of the Christianization of the
    Roman Aristocracy." *JRS* 51 (1961): 1-11.

_____. *Augustine of Hippo. A Biography*. Berkeley/ Los Angeles: University of California Press, 1969.

_____. *The Cult of the Saints: Its Rise and Function in Latin Christianity*. Chicago: University of Chicago Press, 1981.

_____. "The Patrons of Pelagius." *JThS*, n.s., 21 (1970): 56-72.

_____. *Religion and Society in the Age of Augustine*. London: Faber and Faber Ltd., 1972.

_____. "Religious Coercion in the Later Roman Empire; The case of North Africa." *History*, n.s., 48 (1963): 283-305.

_____. "The Rise and Function of the Holy Man in Late Antiquity," *JRS* 61 (1971): 80-101.

_____. *Society and the Holy in Late Antiquity*. Berkeley: University of California Press, 1982.

Butler, E. C. "Cardinal Rampolla's Melania the Younger." *JThS* 7 (1906): 630-632.

Cabrol, Fernand. *Les Eglises de Jérusalem. La Discipline et la liturgie au IVe siècle. Etude sur la Peregrinatio Silviae*. Paris/Poitiers: Librairie Religieuse H. Oudin, 1895.

Cameron, Alan. *Claudian. Poetry and Propaganda at the Court of Honorius*. Oxford: Clarendon Press, 1970.

_____. "The Date and Identity of Macrobius." *JRS* 56 (1966): 25-38.

_____. "Paganism and Literature in Late Fourth Century Rome." In *Christianisme et formes littéraires de l'antiquité tardive en Occident*, ed. Alan Cameron et al. Entretiens sur l'Antiquité Classique 23. Geneva: Fondation Hardt, 1977.

_____. "Rutlius Namatianus, St. Augustine, and the Date of the *De Reditu*." *JRS* 57 (1967): 31-39.

Casson, Lionel. *Travel in the Ancient World*. London: George Allen and Unwin, 1974.

Chapman, John. "On the Date of the Clementines." *ZNW*
     9 (1908): 21-34, 147-159.

Chastagnol, André. *Les Fastes de la préfecture de Rome au Bas-
     Empire*. Etudes Prosopographiques II. Paris:
     Nouvelles Editions Latines, 1962.

_____. "Le Sénateur Volusien et la conver-
     sion d'une famille de l'aristocratie romaine au
     Bas-Empire." *REA* 58 (1956): 241-253.

Chirat, H. "Comptes rendus: *Vie de Sainte Mélanie*, par
     Denys Gorce." *RSR* 38 (1964): 97-100.

Chitty, Derwas. *The Desert A City: An Introduction to the
     Study of Egyptian and Palestinian Monasticism under the
     Christian Empire*. Oxford: Basil Blackwell, 1966.

Clark, Elizabeth A. "Ascetic Renunciation and Feminine
     Advancement: A Paradox of Late Ancient Chris-
     tianity." *Anglican Theological Review* 63 (1981): 240-
     257.

_____. "Authority and Humility: A Conflict
     of Values in Fourth-Century Female Monasticism."
     BZ 76 (1983). Forthcoming.

_____. "Claims on the Bones of Saint
     Stephen: The Partisans of Melania and Eudocia."
     CH 51 (1982): 141-156.

Clermont-Ganneau, Ch. "Deux Nouvelles Inscriptions
     grecques du Mont des Oliviers," *Recueil d'Archéologie
     Orientale* 5 (1903): 163-169.

Colini, Antonio M. *Storia e topographia del Celio nell' anti-
     chità*. Atti della Pontificia Accademia Romana di
     Archeologia, Memorie 7. Roma: Tipografia Poli-
     glotta Vaticana, 1944.

Corbo, Virgilio C., ed. *Richerche archeologiche al Monte
     degli Ulivi*. Pubblicazioni dello Studium Biblicum
     Franciscanum 16. Jerusalem: Tipografia dei Padri
     Francescani, 1965.

Coüasnon, Charles. *The Church of the Holy Sepulchre in Jeru-
     salem*. The Schweich Lectures of the British Acade-
     my, 1972. London: Oxford University Press, 1974.

Courcelle, Pierre. *Les Confessions de Saint Augustin dans le tradition littéraire: antécédents et postérité.* Paris: Etudes Augustiniennes, 1963.

_____. *Les Lettres grecques en occident de Macrobe à Cassiodore.* Paris: E. de Boccard, 1948.

Couret, C. "La Prise de Jérusalem par les Perses en 614." *ROC* 2 (1897): 125-164.

Cox, Patricia. *Biography in Late Antiquity: A Quest for the Holy Man.* The Transformation of the Classical Heritage 5. Berkeley: University of California Press, 1983.

D'Alès, Adhémar. "Les Deux Vies de Sainte Mélanie le Jeune." *AB* 25 (1906): 401-450.

_____. "Sainte Mélanie la Jeune d'après un livre du Cardinal Rampolla." *Etudes* 108 (1906): 221-240.

Davies, J. G. "The Peregrinatio Egeriae and the Ascension." *VChr* 8 (1954): 93-100.

Davies, Stevan L. *The Revolt of the Windows: The Social World of the Apocryphal Acts.* Carbondale, Ill.: Southern Illinois University Press, 1980.

Deichmann, F. W. "Märtyrerbasilika, Martyrion, Memoria und Altargrab." *Mitteilungen des deutschen archaeologischen Instituts. Roemische Abteilung* 77 (1970): 144-169.

Delehaye, Hippolyte. *Etude sur le légendier romain. Les saints de Novembre et de Décembre.* SubsHag 23. Bruxelles: Société des Bollandistes, 1936.

_____. "The Forty Martyrs of Sebaste." *American Catholic Quarterly Review* 24 (1899): 161-171.

_____. "Le Ménologe de Métaphraste." *AB* 17 (1898): 448-452.

_____. *Les Légendes hagiographiques.* 2d ed. Bruxelles: Bureaux de la Société des Bollandistes, 1906.

_____. "Les Ménologes grecs." *AB* 16
(1897): 311-329.

_____. *Les Origines du culte des martyrs.* 2d
ed., rev. SubsHag 20. Bruxelles: Société des
Bollandistes, 1933.

_____. *Les Passions des martyrs et les genres
littéraires.* Bruxelles: Bureaux de la Société des
Bollandistes, 1921.

_____. Review of *Santa Melania Giuniore* by
Mariano Rampolla. *AB* 25 (1906): 204-206.

_____. "S. Melaniae Iunioris. Acta
Graeca." *AB* 22 (1903): 5-50.

_____. "Simeon Metaphrastes." *AER*, 3d ser.,
3 (=23; 1900): 113-120.

_____. "La Vie de Saint Paul le Jeune et
la chronologie de Métaphraste," *RQH* 54 (1893): 49-85.

Demandt, Alexander, and Guntram Brummer. "Der Prozess
gegen Serena im Jahre 408 n. Chr." *Historia* 26
(1977): 479-502.

Demougeot, E. *De l'Unité à la division de l'Empire romain, 395-
410. Essai sur le gouvernement impérial.* Paris:
Librairie d'Amérique et d'Orient Adrien Maisonneuve,
1951.

DeRossi, G. B. "La casa dei Valerii sul Celio et il
monastero di S. Erasmo." *Studi e Documenti di Storia
e Diritto* 7 (1886): 235-243.

_____. "Dei primi monumenti cristiani di
Ginevra, e specialmente d'una lucerna di terra cotta colle immagini dei dodici apostoli," *BACr* 5
(1867): 23-28.

_____. "Nuove scoperte nel cimitero di Priscil-
la per le escavazione fatte nell' a. 1887," *BACr*,
4th ser., 5 (1887): 7-35.

DeSmedt, Carolus. "Vita Sanctae Melaniae Junioris."
AB 8 (1889): 16-63.

Devos, Paul. "La Date du voyage d'Egérie." *AB* 85 (1967): 165-194.

_____. "La 'Servante de Dieu' Poemenia d'après Pallade, le tradition copte et Jean Rufus." *AB* 87 (1969): 189-212.

_____. "Quand Pierre l'Ibère vint-il à Jérusalem?" *AB* 86 (1968): 337-350.

De Waal, Anton. "Aus der Vita Melaniae jun." *RQ* 21 (1907): 28-37.

Dihle, Albrecht. *Studien zur griechischen Biographie.* Abh der Akademie der Wissenschaften, Gött., philol.-hist. Klasse, ser. 3, 37. Göttingen: Vandenhoeck & Ruprecht, 1956.

Dobschütz, Ernst von. "Der Roman in der altchristlichen Literatur." *Deutsche Rundschau* 111 (1902): 87-106.

Dörrie, Heinrich. "Die griechischen Romane und das Christentum." *Philologus* 93 (1938): 273-276.

Draguet, René. "Butleriana: Une Mauvaise Cause et son malchanceux avocat." *Le Muséon* 68 (1955): 239-258.

Dubois, Jean. "Un Témoin de la vie intellectuelle à Saint-Germain-des-Près au IXe siécle: Le Martyrologe d'Usuard." *Revue d'Histoire de l'Eglise de France* 43 (1957): 35-48.

Ehrhard, Albert. *Überlieferung und Bestand der hagiographischen und homiletischen Literatur der griechischen Kirche von den Anfängen bis zum Ende des 16. Jahrhunderts.* TU 50, 51, 52. Leipzig: J. C. Hinrichs, 1937, 1938, 1952.

Ensslin, Wilhelm. "Placidia," *RE* XX.2 (1950): cols. 1910-1933.

_____. "Proklos." *RE* XXIII.1 (1957): cols. 183-186.

Evans, Robert F. *Pelagius: Inquiries and Reappraisals.* New York: Seabury Press, 1968.

Fabre, Pierre. *Essai sur la chronologie de l'oeuvre de Saint Paulin de Nole.* Publications de la Faculté des Lettres

de l'Université de Strasbourg 109. Paris: "Les
Belles Lettres," 1948.

Fabricius, Ulrich. *Die Legende im Bild des Jahrtausends der
Kirche. Der Einfluss der Apokryphen und Pseudepigraphen auf
die altchristliche und byzantinische Kunst.* Kassel: J.
C. Onken Verlag, 1956.

Faye, Eugène de. *Origène: sa vie, son oeuvre, sa pensée.*
Vol. II, *L'Ambiance philosophique.* Vol. III, *La Doctrine.*
Bibliothèque de l'Ecole des Haute Etudes, sciences
religieuses 43, 44. Paris: Ernest Leroux, 1927-
1928.

Ferotin, D. Marius. *Le Liber Ordinum en usage dans l'église
wisigothique et mozarabe d'espagne du cinquième au onzième
siècle.* Monumenta Ecclesiae Liturgica 5. Paris:
Librairie de Firmin-Didot, 1904.

Festugière, A.-J. "Le Problem littéraire de l'Historia
Monachorum." *Hermes* 83 (1955): 257-284.

Feuillatre, E. *Etudes sur les 'Ethiopiques' d'Héliodore.* Con-
tribution à la connaissance du roman grec. Publications
de la Faculté des Lettres et Sciences Humaines de
Poitiers 2. Paris: Presses Universitaires de
France, 1966.

"Fiches et Notules." *Recueil d'Archéologie Orientale* 5
(1903): 177-186.

Fleming, Johannes. "Akten der Ephesinischen Synode vom
Jahre 449, syrisch mit Georg Hoffmanns deutscher
Übersetzung und seinen Anmerkungen." Abh Gött.
philol.-hist. Kl., N.F., 15.1. Berlin: Weidmannsche Buchhandlung, 1917.

Fleschenberg, Otmar Schiffel von. *Entwicklungsgeschichte
des griechischen Romanes im Altertum.* Halle a.S.: Max
Niemeyer, 1913.

Fontaine, Jacques. "Valeurs antiques et valeurs chrétiennes dans la spiritualité des grand propriétaires
terriens à la fin du IVe siècle occidental." In
*Epektasis. Mélanges patristiques offerts au Cardinal Jean
Daniélou,* ed. Jacques Fontaine and Charles Kannengiesser. Paris: Beauschesne, 1972.

Frankenberg, Wilhelm. *Euagrius Ponticus*. Abh Gött.,
    philol.-hist. Kl., n.f., 13.2. Berlin: Weidmann,
    1912.

Fremantle, William H. "Melania (2)." In *Dictionary of
    Christian Biography*, eds. William Smith and Henry
    Wace. Vol. III. London: John Murray, 1882.

_____. "Pinianus (2)." In *Dictionary of
    Christian Biography*, eds. William Smith and Henry
    Wace. Vol. IV. London: John Murray, 1887.

Fuhrmann, Manfred. "Die Mönchsgeschichten des Hierony-
    mus. Formexperimente in erzählender Literatur."
    In *Christianisme et formes littéraires de l'antiquité tar-
    dive en Occident*, ed. Alan Cameron et al. Entretiens
    sur l'Antiquité Classique 23. Geneva: Fondation
    Hardt, 1977.

Gaiffier, Baudouin de. *Recueil d'hagiographie*. SubsHag 61.
    Bruxelles: Société des Bollandistes, 1977.

Garitte, Gerard. *Un Témoin important du texte de la Vie de S.
    Antoine par S. Athanase. La Version latine inédite des
    Archives du Chapitre de S. Pierre à Rome*. Etudes de
    Philologie, d'Archéologie et d'Histoire Anciennes
    3. Bruxelles: Palais des Académies; Rome:
    Academia Belgica, 1939.

Gatti, Giuseppe. "Le casa celimontana dei Valerii e il
    monastero di S. Erasmo." *BullComm* 30 (1902): 145-
    163.

Gaudemet, Jean. "Les Transformations de la vie familiale
    au Bas-Empire et l'influence du Christianisme."
    Romanitas 5 (1962): 58-85.

Geffcken, Johannes. *Christliche Apokryphen*. Religionsge-
    schichtliche Volksbücher für die deutsche christ-
    liche Gegenwart, I.15. Tübingen: J. C. B. Mohr
    [Paul Siebeck], 1908.

Giangrande, Giuseppe. "On the Origins of the Greek
    Romance: The Birth of a Literary Form." *Eranos*
    60 (1962): 132-159.

Gorce, Denys. *La Lectio divina. Des Origines du cénobitisme
    a Saint Benoît et Cassiodore*. Vol. I, *Saint Jérome et la*

lecture sacrée dans le milieu ascetique romain. Paris:
Libraire Auguste Picard; Wépion-sur-Meuse: Monastère du Mont-Vierge, 1925.

_____. *Les Voyages, l'hospitalité et le port des lettres
dans le monde chrétien des IVe et Ve siècles.* Wépion-sur-
Meuse: Monastère du Mont-Vierge; Paris: Librairie
Auguste Picard, 1925.

Gordini, Gian Domenico. "Il Monachesimo romano in
Palestina nel IV secolo." In *Saint Martin et son
temps.* Studia Anselmiana 46. Rome: Herder, 1961.

_____. "Origine e sviluppo del mona-
chesimo a Roma." *Gregorianum* 37 (1956): 220-260.

Goubert, Paul. "Le Rôle de Sainte Pulchérie et l'eunuque
Chrysaphios." In *Das Konzil von Chalkedon: Geschichte
und Gegenwart,* ed. A. Grillmeier and H. Bacht. 3
vols. Würzburg: Echter-Verlag, 1954.

Goyau, Georges. *Sainte Mélanie.* Paris: Lecoffre, 1952.

Gregg, Robert C., and Dennis E. Groh. *Early Arianism: A
View of Salvation.* Philadelphia: Fortress Press,
1981.

Grumel, V. *Traité d'études byzantines. I: La Chronologie.*
Paris: Presses Universitaires de France, 1958.

Guillaumont, Antoine. *Les 'Kephalaia Gnostica' d'Evagre le
Pontique et l'histoire de l'Origènisme chez les Grecs et chez
les Syriens.* Patristica Sorbonensia 5. Paris:
Editions du Seuil, 1962.

Gutschmid, Alfred von. "Die Königsnamen in den apokryphen Apostelgeschichte. Ein Beitrag zur Kenntnis
des geschichtlichen Romans." *Rheinisches Museum* 19
(1964): 161-183, 380-401.

Hadas, Moses, and Morton Smith. *Heroes and Gods. Spiritual
Biographies in Antiquity.* New York: Harper & Row,
1965.

Hägg, Tomas. *Narrative Technique in Ancient Greek Romances.
Studies of Chariton, Xenophon Ephesius, and Achilles Tatius.*
Skrifter Utgivna av Svenska Institutet i Athen, 8°,
8. Stockholm: Svenska Institutet i Athen, 1971.

_____. *The Novel in Antquity*. Berkeley/Los Angeles: University of California Press, 1983.

Hagendahl, Harald. *Latin Fathers and the Classics. A Study on the Apologists, Jerome, and Other Christian Writers*. Studia Graeca et Latina Gothoburgensia 6. Göteborg: Elanders Boktr. Aktiebolag, 1958.

Haight, Elizabeth Hazelton. *Essays on the Greek Romances*. New York: Longmans, Green & Co., 1943.

_____. *More Essays on the Greek Romances*. New York: Longmans, Green & Co., 1945.

Hammond, C. P. "The Last Ten Years of Rufinus' Life and the Date of His Move South from Aquileia." *JThS*, n.s., 28 (1977): 372-427.

Helm, Rudolf. *Der antike Roman*. Berlin: Wissenschaftliche Editionsgesellschaft, 1948.

Hendrikx, E. "Saint Jérôme en tant qu'hagiographe." *La Ciudad de Dios* 181 (1968): 661-667.

Holl, Karl. "Die schriftstellerische Form des griechischen Heiligenlebens." *Neue Jahrbücher für klassische Altertum* 29 (1912): 406-427.

Holum, Kenneth. *Theodosian Empresses: Women and Imperial Dominion in Late Antiquity*. Berkeley: University of California Press, 1982.

Holzhey, Carl. *Die Thekla-Akten. Ihre Verbreitung und Beurteilung in der Kirche*. Veröffentlichungen aus dem kirchenhistorischen Seminar-München II.7. München: J. J. Lentner, 1905.

Honigmann, Ernest. "Juvenal of Jerusalem." *DOP* 5 Cambridge, Mass.: Harvard University Press, 1950: 211-279.

Hunt, E. D. *Holy Land Pilgrimages in the Later Roman Empire, A.D. 312-460*. Oxford: Clarendon Press, 1982.

_____. "Palladius of Helenopolis: A Party and Its Supporters in the Church of the Late Fourth Century." *JThS*, n.s., 24 (1973): 456-480.

_____. "St. Silvia of Aquitaine: The Role of a Theodosian Pilgrim in the Society of East and West." *JThS*, n.s., 23 (1972): 351-373.

Irmscher, J. "Introduction to the Pseudo-Clementines." In *New Testament Apocrypha*, eds. Edgar Hennecke and Wilhelm Schneemelcher; English trans. and ed. R. McL. Wilson. Vol. II. Philadelphia: Westminster Press, 1965.

Jones, A. H. M. *The Later Roman Empire, 284-602. A Social, Economic and Administrative Survey*. 2 vols. Norman, Ok.: University of Oklahoma Press, 1964.

_____. "The Social Background of the Struggle between Paganism and Christianity in the Fourth Century." In *Paganism and Christianity in the Fourth Century*, ed. Arnaldo Momigliano. Oxford: Clarendon Press, 1963.

Jones, C. P. "Apuleius' *Metamorphoses* and Lollianus' *Phoinikika*." *Phoenix* 34 (1980): 243-254.

Kappelmacher, Alfred. "Sulpicius Severus." *RE* IV.A (1931): col. 869.

Kech, Herbert. *Hagiographie als christliche Unterhaltungsliteratur. Studien zum Phänomen des Erbauchlichen anhand der Mönchsviten des Hl. Hieronymus*. Göppinger Arbeiten zur Germanistik 225. Göppingen: Verlag Alfred Kümmerle, 1977.

Kelly, J. N. D. *Jerome: His Life, Writings, and Controversies*. New York: Harper & Row, 1975.

Kerényi, Karl. *Die griechisch-orientalische Romanliteratur in religionsgeschichtlicher Beleuchtung*. Tübingen: J. C. B. Mohr [Paul Siebeck], 1927.

Kirsch, Johann Peter. *Der stadtrömische christliche Festkalendar im Altertum. Textkritische Untersuchungen zu den römischen "Depositiones" und dem Martyrologium Hieronymianum*. Liturgiegeschichtliche Quellen 7/8. Münster in Westf.: Verlag der Aschendorffschen Verlagsbuchhandlung, 1924.

Kötting, Bernhard. *Peregrinatio Religiosa. Wallfahrten in der Antike und das Pilgerwesen in der alten Kirche*.

Forschungen zur Volkskunde 33-35. Münster Westf.: no pub., 1950.

Kretschmar, Georg. "Festkalendar und Memorialstätten Jerusalems in altkirchlicher Zeit." *ZPalV* 87 (1971): 167-205.

Kurtz, Benjamin P. "From St. Antony to St. Guthlac. A Study in Biography." *University of California Publications in Modern Philology* 12.2 (1926): 103-146.

Lagrange, M.-J. "Chronique de Jérusalem." *RBib* 4 (1895): 88-96.

Lang, D. M. "Peter the Iberian and His Biographers." *Journal of Ecclesiastical History* 2 (1951): 158-168.

Lassère, Jean-Marie. *Ubique Populus. Peuplement et mouvements de population dans l'Afrique romaine de la chute de Carthage à la fin de la dynastie des Sévères (146 a.C.-235 p.C.).* Paris: Editions du Centre National de la Recherche Scientifique, 1977.

Lavagnini, Bruno. *Studi sul romanzo greco.* Messina/Firenze: Casa Editrice G. D'Anna, 1950.

LeClercq, Henri. "Mélanie la Jeune (Sainte)." *DACL* XI.1 (1933): cols. 209-230.

_____. "Vigiles." *DACL* 15.2 (1953): cols. 3108-3113.

Leo, Friedrich. *Die griechisch-römische Biographie nach ihrer litterarischen Form.* Leipzig: G. B. Teubner, 1901. Reprint. Hildesheim: Georg Olms Verlagsbuchhandlung, 1956.

Lepelley, Claude. *Les Cités de l'Afrique romaine au Bas-Empire.* 2 vols. Paris: Etudes Augustiniennes, 1979, 1981.

Levin, David N. "To Whom Did the Ancient Novelists Address Themselves?" *Rivisita di Studi Classici* 25 (1977): 18-29.

Lienhard, Joseph T. *Paulinus of Nola and Early Western Monasticism, With a Study of the Chronology of His Works and an Annotated Bibliography, 1879-1976.* Theophaneia 28. Cologne/Bonn: Peter Hanstein Verlag, 1977.

Lipsius, Richard A.   *Die apokryphen Apostelgeschichten und*
     Apostellegenden. Ein Beitrag zur altchristlichen Literatur-
     geschichte. 3 vols. Braunschweig: C. A. Schwetschke
     und Sohn, 1887.

Lorenz, Rudolf. "Die Anfänge des abenländischen Mönch-
     tums im 4. Jahrhundert." *Zeitschrift für Kirchenges-*
     chichte 77 (1966): 1-61.

Luck, Georg. "Die Form der Suetonischen Biographie und
     die frühen Heiligenviten." In *Mullus. Festschrift*
     Theodor Klausner. Jahrbuch für Antike und Christentum
     Ergänzungsband 1. Münster-West.: Aschendorffsche
     Verlagsbuchhandlung, 1964.

McGeachy, John Alexander, Jr.   *Quintus Aurelius Symmachus*
     and the Senatorial Aristocracy of the West. Chicago:
     University of Chicago Libraries, 1942.

McNabb, Vincent. "Was the Rule of St. Augustine Written
     for St. Melania the Younger?" *JThS* 20 (1919): 242-
     249.

Manganaro, Giacomo. "La reazione pagana a Roma nel 408-
     9 d.C. e il poemetto anonimo 'Contra Paganos'."
     Giornale Italiano di Filologia 13 (1960): 210-224.

Mango, Cyril. "Antique Statuary and the Byzantine Be-
     holder." *DOP* 17 (1963): 55-75.

Markus, R. A. "Paganism, Christianity and the Latin
     Classics in the Fourth Century." In *Latin Literature*
     of the Fourth Century, ed. J. W. Binns. London/Boston:
     Routledge & Kegan Paul, 1974.

Martain, Philibert. "Volusien. Une conversion au Ve
     siècle." *Revue Augustinienne* 10 (1907): 145-172.

Matthews, John. "The Historical Setting of the 'Carmen
     contra paganos'." *Historia* 19 (1970): 464-479.

_____. "The Letters of Symmachus." In *Latin*
     Literature of the Fourth Century, ed. J. W. Binns.
     London: Routledge & Kegan Paul, 1974.

_____. "Olympiodorus of Thebes and the History
     of the West (A.D. 407-425)." *JRS* 60 (1970): 79-97.

_____. *Western Aristocracies and Imperial Court, A.D.
364-425.* Oxford: Clarendon Press, 1975.

Mazal, Otto. "Der griechische und byzantinische Roman
in der Forschung von 1945 bis 1960." *Jahrbuch der
österreichischen byzantinischen Gesellschaft* 11/12 (1962/
1963): 9-55; 13 (1964): 29-86; 14 (1965): 83-124.

Mazzarino, Santo. *Antico, Tardoantico ed era costantiniana.*
Bari: Dedalo Libri, 1974.

_____. *Serena e le due Eudossie.* Quaderni di
Studi Romani. Donne di Roma Antica VII. Roma:
Reale Istituto di Studi Romani, 1946.

_____. *Stilicone. La crisi imperiale dopo Teodo-
sio.* Studi Pubblicati dal R. Istituto Italiano per
la Storia Antica 3. Roma: Angelo Signorelli,
1942.

Meckelbach, Reinhold. *Roman und Mysterium in der Antike.*
München/Berlin: C. H. Beck, 1962.

Mertel, Hans. *Die biographische Form der griechischen Heiligenlegenden.* München: C. Wolf & Sohn, 1909.

Milik, J. T. "Notes d'épigraphie et de topographie
palestiniennes." *RBib* 67 (1960): 550-591.

Miralles, Carlos. "*Eros* as *nosos* in the Greek novel."
In *Erotica Antiqua: Acta of the International Conference
on the Ancient Novel*, Bangor, Wales, 12-17 July 1976,
ed. B. P. Reardon. Bangor: no pub., 1977.

Moine, Nicole. "Melaniana." *RecAug* 15 (1980): 3-79.

_____. "Mélanie la Jeune (Sainte)," *DS* X
(1980): cols. 960-965.

Momigliano, Arnaldo. *The Development of Greek Biography.
Four Lectures.* Cambridge, Mass.: Harvard University Press, 1971.

_____. "Introduction. Christianity and
the Decline of the Roman Empire." In *The Conflict
Between Paganism and Christianity in the Fourth Century*, ed.
Arnaldo Momigliano. Oxford: Clarendon Press,
1963.

Monceaux, Paul. "Les Colonies juives dans l'Afrique
    romaine," *Les Cahiers de Tunisie* 18 (1970): 159-184
    (= *Revue des Etudes Juives* 49 [1904]: 1-28).

──────────────. *Enquête sur l'épigraphie chrétienne d'Afrique.*
    Paris: Imprimerie Nationale, 1907.

Moreau, Madeleine. "Le Dossier Marcellinus dans la
    correspondance de Saint Augustin."   *RecAug* 9 (1973):
    6-181.

──────────────. "Sur un Correspondant d'Augustin:
    qui est donc Publicola?"   *Revue des Etudes Augustinien-
    nes* 28 (1982): 225-238.

Morin, Germain. "Les Monuments de la prédication de
    Saint Jerome."   *Revue d'Histoire et de Littérature
    Religieuses* 1 (1896): 393-434.

Mossay, Justin.   *Les Fêtes de Noël et d'Epiphanie d'après les
    sources littéraires cappadociennes du IVe siècle.*   Textes
    et Etudes Liturgiques 3.   Louvain: Abbaye du Mont
    César, 1965.

Murphy, Francis X. "Melania the Elder: A Biographical
    Note."   *Traditio* 5 (1947): 59-77.

──────────────.   *Rufinus of Aquileia (345-411).   His Life
    and Works.*   The Catholic University of America
    Studies in Medieval History, n.s., 6.   Washington,
    D.C.:   The Catholic University of America Press,
    1945.

Nagel, Peter.   *Die Motivierung der Askese in der alte Kirche
    und der Ursprung des Mönchtums.*   TU 95.   Berlin:
    Akademie-Verlag, 1966.

Oost, Stewart Irwin.   *Galla Placidia Augusta: A Biographical
    Essay.*   Chicago/London: University of Chicago Press,
    1968.

Ovadiah, Asher.   *Corpus of the Byzantine Churches in the Holy
    Land.*   Theophaneia 22.   Bonn: Peter Hanstein Ver-
    lag, 1970.

Patlagean, Evelyne.   *Pauvreté économique et pauvreté sociale
    à Byzance 4e-7e siècles.*   Civilisations et Sociétés 48.

Pavlovskis, Zoja. "The Life of St. Pelagia the Harlot: Hagiographic Adaptation of Pagan Romance." *Classical Folia* 30 (1976): 138-149.

Peeters, Paul. "De Codice Hiberico Bibliothecae Bodleianae Oxoniensis." *AB* 31 (1912): 301-318.

_____. Review of *Rufinus of Aquileia (345-411)*, by F. X. Murphy. *AB* 66 (1948): 325-331.

_____. "Une Vie Copte de S. Jean de Lycopolis." *AB* 54 (1936): 359-381.

Pellegrino, Michele. "Sull'antica biografia cristiana: problemi e orientamenti." In *Studi in Onore Gino Funaioli*. Roma: Angelo Signorelli, 1955.

Perry, Ben Edwin. *The Ancient Romances: A Literary-Historical Account of Their Origins.* Sather Classical Lectures 37 Berkeley: University of California Press, 1967.

_____. "Chariton and His Romance from a Literary-Historical Point of View." *American Journal of Philology* 51 (1930): 93-134.

Petri, Remy. *Über den Roman des Chariton.* Beiträge zur klassischen Philologie 11. Meisenheim am Glan: Verlag Anton Hain, 1963.

Pietri, Charles. "Esquisse de conclusion: l'aristocratie chrétienne entre Jean de Constantinople et Augustin d'Hippone." *Jean Chrysostome et Augustine: Actes du Colloque de Chantilly* 22-24 September 1974, ed. Charles Kannengiesser. Théologie Historique 35. Paris: Editions Beauchesne, 1975.

_____. *Roma Christiana. Recherches sur l'église de Rome, son organisation, sa politique, son idéologie de Miltiade à Sixte III (311-440).* Roma: Ecole Française de Rome, 1976.

Piganiol, André. "Le Problème de l'or au IVe siècle." *Annales d'Histoire Sociale* 7 (1945): 47-53.

Plesch, Julius. *Die Originalität und literarische Form der Mönchsbiographien des Hl. Hieronymus.* München: C. Wolf & Sohn, 1910.

Poncelet, Albertus. "Le Légendier de Pierre Calo." *AB* 29 (1910): 5-116.

Priessnig, A. "Die biographische Form der Plotinvita des Porphyrios und das Antoniosleben des Athanasios." *BZ* 64 (1971): 1-5.

_____. "Die literarische Form der spätantiken Philosophenromane." *BZ* 30 (1929/30): 23-30.

Quain, Edwin A. "St. Jerome as a Humanist." In *A Monument to Saint Jerome: Essays on Some Aspects of His Life, Works and Influence*, ed. Francis X. Murphy. New York: Sheed & Ward, 1952.

Radermacher, L. *Hippolytos und Thekla. Studien zur Geschichte von Legende und Kultus.* SB Wien, philos.-hist. Kl 182.3. Vienna: Alfred Hölder, 1916.

Rattenbury, R. M. "Chastity and Chastity Ordeals in the Ancient Greek Romances." *Proceedings of the Leeds Philosophical and Literary Society* 1 (1926): 59-71.

Reardon, B. P. *Courants littéraires grecs de IIe et IIIe siècles après J.-C.* Annales littéraires de l'Université de Nantes 3. Paris: Société d'Edition 'Les Belles Lettres,' 1971.

_____. "The Greek Novel." *Phoenix* 23 (1969): 291-309.

Reitzenstein, Richard. "Des Athanasius Werk über das Leben des Antonius." *SB* Heid. philos.-hist. Kl. 5 (1914).

_____. *Hellenistische Wundererzählungen.* Leipzig: B. G. Teubner, 1906.

Rohde, Erwin. *Der griechische Roman und seine Vorläufer.* Leipzig: Breitkopf und Hartel, 1876.

Rougé, Jean. "Une Emeute à Rome au IVe siècle. Ammien Marcellin, XXVII, 3-4: Essai d'interprétation." *REA* 63 (1961): 59-77.

Rousseau, Philip. *Ascetics, Authority, and the Church in the Age of Jerome and Cassian.* Oxford: University Press, 1978.

Ruggini, Lelia. *Economia e società nell' 'Italia Annonaria'*:
     Rapporti fra agricoltura e commercio dal IV al VI secolo d.C.
     Fondazione Guglielmo Castelli 30. Milano: A.
     Giufrè, 1961.

_____. "Il paganesimo romano tra religione e
     politica (384-394 d.C.): per una reinterpretazione
     del Carmen contra paganos." *Atti della Accademia
     Nazionale dei Lincei*, Memorie, Classe di Scienze,
     storiche e filologiche, 8th ser., vol. 23, fasc.
     1. Roma: Accademia Nazionale dei Lincei, 1979.

Sbordone, Silvia. "Caratteristiche strutturali di alcuni
     Vite di santi dei secoli III-IV." *Koinonia* 2 (1978):
     57-67.

Schanze, Martin, Carl Hosius, and Gustav Krüger. *Ge-
     schichte der römischer Literatur* III. München: C. H.
     Beck'sche Verlagsbuchhandlung, 1922.

Schneemelcher, Wilhelm. "The Acts of Paul." In *New
     Testament Apocrypha*, eds. Edgar Hennecke and Wilhelm
     Schneemelcher; English trans. and ed. R. McL.
     Wilson. Vol. II. Philadelphia: Westminster
     Press, 1965.

Schneider, Alfons M. "Sankt Euphemia und das Konzil
     von Chalkedon." In *Das Konzil von Chalkedon: Geschichte
     und Gegenwart*, eds. Alois Grillmeier and Heinrich
     Bacht. 3 vols. Würzburg: Echter-Verlag, 1951.

Schumacher, Walter N. "Dominus Legem Dat." *RQ* 54
     (1959): 1-39.

Schwartz, Eduard. *Fünf Vorträge über den griechischen Roman.
     Das Romanhafte in der erzählenden Literatur der Griechen.*
     2d ed. Berlin: Walter de Gruyter, 1943.

_____. *Johannes Rufus, ein monophysitischer
     Schriftsteller.* SB Heid. philos.-hist. Kl. 16.
     Heidelberg: Carl Winter's Universitätsbuchhand-
     lung, 1912.

_____. "Palladiana." *ZNW* 36 (1937): 161-204.

_____. "Unzeitgemässe Beobachtungen zu den
     Clementinen." *ZNW* 31 (1932): 151-199.

Schwartz, Jacques. "Quelques Observations sur les ro-
     mans grecs." *L'Antiquité Classiques* 36 (1967): 536-552.

Scobie, Alexander. *Aspects of the Ancient Romance and Its Heritage. Essays on Apuleius, Petronius, and the Greek Romances.* Beiträge zur klassischen Philologie 30. Meisenheim am Glan: Verlag Anton Hain, 1969.

Seeck, Otto. "Cursus Publicus." *RE* IV (1901): cols. 1846-1863.

_____. "Heraclianus." *RE* VIII.1 (1912): cols. 405-406.

_____. *Regesten der Kaiser und Päpste für die Jahre 311 bis 476 n. Chr. Vorarbeit zu einer Prosopographie der christlichen Kaiserzeit.* Stuttgart: J. B. Metzlersche Verlagsbuchhandlung, 1919.

Séjourné, Paul-M. "Chronique de Jérusalem." *RBib* 4 (1895): 437-447.

Siegmund, Albert. *Die Überlieferung der griechischen christlichen Literatur in der lateinschen Kirche bis zum zwölften Jahrhundert.* Abh Bayerischen Benediktiner-Akademie 51. München-Pasing: Filser-Verlag, 1949.

Smith, Morton. "Prolegomena to a Discussion of Aretalogies, Divine Men, the Gospels and Jesus." *JBL* 90 (1971): 174-199.

Söder, Rosa. *Die apokryphen Apostelgeschichten und die romanhafte Literatur der Antike.* Würzburger Studien zur Altertumswissenschaft 3. Stuttgart: W. Kohlhammer, 1932.

Steidle, Wolf. *Sueton und die antike Biographie.* Zetemata 1. München: Verlag C. H. Beck, 1951.

Stuart, Duane Reed. *Epochs of Greek and Roman Biography.* Sather Classical Lectures 4 (1928). Berkeley: University of California Press, 1928.

Tarchnišvili, Michael. *Geschichte der kirchlichen georgischen Literatur.* ST 185. Roma: Biblioteca Apostolica Vaticana, 1955.

Tengström, Emin. *Donatisten und Katholiken. Soziale, wirtschaftliche und politische Aspekte einer nordafrikanischen Kirchenspaltung.* Göteborg: Elanders Boktryckeri Aktiebolag, 1964.

Thélamon, Francoise. "Modèles de monachisme oriental selon Rufin d'Aquilée." *Aquileia e l'Oriente Mediterraneo.* Vol. I, *Testo.* Antichita' Altoadriatiche. Settimana di studi aquileiesi, 7th, Aquileia. Udine: Arti Grafiche Friulane, 1977.

Thompson, E. A. "The Settlement of the Barbarians in Southern Gaul." *JRS* 46 (1956): 65-75.

_____. "The Visigoths from Fritigern to Euric." *Historia* 12 (1963): 105-126.

Thouvenot, R. "Saint Augustin et les païens d'après Epist., XLVI et XLVII." In *Hommages à Jean Bayet,* eds. M. Renard and R. Schilling. Collection Latomus 70. Bruxelles/Berchem: Latomus, 1964: 682-690.

Tillemont, Louis Sebastian Lenain de. *Mémoires pour servir à l'histoire ecclésiastique des six premiers siècles.* Paris: Charles Robustel, 1709.

Vailhé, S. "Répertoire alphabétique des monastères de Palestine." Part 1. *ROC* 5 (1900): 19-48.

Van der Meer, F. *Augustine the Bishop. The Life and Work of a Father of the Church,* trans. B. Battershaw and G. R. Lamb. London/New York: Sheed and Ward, 1961.

Van de Vorst, Carolus, and Paul Peeters. "Saint Phocas." *AB* 30 (1911): 252-295.

Van Esbroeck, Michel. "Encore la Lettre de Justinien. Sa date: 560 et non 561." *AB* 87 (1969): 442-444.

_____. "La Lettre de l'empereur Justinien sur l'Annonciation et la Nöel en 561." *AB* 86 (1968): 351-371.

Villain, Maurice. "Rufin d'Aquilée--La Querelle autour d'Origéne." *RecSR* 27 (1937): 5-37, 165-195.

Vincent, Hugues. "L'Eléona: Sanctuaire primitif de l'Ascension." *RBib* 64 (1957): 48-71.

_____, and F.-M. Abel. *Jérusalem. Recherches de topographie, d'archéologie et d'histoire.* Vol. II, *Jérusalem nouvelle.* Paris: Librairie Victor Lecoffre, 1914.

Vööbus, Arthur. *History of Asceticism in the Syrian Orient.*
    A Contribution to the History of Culture in the Near East.
    Vol. I, *The Origin of Asceticism. Early Monasticism in*
    Persia. CSCO, Subsidia 14 (=184). Vol. II, *Early*
    Monasticism in Mesopotamia and Syria. CSCO, Subsidia 17
    (=197). Louvain: Secrétariat du Corpus SCO, 1958,
    1960.

Wagner, Mary Monica. *Rufinus, The Translator.* The Catho-
    lic University of America Patristic Studies 73.
    Washington, D.C.: The Catholic University of Amer-
    ica Press, 1945.

Walsh, P. G. "Paulinus of Nola and the Conflict of
    Ideologies in the Fourth Century." In *Kyriakon:*
    Festschrift Johannes Quasten, eds. P. Granfield and J.
    A. Jungmann. Vol. II. Münster Westf.: Verlag
    Aschendorff, 1970.

_____. *The Roman Novel. The 'Satyricon' of Petronius*
    and the 'Metamorphoses' of Apuleius. Cambridge: Cam-
    bridge University Press, 1970.

Wehrli, Fritz. "Einheit und Vorgeschichte der
    griechisch-römischen Romanliteratur." *Museum Helveti-*
    cum 22 (1965): 133-154.

Weingarten, Hermann. *Der Ursprung des Mönchtums im nachcon-*
    stantinischen Zeit. Gotha: Friedrich Andreas Perthes,
    1877.

Weinreich, Otto. *Der griechische Liebesroman.* Zürich:
    Artemis-Verlag, 1962.

Wendland, Paul. *Die urchristlichen Literaturformen.* Tübin-
    gen: J. C. B. Mohr (Paul Siebeck), 1912.

Wiesen, David S. *St. Jerome as a Satirist.* Ithaca: Cor-
    nell University Press, 1964.

Wilkinson, John. "Christian Pilgrims in Jerusalem during
    the Byzantine Period." *Palestine Exploration Quarterly*
    108 (1976): 75-101.

_____. "Jewish Influences on the Early Chris-
    tian Rite of Jerusalem." *Le Muséon* 92 (1979): 347-
    358.

Winkler, Jack. "Lollianus and the Desperados." *JHS*
      100 (1980): 155-181.

Winter, Paul. *Der literarische Charakter der Vita beati Hilari-
      onis des Hieronymus.* Zittau: Richard Menzel Nachf.,
      1904.

Yarbrough, Anne. "Christianization in the Fourth Cen-
      tury: The Example of Roman Women." *Church History*
      45 (1976): 149-165.

INDEX

Achilles Tatius, 159.
Aemilius of Beneventum, 144, 240 n. 24.
Alaric, 41, 102-108, 110, 112, 213 n. 147, 234 n. 55.
Albina, mother of Melania the Younger, 10, 16, 18, 32, 45-46, 49, 50, 51, 54, 84, 110-111, 115, 117, 122, 129, 144, 195 n. 13.
Albinus, Ceionius Rufius, 84.
Albinus, Publilius Caeionius Caecina, 84, 195 n. 16.
Alypius of Thagaste, 11, 43, 44, 110.
Ambrose of Milan, 84, 93, 123.
Anastasius, bishop of Rome, 142.
Anicii, gens, 93, 110, 112-113, 211 n. 122.
Antonius Marcellinus, 83.
Antony; *Life of Antony*, 141, 158, 165, 167, 168, 169, 201 n. 2, 256 n. 109.
Apatheia, 143.
Apocryphal Acts, 157, 160, 163, 169.
Apollonius of Tyana, 131.
Aposteleion, 61, 117, 222 nn. 25, 26.
Apronianus, 168.
Apuleius, 131.
Arcadius, 103.
Armenian Lectionary, 228 n. 108.
Artemis, cult of, 161.
Arzuges, 87.
Ascension, Church of, 62, 115, 117, 119, 220 n. 5, 223 n. 32.

Asceticism, role of women, 83, 92-94, 203 nn. 24-25, 208 n. 86; see Melania the Younger, ascetic practices.
Asella, 93.
Atalus, 112.
Athanasius, bishop of Alexandria, 93, 141.
Athanasius, nephew of Cyril of Alexandria, 18.
Augustine, Augustinians, 1, 11, 43, 84, 87, 93, 109, 110-111, 113, 131-132, 144, 145, 148, 216 n. 19, 218 n. 55, 219 n. 58.
Aurelius of Carthage, 11, 43, 110.
Avita, 168.

Barbarian invasion of Italy, 109; of Mediterranean islands, 43-43; of Rome, 38, 41-42, 98, 99, 102-105, 132, 157; of Sicily, 109-110; of Spain, 52, 114.
Basil of Caesarea, 116, 120, 126, 225 n. 50, 234 n. 52.
Biography (genre), 153-155.
Bollandists, 3-4.
Bordeaux Pilgrim, 135.
Brown, Peter, 144.
Butler, Cuthbert, 10, 148-149, 200 n. 60.

Calendar of 354, 126.
Callirhoe, 156, 158.
Cappadocian Fathers, 153.
Cedrenus, George, 137.
"The Cells", 53, 114, 169.
Chalcedon, Council of; Chalcedonianism, 14, 17, 18, 20, 21, 22.
Chareas; *Chareas and Callirhoe*, 158, 159.